Women and the Law in South Africa

WOMEN & THE LAW IN SOUTH AFRICA

empowerment through enlightenment

Unit for Gender Research in Law Unisa

First published October 1998

© Juta & Co Ltd
PO Box 14373 Kenwyn 7790 South Africa

This book is copyright under the Berne Convention. In terms of the Copyright Act, No 98 of 1978, no part of this book may be reproduced or transmitted in any form or by any means, electronic or mechanical, including photocopying, recording or by any information storage and retrieval system, without permission in writing from the Publisher.

ISBN: 07021 4536 X

Edited: John Linnegar and Ken McGillivray
Cover artwork: Juanita Stead
Design & layout: The Nimble Mouse, Kalk Bay
Cover design: Comet Design

Reproduction:
Printed and bound in the Republic of South Africa by
The Rustica Press

Preface

Throughout South Africa's history neither the State nor the public at large, nor the media, were much concerned with the issue of women's rights. Until very recently, women themselves accepted their subordinate status as part of the immutable order of things. They knew that, in the home, the man was the head of the household and his word was law. They knew that gender-based violence happened – and would always happen – because that was the way things were. They accepted that, if they wanted to work outside the home, they would be entering a sphere where working conditions had been set by men for men. Juggling domestic and workplace responsibilities was a woman's problem and nobody else's. After all, if she couldn't manage, she didn't have to work, did she? 'Sexual harassment' was something many women encountered in the workplace, but few had heard of the term or thought to seek a remedy. Moreover, a woman's reproductive life was everybody's business but her own. When the original legislation on abortion was introduced, women were not even consulted.

However, during the last decade, a quiet revolution started taking place which saw women's rights emerge as essential to the establishment of true democracy in this country. The sudden revelation that women comprised more than half the population, and were thus a powerful voting bloc, helped enormously. After women insisted on forming part of the negotiating teams when the Interim Constitution was being prepared, the revolution ceased to be a quiet one. Today, South Africa has a constitution which insists on the equality of all people, and which prohibits discrimination on the grounds of sex and gender. The law-makers and, in some instances, the Courts, have addressed all the issues referred to above. Compared with most countries, the percentage of women in our Parliament is high. South Africa has not only signed and ratified the United Nations Convention on the Elimination of All Forms of Discrimination against Women, but, in June 1998, presented its first report on the country's implementation of the Convention to the CEDAW committee in New York.

If, then, equality has arrived, why do we still need to talk about women's rights or women and the law? There are two reasons. One is that while women's rights receive plenty of attention during a transitional phase in a country's history, they are often conveniently forgotten after that. The second is that although women now have equality on paper, many of them do not know it. If they do not know they have rights, they cannot exercise them. If they do not exercise their rights, they continue to be as powerless as they always have been. This book seeks to remedy that situation. While not seeking to force a certain point of view on anybody, it does tell women that they have choices.

It is for all women. It is
- for the woman who merely wants the equality provisions of the Constitution explained to her in plain language;
- for the woman who is about to enter into a customary-law marriage and wants to know what the advantages and disadvantages of such a marriage are;
- for the woman about to get married who wants to know which kind of matrimonial property system to choose;
- for the woman whose marriage is in trouble and who wants to know how to go about seeking a divorce and what her financial position will be if she does;
- for the woman who wants to know what the ongoing abortion debate is all about;
- for the woman who is being abused and seeks help; and,
- especially, for the woman who is herself engaged in 'legal literacy' and grassroots projects for other women.

I take this opportunity to thank all my former colleagues who helped establish the 'Women and the Law' certificate course at Unisa, and write the study material for it, and all those involved in teaching it. The material written for the course forms the basis of this book. Although free time is a scarce commodity for academics, their dedication to the cause of women is such that somehow they found – and continue to find – the time to do the work. The overwhelming enthusiasm of the students has been their reward. It is our hope that this book will elicit a similarly enthusiastic response.

Lesbury van Zyl
Professor Emeritus
Faculty of Law, Unisa

Contents

Preface　v

Part One: Introduction

How the law has viewed women　2
How women have viewed the law　4
Equality: sameness and difference　5
Women and legal language　5
The law and social change　6
The purpose of this work　7

Part Two: Family law

Introduction　9

Chapter 1: Marriage in the law　11

Introduction　11
Marriage (and divorce) in South Africa: general　12
Civil marriage　13
　Requirements for a legal civil marriage　13
　Invariable consequences of civil marriage　14
Customary marriage　17
　Characteristics of customary marriage　17
　Legal requirements for customary marriage　18
　Consequences of customary marriage　19
　Termination of customary marriage　20
　　Ways of termination　20
　　Grounds for termination of customary marriage　21
　　Consequences of termination　22
　Annulment of customary marriage　24
African civil marriage　24
　Lobolo within an African civil marriage　24
　Termination of marriage and custody of children　25
Islamic marriage　26
　Requirements for Islamic marriage　26
　Consequences of Islamic marriage　28
　Dissolution of Islamic marriage　28
South African law　29
Foreign marriage　31
Cohabitation (living together)　32
　Cohabitation and the law　33
　　Partners, their children and the law　35
Protection in a cohabitation relationship　35
　A cohabitation contract　36
　Drafting of a valid will　36
Conclusion　37

Chapter 2: Financial inequality: husbands and wives 39
Introduction 39
Matrimonial property systems 40
Community of property 41
   During the marriage 42
   At the dissolution of the marriage 45
   Advantages and disadvantages of community of property 48
The accrual system 49
   During the marriage 49
   At the dissolution of the marriage 50
   Advantages and disadvantages of the accrual system 53
Complete separation of property 54
   During the marriage 54
   At the dissolution of the marriage 55
   Advantages and disadvantages of complete separation of property 57
The choice of a matrimonial property system 58
   Changing the matrimonial property system 58
   Summary: the correct choice 59

Chapter 3: Support of the household 61
Introduction 61
Financial support in marriage 61
   Duty of support between spouses 61
   Duty of support between parents and children 62
Maintenance and divorce 64
   Interim relief 64
   Maintenance of former spouse after divorce 64
   Case Study: Mr. and Mrs. Ayyad 65
   Types of maintenance 66
   Maintenance of children after divorce 69
Enforcement of maintenance 70
   Enforcement under the Maintenance Act and the Child Care Act 70
   Types of enforcement 71
Conclusion 72

Chapter 4: Child law 75
Introduction 75
The legal subject 75
Legitimacy and illegitimacy 76
Parental authority 76
   Legitimate children 77
   Illegitimate children 78
   Termination of parental authority 79
Duty of support 79
Children and divorce procedure 79
   Alternative dispute resolution 79
   The family advocate 81
Conclusion 82

Chapter 5: Divorce law   83
Introduction   83
Grounds for divorce   83
    Irretrievable breakdown   83
        Mental illness or continuous unconsciousness   84
        Divorce and religious marriages   84
Consequences of divorce   85
    Property   85
    Maintenance   85
    Children   86
Interim relief: rule 43 of the Uniform Rules of Court   86
What will happen when you decide to divorce?   87
    Entering into a divorce settlement   88
    Case Study   88
    Divorce settlement: checklist   89

Part Three: Women and Violence

Introduction   91
    What 'violence' means   92

Chapter 6: Common forms of violence encountered by women   95
Violence through assault   95
    Assault with intent to do grievous bodily harm   97
    Indecent assault   97
    Assault within the family circle (domestic violence)   98
Violence through rape   104
    Proving rape in Court   109
    In camera hearings   111
Violence through incest   112

Chapter 7: Private defence (self-defence)   115

Chapter 8: Remedies in law   117
Criminal proceedings   118
    Outline of the legal process   120
    The trial procedure   121
Civil remedies   123
    Interdicts   123
    Damages   125
    Other legal options   127

Chapter 9: Support systems in the community   129
The South African Police Services   129
Community-based support systems   130
Conclusion   131

Part Four: Women and Employment

Introduction   133

Chapter 10: What is sex discrimination?   135
The concept of sex discrimination   137
   Liberal human rights model   138
   Radical human rights model   139
Direct and indirect discrimination   140
Conclusion   142

Chapter 11: Enforcement of equality in the workplace: the Constitution and the Labour Relations Act   143
Introduction   143
The Constitution of the Republic of South Africa Act 108 of 1996   143
Equality in the workplace: the Labour Relations Act 66 of 1995   147
   Automatically unfair dismissals   147
   Residual unfair labour practice   150
Conclusion   152

Chapter 12: Equality for women in the workplace: affirmative action   153
Different ways of implementing affirmative action   154
Affirmative action programmes from the First World   155
   The United States of America   155
   The United Kingdom   156
   Australia   157
Affirmative action programmes in South Africa   158
Conclusion   160

Chapter 13: 'Equal pay for equal work'   163
The comparator   164
The bases of comparison   164
   Like work   164
   Equivalent work   165
   Equal value/comparable worth   165
The meaning of 'equal pay'   166
Justifiable grounds for pay disparity   166
Suggestions for implementing equal remuneration   167

Chapter 14: Sexual harassment in the workplace   169
Definition of sexual harassment   171
   Quid pro quo harassment   172
   Hostile environment harassment   172
The requirement of fault   173
Policies to prevent sexual harassment   174

Chapter 15: Pregnancy rights in the workplace   177
Maternity leave   178
Payment of benefits during maternity leave   179
Protection of employees before and after the birth of a child   180
Protection against dismissal   180
Conclusion   182

Part Five: Women and Health
Introduction   183

Chapter 16: Procreation rights   185
Assisted reproduction   185
   Artificial insemination   186
   In vitro fertilisation   186
Regulation of assisted reproduction in South Africa   187

Chapter 17: Surrogate motherhood   189
Reasons for using a surrogate mother   189
Forms of surrogacy   190
Altruistic vs commercial surrogacy   192
Validity and enforceability of surrogacy contracts   192
   Breach of contract   193
   Recommendations of the Law Commission   193

Chapter 18: Unwanted procreation   197
Abortion   197
   The present abortion law in South Africa: Choice on the Termination of Pregnancy Act 92 of 1996   198
   A critical evaluation of the new Act   203
Sterilization   204
Conclusion   205

Chapter 19: AIDS and women   207
Background to AIDS   207
Detection and prevention of AIDS   209
Prostitution and HIV/AIDS   211
Marriage and HIV/AIDS   212
Pregancy and HIV/AIDS   212
Conclusion   213

© JUTA & CO, LTD

XI

Part Six: Women, human rights and democracy

Introduction   215

Chapter 20: Women and the Constitution   217
What is a constitution?   218
   Democracy   218
   Constitution   219
   State authority   220
Constitutional history of South Africa   220
   The right to vote   221
   The rights of women   221
   After 1990   221
   The elections of 1994   222
   Women in the process   222
Structure and framework of the final (1996) Constitution   222
   Framework of the Constitution   223
   Legislature   224
   Executive   224
   Judiciary   225
Implications of the 1996 Constitution for women   226
   General implications   226
   The Bill of Rights and the principle of equality   226
   Control and enforcement   231

Chapter 21: International conventions of particular importance to women   235
Convention on the political rights of women   236
Convention on consent to marriage, minimum age for marriage, and registration of marriages   236
Convention on the nationality of married women   237
Convention on the Elimination of all forms of Discrimination Against Women (CEDAW)   238
   Enforcement of CEDAW   241
   Draft optional protocol to CEDAW   242
   The Beijing Declaration and Platform for Action   243

Chapter 22: National machinery for the advancement of women   245
The office on the status of women   245
   The Women's Budget   246
Commission on Gender Equality   247
   Powers and functions of the Commission   247
   An assessment of the Commission's powers of enforcement   249
The Human Rights Commission   249
The Public Protector   250
The Truth and Reconciliation Commission   250
How women's human rights issues may be brought to Court   251
Conclusion   251

Appendix   255

Glossary   261

Table of Cases

B v B 1983 (1) SA 496 (N)   13
Beaumont v Beaumont 1987 (1) SA 967 (A)   56

Clark & Co v Lynch 1963 (1) SA 183 (N)   50

Elliso v Brady 924 F2d at 878   173

Fraser v Children's Court, Pretoria and others 1997 (2) SA 261 (CC)   78

Gliksman v Talekinsky 1955 (4) SA 468 (W)   63

Incorporated Law Society v Wookey 1912 AD 623   3

J v M Ltd (1989) 10 ILJ 755 (IC)   171–2

Katz v Katz 1989 (3) SA 1 (A)   68
Kroon v Kroon 1986 (4) SA 616 (EC) 67
Krös, ex parte 1986 (1) SA 642 (NC)   59

J Mampuru v PUTCO
    (unreported, Industrial Court No NH11/2/2136)   171–2
Moola v Aulsebrook 1983 (1) SA 687 (N)   30

Re: Bradwell, 1873   3
Roe v Wade 410 US 118 (1973)   201, 214
Ryland v Edros (2) SA 690 (C)   29

S v Chapman 1998 (3) SA 345 (SCA)   108
S v K 1966 (1) SA 366 (RA)   107
S v Marx 1962 (1) SA 848 (N)   96
Singh v Singh 1983 (1) SA 781 (C)   47
Sperling v Sperling 1975 (3) SA 707 (A)   31

Table of Statutes

South Africa
Abortion and Sterilization Act 2 of 1975   197, 200–1, 204
Abortion and Sterilization Amendment Act 18 of 1976   197
   38 of 1980   197
   48 of 1982   197

Basic Conditions of Employment Act 3 of 1983   178–80, 182
Births and Deaths Registration Act 51 of 1992   29, 76

Child Care Act 74 of 1983   70, 190, 195
Children's Status Act 82 of 1987   180, 190, 195, 204
Choice on the Termination of Pregnancy Act 92 of 1996   197–8, 200, 204
Commission on Gender Equality Act 39 of 1996   247
Compensation for Occupational Injuries and Diseases Act 130 of 1993   35
Constitution of the Republic of South Africa Act 200 of 1993   222
Constitution of the Republic of South Africa Act 108 of 1996   82, 91–3, 133, 143–5, 147, 153, 182, 190, 195, 200, 203, 217, 235
Criminal Procedure Amendment Act 86 of 1996   111

Divorce Act 70 of 1979   46–7, 56, 66, 83, 85

Gender Equality Act 34 of 1996   247, 249
General Law Fourth Amendment Act 132 of 1993   43

Human Tissue Act 65 of 1983   249

Interpretation Act 33 of 1957   5, 226

KwaZulu Code of Zulu Law Act 16 of 1985   17, 19, 21–2, 24

Labour Relations Act 66 of 1995   133, 137, 143-4, 147–8, 150, 152, 158–9, 163, 166, 180-2
Law of Evidence and Criminal Procedure Amendment Act 103 of 1987   105

Maintenance Act 23 of 1963   68, 70–1
Maintenance of Surviving Spouses Act 27 of 1990   46
Marriage Act 25 of 1961   26, 29
Matrimonial Property Act 88 of 1984   42–3, 51, 54, 58
Mediation in Certain Divorce Matters Act 24 of 1987   81

Natural Fathers of Children Born out of Wedlock Act 86 of 1997   78

Prevention of Family Violence Act 133 of 1993   35, 106, 121, 123
Public Protector Act 23 of 1994   250

Reciprocal Enforcement of Maintenance Orders Act 80 of 1963   72

Sexual Offences Act 23 of 1957   107, 211

Unemployment Insurance Act 30 of 1966   179

Australia
Affirmative Action (Equal opportunities for Women) Act 1986   157

Canada
Ontario Human Rights Code   174

The United States of America
Civil Rights Act of 1964   155

United Kingdom
Equal Pay Act 1970   164–7
Sex Discrimination Act 1975   156

Zimbabwe
Age of Majority Act   6

PART ONE:
Introduction

In writing this book, we are following the example of other countries throughout the world which, during the past few decades, have been writing about women and the law. You may ask why a publication on this topic is necessary – the law treats men and women alike, surely?

As you read this introduction, think about the following questions:
- What are your personal experiences of the legal system in South Africa?
- Have you ever had to go to the law courts? Why?
- Do you know any women who have experienced problems with the law in South Africa?
- Do you think the legal system in South Africa is fair to all people?

For the first time ever, during the 1970s, in countries such as Norway, the United States and Great Britain, women started to analyse and write about the law from a woman's perspective. Consequently, today we have a large body of writing of this genre, known as feminist jurisprudence.[†‡] In North America alone, there are over 20 journals devoted exclusively to the subject of women and the law.

Lawyers have boasted that the law is rational, objective and impartial, but women writers have pointed out that until very recently no women were present when laws were made or when they were interpreted or administered. Laws were made by men for men. Instead of being unbiased, these laws reflected the male view of the world and male bias, though perhaps an unconscious one. In particular, the laws dealing specifically with women reflected the male view of women and of women's needs. Women themselves were not canvassed for their opinions.

To redress this imbalance and to make laws equal for men and women, it was decided to start focusing on women and the law with the purpose of:
- examining the legal position of women, and
- improving that legal posittion.

---

‡ Throughout this work the [†] symbol indicates that the word or expression it follows is defined or explained in the Glossary, which commences on page 261.

Those of us writing on this subject therefore make no claim to be impartial and unbiased: on the contrary, we claim that a bias in favour of women is necessary in order to counteract or counterbalance the male bias of the past. Our main focus is not on the law but on the woman and how she experiences the law. Our emphasis is therefore not on 'the law in the books' but on 'the law in practice'.

In many African countries, researchers have interviewed women in their homes or in local gathering places to find out how the law affects their lives. This is far more effective than reading court records and reported cases, because most women will never go to court in their lifetime.

Perhaps, now, you will also understand why we do not write about the law according to its usual divisions of public/private or substantive/procedural. Instead, we look at the law from a woman's point of view, concentrating on those aspects of it which are of special importance to women.

How the law has viewed women

When women first started setting their sights on emancipation or freedom, they looked to the law for help. Two methods which they used were, first, to lobby for changes in legislation and, secondly, to try to establish their rights by bringing cases to court. This was not easy, however, for the law has always been a conservative profession with its own particular view of women and their role in society. This view is shown by two Roman law[†] rules which still formed part of our law until as recently as 1971. These rules prohibited a woman from 'standing surety' (ie promising to pay the debt of her husband or another person if necessary), on account of the assumed weakness of her sex and the ease with which she might be influenced by other persons.

In the past, in its traditional division of society into public and private spheres (in public society and in private life), the law saw men as belonging primarily to the public sphere, holding that the private domain of the family was the proper place for women. Thus as recently as 1980 Lord Denning, an English judge, wrote in his book *The Due Process of Law*:

> 'No matter how you may dispute and argue, you cannot alter the fact that women are quite different from men. The principal task in the life of women is to bear and rear children: ... He is temperamentally the more aggressive and she the more submissive. It is he who takes the initiative and she who responds ... .'

Until recently, it was believed that because what happened in the family was private, the State should not intervene in or make laws about the family. This placed women who suffered domestic abuse,[†] for example, at a severe disadvantage. These days, fortunately, people are more aware of the dimensions and seriousness of domestic violence, and therefore of the need for State or other intervention.

Women have not been helped by the fact that most judges and practising lawyers have been white middle-aged males who were perfectly content with the laws as they were. The belief that the private sphere or the home was the proper place for women meant, too, that women had to struggle long and hard before they were permitted to enter professions such as medicine and the law. In the United States in 1873, in the case of *Re: Bradwell*, in rejecting a woman's application for a licence to practise law, Judge Bradley stated:

> *'The civil law, as well as nature herself, has always recognised a wide difference in the respective spheres and destinies of man and woman ... The natural and proper timidity and delicacy which belongs to the female sex evidently unfits it for many of the occupations of civil life.'*

In South Africa and in several other countries, the courts at first sought to exclude women from the legal profession by stating that only 'persons' might practise law and that women were not 'persons' in terms of the applicable laws!

INCORPORATED LAW SOCIETY V WOOKEY 1912 AD 623

Madeline Wookey wanted to be registered as a candidate attorney, but the Law Society refused to register her articles. After the Provincial Division ordered the Law Society to register her, they appealed against the order.

The Appeal Court ruled that the word 'persons' included only male persons and that Miss Wookey was not entitled to be enrolled as a candidate attorney.

Over the last 20 years, however, women have made great progress in their search for emancipation and equal rights. In South Africa this quest has led to full gender† equality being written into the Constitution of 1996 (discussed more fully in Part Six: Women, human rights and democracy). But does this mean that there really will be full equality now? For this to happen, law reform on its own is not enough; social attitudes will have to change too.

We have spoken of gender equality being entrenched in the Constitution. What is meant by the term 'gender'? When we speak of the differences between the sexes, we refer to the biological differences between men and women. Gender differences, however, have a cultural aspect; they are the differences between men and women which society has constructed. Society has created certain beliefs about what femininity and masculinity are, and about how women and men should, for example, dress and behave. Because these beliefs are created by our society, in the form of social constructs,† we believe it is possible to change them in the pursuit of greater gender equality.

GENDER ROLES IN OUR SOCIETY

1 Study the jobs listed below. Tick alongside all the jobs you usually do during one week.

A job for money with a regular salary	Ironing
Laundry (washing clothes)	Cooking food
Cleaning the house	Washing dishes
Sweeping the floor	Shopping for food
Shopping for clothes	Bathing children
Taking care of children	Dressing children
Feeding children	Cleaning the car
Feeding the family	Buying petrol/oil
Repairing the car	Paying bills
Gardening	

2 What other tasks do you perform for your family every week?
3 What kind of jobs does your mother do, or did she do, in your home?

HOW WOMEN HAVE VIEWED THE LAW

As we have seen, women played hardly any role in the making of laws or in the administration or practice of the law until very recently. For this reason, although the law has impinged on or affected their lives as it does the lives of everybody, women have often experienced the law as something incomprehensible, unfamiliar and even frightening. Male-dominated courts are a strange world to many women. Many women also live far away from a court and lack the resources and the time to bring a case to court. Moreover they may encounter resistance from their husbands if they even try.

In Africa, women often prefer to settle their disputes in informal arenas such as the tribal court or the family, which do not frighten them and where they are given more of a voice. However, informal dispute settlement† also holds dangers for women; those presiding over hearings are likely to have their own prejudices and may have very conservative ideas about women's place in society. It has been found, too, that informal dispute settlement is unsatisfactory where there is an unequal power balance between the people or groups involved – as there usually is in disputes between husband and wife. For example, whenever one spouse has more money, a better education, a better job, and more work experience, that spouse has more power in the marriage. Since it is usually the husband who is in this powerful situation, the woman is the more likely party to lose the dispute.

Equality: sameness and difference

Early campaigners for women's rights strove to obtain equality with men. Men were the norm and, although the circumstances of women's lives were very different from those of men, women realized that if they wanted equality they would have to comply with that norm. They accepted that in the workplace, for example, employers would make no allowances for the 'double shift' (or two jobs) of women who were both employees and homemakers. Women, who carry a far heavier burden of child-raising than men do would receive no special treatment from their employers in the workplace.

More recently, however, it has come to be realized that treating people equally whose life circumstances are different does not always result in equality. The call today is for *actual equality* or equality of result rather than *formal equality*; for formal equality simply takes it for granted that everybody is the same. This means that it may be necessary to treat people differently in order to obtain true equality between men and women. Thus affirmative action,† provided for in our Constitution, may be essential before there is true equality in the workplace. This question is discussed more fully in Part Four: Women and employment.

Women and legal language

Until very recently legal language used to make it clear that the law regarded women as less important than men. The Interpretation Act 33 of 1957 provides:

> 'In every law, unless the contrary intention appears – words importing the masculine gender include females.'

This means that, for example, when pronouns such as 'he' and 'him' are used, the words 'she' and 'her' are also implied. In criminal law† and the law of delict,† a test for determining negligence is whether 'the reasonable man' would have foreseen or predicted the result.

Textbooks on these subjects are full of references to this 'reasonable man', who is also defined as the 'careful father of the family'. Nowhere is there any reference to the 'reasonable woman'!

The Constitution represents a significant advance from this position, for its drafters were careful to use gender-neutral language at all times. Thus the Bill of Rights speaks at various places of 'everyone', 'every citizen' and of 'all people'.

Indeed, it goes even further than that in striving for balance, and provides, for example, that:

'The national Assembly must elect a woman or a man from among its members to be President'

and

'a Provincial Legislature consists of women and men elected as members'.

It is likely that under the influence of the Constitution, the law will in future employ only gender-neutral language. However, general society and the media still need to be educated in this respect: how often do we not read about 'the *man* in the street'.

THE LAW AND SOCIAL CHANGE

As we have seen, gender equality has now been written into the Constitution; but this is not enough to ensure full gender equality. Women cannot heave a sigh of relief yet, because their struggle for emancipation is not over. It is up to people who believe in equality to ensure that this equality becomes a practical reality and does not remain 'the law in the books'. In other African countries there was a tendency to push women's issues into the background once independence was achieved. United Nations statistics tell us that women constitute just over half the world's population, do two-thirds of the world's work, earn one-tenth of the world's wages and own one-hundredth of the world's property. These statistics illustrate how far women still have to go to catch up with men.

Sometimes the law is slower than social change, but sometimes runs ahead of it. An example of the law running ahead of society was the Age of Majority Act in Zimbabwe, which fixed the age of majority at 18 years for all persons. This led to an enormous outcry and questions from members of the public, especially from fathers who possibly stood to lose *lobola* payments for their daughters or payment of damages if their daughters were seduced when they were older than 18.

In South Africa, the gender equality provisions of the Constitution are probably also ahead of social reality. In 1993, even before the Constitution came into operation, the husband's position as head of the household was abolished by legislation. Husbands and wives now head the household jointly. But how many husbands and wives are aware of this?

These difficulties explain why people need to be informed about the law and legal change, or, put differently, why there is a need for legal literacy.[†] This means inter alia that, before a law is changed, the changes should be widely publicized and the reasons for the changes explained clearly. Both women and men need to be told about women's improved legal status.[†] In addition, the impact of the changes on the lives of people should be studied.

It is a good start for women to be informed about their rights, but it is not enough. For one thing, there is a need for better representation of women in the legal profession – for more women to practise law and for more women to become judges. At present, approximately 12% of advocates and 15% of attorneys are women. Of the 18 Appeal Court judges, none is a woman, and only 10 of the 186 permanent High Court judges are women. Of the 11 judges appointed to the new Constitutional Court, only two are women.

THE PURPOSE OF THIS WORK

Finally, if the legal system is really to reflect the views and concerns of women, it is essential that far more women should serve at all levels of government. Only then will women's issues (such as day care for the children of working women) be given the priority that they deserve. However, such representatives should be carefully chosen, for not all women will serve women's interests well. Some, for example, will follow their party's line in order to further their own careers. What are needed are women, and men, who not only know what the important women's issues are, but are also concerned about them.

> **SUGGESTED READING**
>
> Desireé Hanson & Beatie Hofmeyr. *Women's Rights: Towards a Non-sexist South Africa.* 1992. No 7 in the *Developing Justice* series of titles published by the Social Justice Resource Project and the Legal Education Action Project, Institute of Criminology, University of Cape Town, Private Bag, Rondebosch, 7700
> Saras Jagwanth, Pamela-Jane Schwikkard and Brenda Grant (eds). *Women and the Law.* 1994. HSRC Publishers, Pretoria

PART TWO:
Family Law

INTRODUCTION

The first branch of the law that we are going to look at is family law. There is a good reason for this: until recently, the lives of most women revolved largely around their families and their homes. To put it in another way, women traditionally spent most of their lives in the private, not the public sphere. You will remember that we discussed the public/private division in the introduction to Part One. Today though many women are active in the public sphere also, doing paid or voluntary work, their relationships with their family are still important to them.

Family law has seen huge changes over the last 30 years or so. Most of these changes have been to women's advantage. But further reform is still needed. Whereas, for instance, South African law was recently changed to make both husbands and wives heads of the household and guardians[†] of their children, these reforms have not helped women married by African customary law or by Islamic law, because these forms of marriage are not recognized by South African law. As we discussed in Part One, legal change does not always guarantee social change. People's attitudes also need changing.

There are several important decisions that most women have to make during their lives. One of these decisions will be whether it is better for them to marry, remain single or simply to live together with a partner. If they live together without marrying, how will this affect their children? If they do decide to marry, women need to know which of the property systems governing marriage is best for them. If they do marry, should they marry by South African law, or according to African customary or Islamic law? They need to know what rights and duties flow from those types of marriages.

It is also important to know which decisions each parent may make about bringing up their children, and what responsibilities each parent has towards the children. Also it is important to know what financial support husbands and wives must give each other and their children. What remedies does the law provide if someone does not give the support he or she is required to give?

After divorce, most disputes have to do with children and maintenance. Who gets custody† of the children? What visiting rights does the parent have who does not get custody? Who must give financial support to whom after a divorce? If a parent gives support, how much should be given? These are some of the questions that we try to answer in this part.

CHAPTER ONE:
Marriage in the law

INTRODUCTION

We sometimes take for granted the word 'marriage' when we talk about 'a married couple'. We forget that the concepts 'marriage' and 'husband' and 'wife' differ from culture to culture. There are some societies which allow polygyny,[†] whereas others don't. There are cultures which allow concubinage within marriage (having mistresses and a wife) while others don't. There are even cultures which allow polyandry.[†] South African society is composed of many people, speaking many different languages, with many different perspectives on why, when and how a man takes a female life partner or partners, or why, when and how a woman becomes betrothed.

The *Oxford English Dictionary* states that the words 'to marry' mean 'to constitute as man and wife, according to the laws and the customs of the nation'. This definition points to two very important elements when we talk about marriage. First, it refers to the fact that there are laws which govern:

- how a marriage may be contracted;
- with whom it may be contracted;
- how that marriage is conducted; and
- what the special responsibilities and privileges are of the people involved.

Secondly, this definition points out that there is an element of traditional custom involved. Each nation and each culture bases the act of union (marriage) on what is accepted in that society.

As an *individual*, a woman is subjected to all the laws of the land. In our introduction to Part One, we explained that this work has been written to highlight some of the disadvantages women experience in the realm of the law. It would be impossible here give a full account of the responsibilities and rights of women. However, a woman's status as a married person affects her legal rights and duties in many ways. The clue to this fact is to be found in the denotations of 'man' and 'woman'.

The original meaning of the word 'husband' is 'the owner or the tiller of the land'. On the other hand, the original meaning of the word 'wife' is simply 'a woman'. The very difference in focus between these two definitions indicates that a division occurred between how men and women are viewed. The man was perceived to be a 'do-er', one who does something important. He was the tiller of the soil, a farmer. The man was also seen to be a possessor – or owner of things – in this instance, land. The woman, on the other hand, was not identified by what she owned, nor by what she did. She was merely identified by her gender – that she was female.

We have a different perspective on the same theme in the Jewish-Christian chronicle of religious events and prophecy, called the Bible. The Bible recounts how God made Adam, the first man, in His own image to be 'the master of the earth'. *(Genesis 1: 26)*

Once again, the male of the species is referred to as the doer and the owner. God then declared that it was not good that man should be alone and said that He would make Adam a helpmate – a wife, Eve *(Genesis 1: 18)*. She was still only an assistant to the man.

Marriage (and divorce) in South Africa: general

In any country there are many problems linked to the concept of marriage. In addition, South Africa with its many cultures, has some unique problems of its own because of its unique history. For example, Roman-Dutch law has tended to prescribe a certain form of marital union as the basis for our society. Other systems of marital union – derived from non-Roman-Dutch law origins – do not fit into that system of law. Below you will read about customary marriages and other types of marriage that occur in South Africa. You will also read about the problems that can occur because these systems of marriage are not accepted and recognized by South African law. The focus of Part Two will, however, be on civil marriages as they are at present the only type of marriage which is fully recognized.

Another problem is the concept of divorce. As with the concept of marriage, so the concept of divorce is different in other cultures, in other nations, in other religions. Even within the same nation, huge differences of perspective exist. For example, the Protestant faiths, accept the fact that a marital union need not necessarily be a life-long one; they allow divorce in certain circumstances. The Catholic faith, on the other hand, rejects the whole concept of divorce. In Catholic law, it is not possible for a divorced person to remarry since the first marriage is not over.

CIVIL MARRIAGE

Requirements for a legal civil marriage

In this section, we discuss the requirements for a legal marriage in South Africa and the invariable consequences† of marriage, as stated by the law.

In South Africa, marriage is a legally recognized voluntary union between one man and one woman which lasts until death or until a court order is made which ends the marriage. Not all persons may marry or may marry each other. Certain persons may not marry at all. These are:
- persons who are not of sound mind (that is, insane persons);
- persons below the age of puberty (which in our law means 12 years for girls and 14 years for boys), and
- persons who are already married.

Although children under the age of puberty may not marry at all, people do not have to wait until they are majors† to get married. If boys over the age of 14 but below the age of 18 or girls over the age of 12 but below the age of 15 wish to get married, they have to obtain the permission of their parents and also of the Minister of Home Affairs. Boys over the age of 18 but below the age of 21 may marry if they have their parents' consent, and so may girls over the age of 15 but below the age of 21. If the parents are absent, insane or otherwise not competent to consent, or if there is no parent, the couple wishing to get married may ask the Commissioner of Child Welfare for special permission. If this application is turned down for some reason, or if the parents or one parent unreasonably refuses to consent, the couple may apply to the High Court for permission to marry.

> ### *B v B* 1983 (1) SA 496 (N)
>
> In this case a Muslim girl of 16 asked the Court for permission to marry a 22-year-old man who had converted to Islam. The girl's parents did not want the couple to marry because of their daughter's youth and because they did not want her to marry a convert.
> The Court decided that the parents were unreasonably withholding their consent to the marriage and gave the couple permission to marry.

In South African law, some people may not marry each other:
- persons of the same sex are not allowed to marry each other;
- persons who are too closely related to each other by blood relationship or by a previous marriage also may not marry each other. For

example, a grandfather cannot marry his granddaughter, and an aunt cannot marry her nephew;
- an adoptive parent and his or her adopted child also may not marry each other.

The marriage ceremony may be either civil or religious, but there are some conditions:
- it must be performed by a marriage officer who may be a magistrate, or a minister of a specific religion, for example a Catholic priest or father or a Jewish rabbi;
- the marriage must take place in a church or a building used for religious services or in a public office or private home, with open doors;
- at least two witnesses must be present.

Each person must agree to marry the other (give consent) in the presence of the marriage officer. Usually the man and woman give their consent as part of the marriage ceremony. The marriage officer must ask each of the parties to state that, as far as they know, there is no reason why they should not marry each other. The marriage officer then tells the couple to take each other's right hand and declares that they have been lawfully married.

There are certain consequences which automatically follow after two people get married. These are called the 'invariable consequences of marriage'.

Invariable consequences of civil marriage

When two people marry, certain consequences follow automatically according to South African common law. The law does not allow the couple to change these consequences, which are:
- Neither the husband nor the wife may marry somebody else while in the marriage. It is a crime in South African law to enter into another marriage while the first still exists.
- Because of the marriage there are certain people whom the spouses may not marry after the dissolution of the marriage by divorce or death. For example, the husband may not marry his ex-wife's mother, grandmother, or daughter after the end of the existing marriage.
- The husband can inherit from the wife unless she has made a will† which says that he may not inherit from her. The wife can inherit from her husband unless he has made a will which says that she may not inherit from him.
- If the couple had a child before they were married, the child is considered illegitimate† until the couple get married. Only then does the child become legitimate,† with the result that the parents

both have legal control over the child. Only the mother has legal control while the child is illegitimate.
- If the husband or the wife was younger than 21 years at the time of entering into the marriage, the marriage confers the status of majority† on him or her. This means that he or she becomes an adult in the eyes of the law, and he or she can enter into any contract or litigation† as if he or she were 21 years old.
- While the husband and wife are married, they must provide each other with support – that is, they must help each other to get things such as food, clothing and accommodation. (See further Chapter 3: Support of the household, below.)
- The couple must live together, help each other, be faithful to each other, and have sexual intercourse with each other. However, the duty to have sexual intercourse with each other does not mean that the husband can force the wife to have sex with him. If she says No and he still has sex with her, he can be charged with rape. (See Part Three: Women and violence.)
- If a husband has sexual intercourse with a woman other than his wife, his wife can sue the other woman on the ground of adultery; the husband can do the same if his wife has sexual intercourse with another man.
- A wife cannot be forced to tell the Court anything which her husband told her about what he said or did to somebody or about a crime which he committed. The same applies to things which a wife tells a husband.

Many things about the woman's and the man's position in law are not affected by their marriage. The most important of these are:
- Usually when a woman marries she takes her husband's surname – Miss Khumalo marries Mr Sithebe and becomes Mrs Sithebe. But the law does not force her to do this. If she wishes, the wife can keep her own surname or she can add her husband's surname to her own (that is, she can become Mrs Khumalo-Sithebe if she wishes). If she was married before, she may even keep her previous married name or add it to her husband's surname.
- If a person marries, this does not mean that the will he or she made before the marriage is automatically changed. If, for example, a woman makes a will in which she leaves everything to her brother and then she marries, her brother will inherit everything if she dies and her husband will get nothing. If she wants her husband to inherit from her, she must change her will.
- A wife does not automatically follow her husband's domicile. The law says that your domicile is where you are present and intend to stay indefinitely. When people are married, the domicile of both the husband and wife is usually the place where they live together.

- A wife does not acquire South African citizenship if she marries a South African man and she does not lose her South African citizenship if she marries a foreigner. The same applies to a husband: he does not acquire South African citizenship just because he marries a South African and he does not lose his South African citizenship just because he marries a foreigner.

Remember also the following:
- A husband does not have marital power† over his wife nowadays (as he used to in the past). The wife now has the same legal status† as her husband has.
- The husband is no longer the head of the family. Both spouses together can now decide where the couple must live and what standard of living they must have.

All the above consequences and rights apply where two people marry in a civil court or by church practice.

There are several issues which can arise during marriage that will affect women and the family, and these are the topics covered in this part. They are important during marriage and can even continue after the spouses have been divorced.

Examples of such issues are listed below:

A. During the marriage the spouses may have these problems:
- Which assets are owned by which of the spouses?
- How can a spouse deal with and control her or his assets and/or the spouses' assets?
- Who will control the money affairs of the household?

B. If spouses decide to divorce, they have to think about these problems:
- What happens to the children until the parents are divorced?
- Who will pay maintenance until they are divorced?
- Who will pay the costs which must be paid to the lawyers even before the divorce proceedings commence?

C. When the spouses get divorced, they may be faced with these problems:
- Who has custody of the children?
- Will the other parent be able to see the children (have access)?
- Who will pay maintenance for the children?
- Will maintenance be paid by one spouse to the other?
- How will the assets be divided?
- Who will pay for the costs of the divorce?

How these issues are to be dealt with in a civil marriage will be discussed in chapters 2 to 5.

Before we deal with them, we shall look at other types of marriage which have different rules and legal consequences to civil marriages. We shall concentrate on customary marriage, African civil marriage, Islamic (or Muslim) marriage and foreign marriage. Customary marriages and marriages by religious rites† are not currently recognized as valid marriages according to South African common law, but this may well change in the wake of the new Constitution.

CUSTOMARY MARRIAGE

African people can marry either according to African law and custom or by civil or Christian rites. The requirements and consequences of these types of marriage differ. In our discussion of customary marriages, we focus on the main issues. Customs may vary from area to area. For example, in KwaZulu-Natal the KwaZulu Code of Zulu Law Act 16 of 1985 governs customary marriages. That Code is a written statement of the law. In other areas customary marriages are governed by unwritten laws.

We focus first on the characteristics and requirements, and then on the consequences and the termination (or ending) of customary marriages. Finally, we look at the question of the annulment† of customary marriages.

Characteristics of customary marriage

A feature or characteristic of a customary marriage is its group nature. It concerns more people than just the man and woman getting married: the families of the spouses are also involved in arranging the marriage. For example, members of the families negotiate or decide on the terms of the marriage.†

Lobolo or dowry is another characteristic of a customary marriage. This idea has different names in different African languages (*lobolo*, in Zulu, *bogadi* in Tswana, etc), but in this work we will use the term *lobolo* because it comes from the Code of Zulu Law, which is a written document and which is familiar in South Africa. *Lobolo* consists of the marriage goods that the man and his family give to the family of the bride. Traditionally, cattle were given as *lobolo*, but nowadays it more often takes the form of money. The *lobolo* is a symbol or token of the bridegroom's appreciation for the bride leaving her family to join his. Sometimes the bride is also required to give gifts to the bridegroom's family members or to bring household goods (such as a trousseau and domestic appliances) for the home she will share with the bridegroom.

Another feature of customary marriage is the possibility of a *polygynous* marriage. This means that a man may be married to more than one wife at the same time but women are not allowed to marry more than one husband at a time.

The last characteristic of a customary marriage is its focus on *having children*. If a husband or a wife is not able to have children, a substitute may in some cases be found to have children for the family.

Legal requirements for customary marriage

The different legal requirements for a customary marriage relate to age, blood relationship, spouses from other marriages, consent, *lobolo* and registration. Each of these is explained in more detail below.

Traditionally there were no specific age requirements for a customary marriage. However, the man and woman must at least have reached puberty† before they can marry. In some groups which practise circumcision, young people can marry only after going through the initiation or puberty ceremonies.

Most societies have rules prohibiting marriages between persons related by blood, and this is the same with traditional African societies. These rules vary greatly between the different cultural groups and we cannot deal with them in detail here. In general, though, the Zulu, Xhosa, Swazi and Ndebele do not allow marriage to blood relatives of any kind. In contrast, the Batswana, Basotho and Bapedi consider marriages between cousins desirable. The preferred marriage among these people is one between a man and his mother's brother's daughter (*malome*), his female cousin.

Traditionally the family groups of the bride and bridegroom agreed to the customary marriage. The individual and expressed consent (agreement) of the bride and bridegroom was not essential. This position has since changed as follows:

- The consent of the husband-to-be is required. In addition, if the man is younger than 21, his father must also consent to the marriage.
- The consent of the bride-to-be is required no matter what her age. In KwaZulu-Natal her expressed consent must take the form of a declaration to an official witnesss at the celebration of the customary marriage.
- The consent of the father or guardian of the woman is also required, irrespective of her age.

The giving of *lobolo* by the husband-to-be to the bride's family is an important requirement for the existence of a customary marriage. The customs concerning *lobolo* vary. Among some people, the amount of *lobolo* is decided by custom, among others, the two families decide on the amount of *lobolo*. In urban areas nowadays, the *lobolo* may take the form of money and is negotiated between the families. The status of the bride and her education are important factors in deciding the amount of *lobolo*. Some people require that the full *lobolo* be handed over before the marriage ceremonies can take place. Others require that part be handed over at the time of the marriage ceremonies. The rest can be handed over later, perhaps even years after the marriage ceremonies.

The registration of customary marriages is compulsory in KwaZulu-Natal and the former Transkei. In other parts of South Africa registration is not compulsory. However, registration is strongly recommended because the certificate issued on registration serves as useful proof of the existence of the customary marriage. Proof is often required by officials, employers and institutions – for example when persons apply for loans or pensions. Proof of a customary marriage is also necessary to decide whether a man is liable for the maintenance of his children born of a customary marriage. (See Chapter 3: Support of the household, below.) Registration is also required where a wife and children in a customary marriage claim compensation from a person who has unlawfully caused the death of the husband and father.

Consequences of customary marriage

The consequences of a customary marriage can be divided into personal consequences and property rights, which are explained below.

In terms of customary law the husband becomes head of the family that results from a customary marriage. He is regarded as a major, an adult in the eyes of the law. This means that he has the right to enter into transactions such as buying a motor car or household furniture on his own; he does not need to have his wife's consent. In legal terminology, his ability to enter into such transactions is known as contractual capacity. He can also institute an action† in court or defend a court case governed by customary law.

The position of the wife in a customary marriage differs from that of her husband. In KwaZulu-Natal the Code of Zulu Law regards her as a major too, with full legal capacity to enter into contracts and to institute an action in court. However, she cannot decide on family matters; these must be decided by the husband as head of the family. In all other areas of South Africa (that is, outside of KwaZulu-Natal), the wife of a customary marriage who is living with her husband is regarded as a minor.† This means that she is under the guardianship of her husband. She cannot enter into a contract without the assistance of her husband. She also cannot appear in court without his assistance. Her position is the same as that of a child under the age of 21. (See Chapter 4: Child law, below.)

The contractual capacity of the wife in a customary marriage is therefore limited in comparison to that of her husband. She does not have the same rights as her spouse. In daily life, however, women often buy and sell and enter into many transactions as if they were free to do so. Their husbands may also allow them to do these things. Women should, however, make sure that they do have their husband's consent for important and costly transactions, such as buying a house or a motor car.

Each customary marriage creates a separate property unit,[†] known as a 'house'. In customary law the husband administers all property acquired by him or by his wife or children. Although he has considerable freedom to use and dispose of the house property, custom requires him to consult his wife on important issues. He must, furthermore, use the property for family purposes. If he misuses or wastes the property, the wife should consult her husband's senior family members. However, if a husband disregards the advice of his family, there is almost nothing a wife can do to stop him from administering the family property badly. In such a case she usually requests that her family negotiate with the husband's family.

Termination of customary marriage

It is better not to refer to the dissolution or breakup of a customary marriage as a divorce, since the marriage concerns two families. It is referred to rather as a termination or ending of the marriage. In this section we deal first with the ways in which a customary marriage is dissolved. Then we consider the grounds for and consequences of the breakup of the marriage.

Ways of termination

Customary law allows for the termination of a customary marriage by a court order or by agreement between the two families.

Traditionally, the indigenous[†] courts were not involved in the dissolution of a customary marriage. The courts were approached only when the parties could not agree about what should happen to the *lobolo*. Today, in all areas where the registration of a customary marriage is compulsory (that is, in KwaZulu-Natal and the former Transkei), only a court such as a magistrate's court can terminate a customary marriage.

If the wife leaves and returns to her family, the husband can take legal action against the wife's father or guardian. The husband asks for his wife to return to him or, failing this, the return of the *lobolo* he paid.

The wife and her father can also institute an action against the husband in order to end the customary marriage and to declare forfeiture[†] of the *lobolo*. This means that the husband loses the *lobolo* he paid. In KwaZulu-Natal, the wife's father cannot institute the action without the woman. However, it seems that the wife can institute the action without her father's assistance.

Sometimes, the marriage can be ended outside the court system. In all areas where the registration of a customary marriage is not compulsory, the marriage can be terminated without the interference of the Court. This can be done by mutual agreement between the families. They will also agree about what is to happen to the *lobolo*. There does not have to be a specific ground or reason for ending the marriage, which means that a customary marriage can also be terminated unilaterally†. It follows that the husband can terminate it without consulting his wife. It also means that the wife and her father can initiate the termination of the customary marriage without consulting the husband.

Also, the death of a spouse will affect the marriage. Traditionally, the death of the husband or the wife did not terminate the marital union between the two families. The deceased spouse could be replaced by a family member. For example, if the wife had died, the woman's sister would join the man's family. The woman, however, had a choice whether she wanted to join the man's family; unfortunately, though, the system was sometimes abused and women were forced to join the man's family.

Nowadays it is accepted that the death of the wife in a customary marriage terminates the marital union. The husband cannot claim a substitute for his deceased wife, although her family may supply one. The property of the wife continues to exist as a separate property unit of her family, whether a substitute is provided for her or not.

The death of the husband does not necessarily dissolve the customary marriage. His widow can remain a wife in the household. Should she still be of childbearing age, she can bear children for her deceased husband's family. Those children will be fathered by a male relative of the husband. This custom is generally known as *ukungena*. A widow is not forced to participate in this custom and her consent is required for it. In urban areas many wives are not keen to practise this custom; instead, they choose to terminate the customary marriage unilaterally after the death of their husbands. After their father's death children born during the customary marriage become the wards† of his heir†, who then assumes the same rights of the father. The same applies in respect of children born from the *ukungena* custom. In KwaZulu-Natal, the husband's death ends the customary marriage in terms of the Code of Zulu Law.

If the widow stays in her deceased husband's household but later decides to marry someone from outside the husband's family, the *lobolo* paid for her can be paid to her in-laws instead of the blood family.

Grounds for termination of customary marriage

Traditionally, there were no fixed or established grounds, or reasons, for the termination of a customary marriage. Anyone could unilaterally terminate the marriage, even without reason. Nowadays, the courts recognize the following as grounds that may terminate a customary marriage:
- adultery by the wife, but only where her conduct amounts to repudiation† or makes the marriage impossible;
- intentional or malicious desertion† by the husband or wife;
- refusal to have sexual intercourse.

In KwaZulu-Natal and the former Transkei, if the man or woman is in prison for at least five years, it is also a ground for termination of a customary marriage.

In addition, the wife may terminate the customary marriage on the following grounds:
- severe cruelty or ill-treatment by her husband;
- accusations of witchcraft or other serious allegations† made against her by the husband.

Consequences of termination

A main consequence of the end of a customary marriage is that the personal marital relationship between the spouses is terminated. Further, when the man and the woman got married, a property unit was immediately created, but what happens to this property when the marriage ends? Usually there are also children of the marriage: what happens to them? There is also the question of what happens to the *lobolo*. We address these questions separately below.

Because of the polygynous nature of the customary marriage, the husband's status is not seriously affected if his customary marriage is terminated. He remains a major with full legal capacity.

On termination of the customary marriage, the position of a wife, however, does change. She is no longer under the guardianship of her husband. If she is 21 years of age or older, she becomes a major. (Remember that in KwaZulu-Natal she becomes a major on entering into a customary marriage, so termination of her marriage does not affect her legal status in that province.)

Traditionally, the children remained members of the household established by the customary marriage. Although infants were allowed to accompany their mother to her family, they were expected to return to their father's family when they were about eight years old. This position has changed in recent times.

In KwaZulu-Natal the Code of Zulu Law provides that the children fall under the guardianship of the husband. The Court may, however, make an order regarding their custody† and maintenance. The court may, for example, place the children under the custody of their mother. This would be the case when a husband, for example, fails to provide support for the family, or where he is violent, or a chronic alcoholic.

Elsewhere in South Africa, the parents themselves may agree on the arrangements that should be made for the children. Where they cannot come to an agreement, the Court can be approached to make an order. The Courts have accepted the principle that the children belong to the husband's family. However, on the basis of the children's best interests the Court can make a different order about their custody and maintenance. Where the custody of a child is taken from the father, he still retains all other rights in respect of that child, for example, the right to the *lobolo* for his daughter

The house, as the property unit that was established when the customary marriage began, continues to exist after termination of a customary marriage. The children are maintained from this unit. The wife, however, loses all the rights and powers she had in respect of house property. She also cannot claim maintenance from house property. (See Chapter 3: Support of the household, below.)

There are also consequences with regard to *lobolo*. You will recall that *lobolo* is given by the husband to the wife's family. The *lobolo* does not become part of the property unit established by the customary marriage, because it was given to the wife's family. The *lobolo* is therefore either returned to the husband or forfeited by him, depending on who is to blame for the breakdown of the marriage. In some cases, only part of the *lobolo* is returned to the husband. The following factors are taken into account when deciding what should happen to the *lobolo*:
- the amount of blame on either side;
- the number of children born, especially sons, and
- the portion of *lobolo* already delivered.

The person who is to blame for the breakdown of the customary marriage forfeits the *lobolo*. Therefore, where the husband is to blame, the *lobolo* remains with the wife's parents. In the days when *lobolo* took the form of cattle, it was customary to return at least one beast to the husband. This was to prove the end of the marriage because there would be no termination of the marriage if the wife's family kept all the *lobolo*. If the husband has not delivered all the *lobolo* by the time the marriage is dissolved, he still owes the outstanding part.

Where the wife is to blame for the breakdown of the customary marriage, her family should return the *lobolo* to the husband. However, certain deductions are allowed. At least one beast is allowed for every child of the wife, even if the child was not born alive. If the wife has had more children than the number of *lobolo* cattle, at least one beast should be returned to the husband as proof of the dissolution. Usually, the duration of the customary marriage is also an important consideration when deciding how many cattle must be returned to the husband. If the marriage has lasted a long time, then only one beast is returned to the husband as proof of the end of the union.

If the parties cannot agree about the *lobolo*, the Court may be approached for a ruling. In such a case the Court is not being asked to dissolve the marriage; it merely has to decide about the *lobolo*.

Annulment of customary marriage

At present the Code of Zulu Law expressly provides for the annulment of a customary marriage in KwaZulu-Natal. The following grounds are prescribed:
- Insanity of one spouse at the time of the celebration of the marriage. The other spouse must have been unaware of the insanity and must institute the action within a reasonable time after the celebration.
- Impotence† or another permanent physical defect preventing consummation† of the marriage. This means that the man or woman is not physically able to have sexual intercourse.
- The wife was a spouse in another customary or civil marriage at the time of the celebration of the customary marriage.
- The customary marriage did not meet the prescribed legal requirements stipulated in the Code of Zulu Law.

In the cases mentioned above, the customary marriage will be annulled. This means that the marriage did not exist.

AFRICAN CIVIL MARRIAGE

Since 2 December 1988 an African civil marriage in South Africa has had the same legal consequences as any other civil marriage in the country. (In this work, we are not going into the complex legal position that existed before this date.)

Africans wishing to enter into a civil marriage must meet the general legal requirements for civil marriage. The following additional requirements apply:
- A man and a woman married to one another in a customary marriage may marry each other in a civil marriage.
- A man who wants to enter into a civil marriage must make a declaration to the marriage officer stating that he is not a spouse in an existing customary marriage with another woman.
- A man or a woman married in terms of customary law may not enter into a civil marriage unless the customary marriage is first dissolved or unless the man or woman marries his or her spouse in the customary marriage.

Lobolo within an African civil marriage

Lobolo can also be given when Africans enter into civil marriages, but the giving of *lobolo* is not a requirement for the validity of the civil marriage. In this way the traditions of customary marriages are continued in civil marriages, too. Thus the civil marriage acquires a dual or double validity: it is valid in terms of traditional customs and in terms of modern law. Traditionally, the main purpose of *lobolo* was to provide security for the woman in case her marriage should end due to her husband's fault. The cattle given as *lobolo* would be kept with her father's herd but would be considered to be hers. If the marriage was terminated due to the husband's fault, he would not get the cattle back and the woman would return to her blood family. She would then be supported by the proceeds of 'her' cattle. Nowadays *lobolo* often takes the form of money and, unfortunately, the money is not kept apart for use in the event that the marriage ends through the husband's fault. It is often used up quickly by her parents.

The relation between the African civil marriage and *lobolo* is one of potential conflict. A civil marriage is primarily a union between the husband and wife as individuals. On the other hand, *lobolo* is a concern of the two family groups, and especially affects the family of the wife as the receivers and beneficiaries of *lobolo*. *Lobolo* therefore gives the wife's family an interest in the civil marriage, which means that the civil marriage is not a matter merely between two individuals.

There are several other issues regarding *lobolo* in African civil marriages. First, *lobolo* is recognized by law as not being opposed to the principles of public policy or natural justice. This implies that the courts have to recognize *lobolo*, even in a civil marriage. The viewpoint of the civil courts is that a *lobolo* agreement is peculiar to indigenous law and is consequently governed by indigenous law. Yet *lobolo* itself is regarded as supplementary to the civil marriage and consequently subject to the principles governing the civil marriage. In cases of conflict the demands of the civil marriage enjoy priority over any rights and duties anyone may have in respect of a *lobolo* agreement.

Since *lobolo* is regarded as supplementary to the civil marriage, it has no effect on the validity of the marriage. This means that the civil marriage is valid whether *lobolo* has been given or not. Where the bride is a minor and her father's or guardian's consent is necessary for the civil marriage, he cannot make his consent subject to a *lobolo* agreement.

Lobolo also requires an express agreement between the people involved. This means that a *lobolo* agreement cannot be implied or assumed merely because the people involved are Africans.

Termination of marriage and custody of children

When Africans in a civil marriage divorce, the dissolution of the marriage is considered separately from the *lobolo* agreement – the Court does not decide the question of *lobolo*. If the husband wants the return of the *lobolo* or part of it, he has to claim it in a magistrate's court.

Traditionally, *lobolo* played an important role in regard to the guardianship of children: the children used to belong to the family who gave the *lobolo* – that is, to the husband's family. Children of a woman with no *lobolo* belonged to her family. In civil marriages, on the other hand, the Courts have decided that the guardianship and custody of the children are decided by common law and not by indigenous law. This means that in a civil marriage *lobolo* does not decide the guardianship or custody of children born to the wife.

In conclusion, it should be noted that the African civil marriage is a blend of different cultures: customary marriage traditions and common-law rights. Many of the customs and traditions of different cultures can be mixed well in order to create a beautiful and meaningful wedding ceremony and married life. Many customs are very similar. For example, in many European cultures, a similar idea to *lobolo* is that of a dowry. In this case the woman is given gifts by the man she will marry. Sometimes this dowry is a diamond engagement ring; sometimes other gifts. In the Middle East, the woman often receives gifts in the form of gold jewellery from the man and his family.

ISLAMIC MARRIAGE

Muslim family law is part of a system of Islamic law (*Sharia*) based on religion. In South Africa, however, a marriage concluded according to a system of religious law only is not recognized as valid. For the marriage to be valid, it also has to be concluded according to the requirements of South African civil law. Marriages in accordance with Islamic law are denied recognition in South Africa on the ground that they are not celebrated in terms of the Marriage Act 25 of 1961 and because they are actually, or potentially, polygynous.

In Islam, the law is based on the Holy Koran (or Quran). The Holy Koran consists of the exact words of Almighty God, Allah. Apart from being a collection of the practices and traditions of the prophet Mohammed, the Koran contains the commandments which govern all aspects of a Muslim's life.

In South Africa there are many people, especially from the Indian and so-called coloured population, who believe in and follow Islam. While Islamic law, including its marriage law, is not legally recognized in South Africa, the followers of Islam are not forbidden to live according to the rules of Islamic law, and many do so. Many female Muslims therefore obey the rules of Islamic law. In this section we look only at the Islamic laws of marriage.

Requirements for Islamic marriage

Before Muslims marry, they enter into a betrothal, which is the same as an engagement in other cultures. In other words, the betrothal is a promise by a man and a woman to marry each other in the future. The betrothal takes place when the man offers to marry the woman and the woman (or somebody who is legally entitled to act on her behalf, such as her father) accepts the offer. Offer and acceptance must take place at the same meeting.

After the betrothal comes the marriage. According to Islamic law, marriage is a contract, but the contract does not have to be in writing. A marriage ceremony must take place and two witnesses must be present at the ceremony. Both the future husband and the future wife must consent to the marriage and both of them must have the capacity to act. They do not, however, have to be adults; minors who have reached puberty may marry with the consent of their parents.

People who are within certain relationships may not marry each other. These prohibitions can be either permanent or temporary. The permanent prohibitions of marriage are based on three grounds: kindred, affinity and fosterage† relationships.

- Kindred or blood relationship: if the man and woman are related by blood, they cannot marry.
- Affinity relationship: if the man and woman are related to each other by marriage, they cannot marry.
- Fosterage relationship: the man and woman cannot marry if they are connected by a foster relationship.

Temporary prohibitions arise only because of the special circumstances in which the parties find themselves, and if the situation changes, the two people can marry. An example of a temporary impediment† is where a man who has four wives wants to marry another woman. He cannot do so because of the Islamic rule that a man may not have more than four wives at any one time. If one of his wives dies, however, the temporary prohibition ends and he may marry another woman.

In Islamic custom, marriage is compulsory for a man if the following conditions are met:
- he has the money to pay the dowry for a wife and to support a wife and children;
- he is healthy;
- he may be tempted to have sexual intercourse outside of marriage if he does not marry (extramarital sexual intercourse is against the beliefs of Islam).

On the other hand, marriage is forbidden for a man who cannot maintain a wife and children or who suffers from a serious illness. It is undesirable, although not forbidden, for a man to marry if he has no sexual desire, if he does not love children, or if it will cause him to forget some of his religious duties.

The spouses may enter into an agreement before the marriage in which they agree on some of the consequences of marriage, particularly matters which they think are important for the regulation of their future relations. Such agreements form part of their marriage contract.†

Consequences of Islamic marriage

An Islamic marriage is automatically out of community of property. This means that the husband and wife keep their own property and do not share in each other's property.

The most important legal rights which marriage creates between the spouses are those of mutual inheritance, the bride price (*mahr*), support or maintenance, and obedience. They are discussed briefly below.

- Inheritance: when one spouse dies, the other spouse is entitled to receive a part of the deceased's assets.
- *Mahr*: to give the wife financial security, the husband must pay her a reasonable amount (depending on the agreement between the two parties) as dowry. The dowry is a sum of money or other property which becomes payable by the husband to the wife as a consequence of marriage. The dowry then becomes the wife's property. (Note that it is different from *lobolo* in African customary marriages because the dowry belongs to the wife, not to her family.)
- Maintenance: there is an obligation on the husband to give the wife housing, food and clothing as soon as she moves into his house.
- Obedience: obedience is a right which the husband can demand of the wife; he undertakes to maintain her and she has to be obedient. She does not, however, have to obey him if what he asks her to do is against Allah's laws, because obedience to Allah comes first.

Having children is considered to be one of the aims of marriage in Islam, and birth control is usually forbidden because it is said to amount to losing one's trust and faith in Allah. Islam forbids abortion completely in family planning, and it is considered a crime. (The issues of birth control and abortion under South African law are discussed in more detail below in Part Five: Women and health.)

Dissolution of Islamic marriage

An Islamic marriage comes to an end when one of the spouses dies. It can also come to an end through divorce. As was pointed out above, marriage in Islam is a contract. If this contract does not work, it can be revoked by way of divorce. The divorce may be given orally or in writing, but it must happen in the presence of witnesses. The divorce takes place in the following ways:

- by way of repudiation by the husband (*talaq*);
- by agreement between the husband and wife, or
- by a judicial order†.

Divorce at the request of the wife (*khule*) is allowed if the wife has provided for this right in the original marriage contract. If she has not done so, she can still divorce her husband, but only on limited grounds and she may lose her dowry.

If the divorce takes the form of repudiation by the husband, then he must exercise his right of repudiation on three successive occasions before the divorce becomes final. Before that, the divorce is still revocable[†] and the husband may resume the marital relationship with his wife even without her consent.

After divorce, the husband must pay maintenance for his former wife for three months, or if she is pregnant, until the child has been born. For his sons born of the marriage, he must pay maintenance until they reach majority and for his daughters until they marry.

The father has guardianship of his children even after divorce. A different rule applies in respect of custody. The mother has custody of her sons until they reach the age of seven and of her daughters until they reach puberty. Thereafter, custody passes to the father.

The wife may not marry again for a certain period after the dissolution of her marriage by divorce or death. This waiting period is called the *iddat*. A child born during the *iddat* is the child of the former husband. If either former spouse dies during this period, the other former spouse inherits from him or her.

South African law

The fact that South African law does not recognize Islamic marriage causes a number of problems. We discuss only a few of them here. The reasons for non-recognition are that the man and woman do not marry in accordance with the formal requirements of the Marriage Act and because the Islamic marriage law permits polygyny.

South African law provides that an Islamic marriage is void and has no consequences in law – it is as if the parties were unmarried. The wife does not have a claim for financial support (see Chapter 3: Support of the household, below), she has no right to claim any property from her husband, and she cannot inherit from him unless she is a beneficiary in his will. In terms of a very recent change to our law, brought about by a 1996 amendment to the Births and Deaths Registration Act 51 of 1992, the children born from the marriage are registered as legitimate (see Chapter 4: Child law, below, on the difference between legitimate and illegitimate children). Until the amendment became law, children born from a Muslim marriage were registered as illegitimate because their parents' marriage is not recognized. However, it should be noted that in 1997 one division of the High Court (the Cape Provincial Division)[‡] decided to recognize the Islamic conse-

---

[‡] *Ryland v Edros* 1997 (2) SA 690 (C)

quences of a Muslim marriage in which the husband had only one wife. The wife was therefore able to claim, amongst other things, maintenance from her husband after divorce. It is very important to remember that, at present, this recognition operates only in the Western Cape. The general rule of South African law still is that Muslim marriages are not recognized and no consequences (either in common law or Islamic law) are attached to them by the courts.

In certain circumstances, South African law does attach some consequences to an Islamic marriage, though. This is when the marriage qualifies as a putative marriage.† A putative marriage is therefore an exception to the rule which says that a void marriage does not have the ordinary consequences of a marriage. To be a putative marriage, two requirements must be met. The first requirement is that one or both of the parties must, at the time of the marriage, be unaware of the fact that their marriage is void, and must believe in good faith (*bona fide*) that they are lawfully married. The other requirement is that some kind of ceremony must have taken place.

Although the putative marriage is void from the time concluded, it has some of the legal consequences of a valid marriage. The Court may not, however, declare a putative marriage to be a valid marriage – it can only declare that the relationship is a putative marriage and that the law attaches certain consequences to it. These consequences apply from the date of the marriage until both parties discover that their marriage is invalid.

If both parties were *bona fide* at the time when the marriage was entered into and they married without an antenuptial contract† in which community of property† was excluded, the marriage is regarded as being in community of property. If only one of the couple was *bona fide*, the marriage will be regarded as being in community of property if this will benefit the *bona fide* party. If the marriage was by antenuptial contract, the marriage will be regarded as being out of community of property† if both parties were *bona fide* or if this will benefit the *bona fide* party.

MOOLA V AULSEBROOK 1983 (1) SA 687 (N)

In this case a man and a woman were married according to Islamic rites. They did not know that their marriage was invalid because it was not contracted according to the requirements of South African law. The couple had seven children. After the husband's death, the wife asked the Court to state that her marriage was a putative marriage.

The Court did so and also decided that the children born of the marriage were legitimate.

In addition, the children born of a putative marriage are automatically legitimate.

In a number of ways, the Bill of Rights in the 1996 Constitution can perhaps help Muslims to have their marriages recognized as valid. First, the Constitution permits Parliament to enact laws which will recognize marriages concluded under different systems of religious law. If such legislation is passed, marriages celebrated under Islamic law may be covered in the legislation and they will then be valid. Secondly, even if such legislation is not passed, Muslims can try to have their marriages recognized by relying on the guarantee of freedom of religion contained in the Bill of Rights. Thirdly, Muslims may rely on the clause which forbids discrimination on the ground of culture as it can be argued that polygyny is part of Muslim culture and should therefore be protected. On the other hand, however, it can be argued that polygyny discriminates against women and because the Bill of Rights forbids discrimination based on sex, Islamic marriages should not be recognized. This problem will have to be decided by the Courts in future. (See Chapter 20: Women and the Constitution, below.)

FOREIGN MARRIAGE

Many marriages in South Africa are between persons who are not South African citizens or are not permanently resident in South Africa at the time of the marriage. A South African may marry someone from another country who is visiting South Africa, or a South African may marry someone else in another country. The possibility therefore exists that, if they decide to divorce, another legal system may be applied to decide what portion of the estate the husband and wife will each receive.

> ### SPERLING V SPERLING 1975 (3) SA 707 (A)
>
> In this case a couple had married in Germany without having entered into an antenuptial contract. Thereafter they emigrated to South Africa. On their divorce in South Africa the question arose whether they were married in or out of community of property.
>
> The Court decided that, because the husband was domiciled in Germany when the couple married, German law had to be applied to determine how the couple were married. German law says that all marriages are automatically out of community of property unless the spouses have an antenuptial contract, and therefore, the couple were deemed to have been married out of community of property.

The general rule in South Africa is that, if there is no antenuptial contract, the property rights of the husband and wife will be determined once and for all by the law of the husband's domicile at the date of the marriage. For example, if a man whose domicile is in South Africa marries a woman from the United States, the laws of South Africa apply. But if a South African woman marries a man whose domicile is Zambia, the Zambian laws apply. There are exceptions to this rule, but they will not be discussed in this work.

If an antenuptial contract was drawn up at the time of marriage, the terms of that contract regarding the applicable law will apply.

Cohabitation (living together)

The last type of relationship dealt with in this chapter is cohabitation. The word 'cohabitation' is one of many words that are used for a relationship where a couple simply live together without getting married in a marriage ceremony prescribed by law. Other words or phrases which we might use for such a relationship include 'living together', 'live-in relationship', 'shacking-up', 'common-law marriage', 'concubinage', 'extra-marital cohabitation', 'unmarried partnership', and 'private or free marriage'. However, for the purposes of our discussion, we use the most common terms, namely 'cohabitation' and 'living together'.

Traditionally, cohabitation was defined as the relationship between a man and a woman who simply live together as husband and wife but who do not officially marry because they do not wish to or are not allowed to marry for some reason. A more modern definition describes cohabitation as the relationship of two people who live together as a couple because they do not wish to or are not allowed to marry. In an increasingly liberal society, this definition is perhaps more correct for it not only refers to the living together of a man and a woman, but is wide enough to include the living together of two men or two women.

In this discussion of cohabitation, we are not talking about two people living together in a casual affair or roommate situation, but rather about couples living together in a stable and long-term relationship similar to that of marriage.

People live together for different reasons. Some do not wish to marry, while others are not allowed to marry according to the law. When partners are asked why they do not wish to marry, they often give the following reasons:

- 'We regard our living together as a trial marriage.'
- 'Living together is the only relationship which offers freedom and equality.'

- 'My previous marriage failed and ended in divorce. Emotionally I am terrified of making another mistake and afraid of another divorce.'

Another category of partners living together are those who are, according to the law, not allowed to marry for one of the following reasons:
- one or both of the partners may be under age (too young) and unable to marry without their parents' consent, and their parents will not consent to their marrying;
- one or both partners may still be married to someone else and therefore not be allowed to marry again until they are divorced;
- the partners are of the same sex.

Thirty or 40 years ago very few people lived together outside marriage. It was considered immoral to 'live together in sin'. However, cohabitation relationships have increased in the past few decades. All round the world, societies have changed their attitudes towards cohabitation. Even in South Africa (traditionally seen as a very conservative society), disapproval of these relationships has decreased.

Cohabitation and the law

The dramatic changes in societies' attitudes have led many countries to give legal recognition and protection to cohabitation relationships. The position in South Africa is different. Despite increasing acceptance by society and tolerance by the law, cohabitation outside marriage is still not recognized or protected by South African law. Therefore we must ask: what is the position of the partners in a cohabitation relationship and what is the legal position of their children?

Before discussing the consequences of a cohabitation relationship for the partners, it would be sensible to look again at some of the consequences of marriage. (See the introduction to this section and the section on the invariable consequences of marriage above, and Chapter 2: Financial inequality, below.)

Remember that the law in South Africa regards marriage as the foundation of family life and the foundation of the State itself. Therefore marriage is recognized by law and automatically has certain legal consequences. For example:
- Reciprocal rights and duties† flow from a marriage. The husband and wife are required by law to be faithful to each other, to give each other company and support, to have sexual intercourse with each other and to support one another financially.
- Husband and wife have a right to inherit from each other.
- Children born of the marriage are legitimate (see Chapter 4: Child law, below).

- The property and assets can be divided by the Court in the case of divorce.
- The spouses have a right to share in each other's future pension benefits, even in the case of divorce.
- Each has the right to claim maintenance from the estate of the other if the marriage is ended by death (see Chapter 3: Support of the household, below).

Since South African law does not recognize a cohabitation relationship as a marriage (no matter how long partners live together), cohabitation does not have any of these legal consequences, that is, partners living together have none of the rights and duties that flow from a legal marriage.

This attitude of the law towards cohabitation may result in serious practical problems not only during the relationship, but also if and when the relationship breaks up, or when the relationship is ended by the death of one of the partners. Let us investigate some of the problems which could face partners in these different phases of their cohabitation relationship.

During the relationship:
- Partners do not have the right to each other's company, support and faithfulness, as in the case of a married couple.
- Since a duty of financial support does not exist, partners in a cohabitation relationship are not obliged to support each other even if one of them is injured or if one becomes seriously ill. (See the section on protection in a cohabitation relationship below.)

When the relationship breaks up:
- Partners do not have a right to maintenance after the relationship has broken up.
- When the partners break up, there is no equal division of property and assets by a court of law. For example, if one partner pays all the day-to-day living expenses and the other partner buys the furniture, the furniture will belong to the one who bought it and the other partner will have no right to compensation for any expenses. (See the section on protection in a cohabitation relationship below.)
- Partners do not have a right to share in each other's future pension benefits (unless specifically chosen by the partner).

When the relationship is ended by death:
- Neither partner has an automatic right to inherit from the other. He or she will inherit only if named as heir in the other's will. If one partner dies without leaving a will, the other partner will inherit nothing.
- If one of the partners dies, the other partner has no claim for maintenance from the estate of the deceased.

- If one partner is killed at the hands of a third party, the other partner has no right to sue the third party for damages.

Although we have said that in general the law does not recognize cohabitation relationships, in some exceptional cases, partners who live together are not entirely ignored by the law. For example, in terms of the Compensation for Occupational Injuries and Diseases Act 130 of 1993, and the Prevention of Family Violence Act 133 of 1993, the definitions of 'dependant' and 'parties to a marriage' are so wide that they may also include a partner in a cohabitation relationship.

Partners, their children and the law

Children born of a cohabitation relationship are illegitimate as they are born of parents who are not married to each other. These children remain illegitimate unless the partners marry each other. Because the children are illegitimate, only the mother has legal control (parental authority) over them, even if the father admits that he is their biological father (see Chapter 4: Child law, below).

If the relationship breaks up, the mother still has parental authority over the children and remains their only custodian and guardian. The father has no legal rights with regard to the children unless the Court gives him rights. Even if he is given no rights he still has to support the children financially. Many people view this position as unfair and it may be attacked as unconstitutional.

Protection in a cohabitation relationship

Because the law does not give much protection to them, partners living together may attempt to protect themselves and their interests by several methods. These include sensible planning before entering into a cohabitation relationship, drawing up a cohabitation contract, drafting a will and obtaining legal advice.

Sensible planning before entering into the relationship is very important. It is suggested that the cohabiting partners should try to improve their legal situation by making fair arrangements about the financial and other consequences of their relationship because the partners know their own circumstances best. The following aspects of their relationship should be formalized:
- living arrangements and household tasks (such as laundry, cooking);
- the sharing of day-to-day expenses (such as buying food, paying bills);
- the making of major purchases (such as a car, major appliances);
- insurance;
- renting and buying property;

- having children;
- making a will or wills.

One possibility would be to draw up a cohabitation contract. This would be especially important in the case where only one of the partners is gainfully employed. The planning of a cohabitation relationship can be very complex and we advise partners who are living together or who are thinking of living together to seek legal advice if they want to plan their cohabitation relationship sensibly.

A cohabitation contract

A cohabitation contract is a written agreement between partners who are already living together or are planning to live together which clarifies their financial arrangements (money matters) and other matters and states what will happen if their relationship ends. In the absence of the regulation of their relationship by law, the cohabitation contract gives the partners an opportunity to establish their own rules when they enter into such a relationship.

The contract should be acceptable to both parties. It should be in writing and be signed by both parties and witnesses. The contract is ended if the partners marry each other. In general, the most important matters to consider in such a contract are as follows:
- income and expenditure;
- how expenses are to be divided – equally or *pro rata*[†];
- how property and assets are to be owned – together or separately;
- how property and assets are to be divided if the relationship ends;
- provision for the payment of maintenance if the relationship ends;
- the payment of future pension benefits to a partner if the relationship ends;
- an agreement that the father will have reasonable access to the children if the relationship ends.

When it comes to drawing up the cohabitation contract, we also advise partners to obtain legal advice. Often a home-made contract will not satisfy the requirements of the law and will therefore be unenforceable. That is, its contents may be incapable of being enforced by a court of law. This will be the case, for instance, if the contract, or any aspect of it, is contrary to public morals, for example if it rewards extramarital sexual services (the so-called 'money-for-sex' contracts).

Drafting of a valid will

The partners in a cohabitation relationship should have valid wills drawn up to ensure that their partners receive some benefit after their death. If a valid will is left in which a partner is named as heir, the estate will be settled according to the deceased's wishes. However, a partner must bear in mind that a will can be changed at any time without his or her consent or knowledge, so even this option does not guarantee complete security.

Conclusion

South African law regards marriage as the foundation of family life and hence the foundation of the State itself. Therefore the law regulates marriage and its consequences and ignores the cohabitation relationship. Our law still takes the view that a couple has a choice whether to get married or not. If they choose not to, they also choose not to be protected by the law and must suffer the consequences. It is therefore vital that cohabitants should create protection for themselves.

Case Study: Sarah, Johannes and Jantjie

Sarah had never been happy from the day she got married. She was too young – only 18 – when she and Johannes decided to marry. He was handsome and dashing – a fast talker and a fast driver. In fact, even the decision to get married was taken at a fast pace. He proposed one Saturday and three weeks later they were married in the magistrate's court in Cape Town. Sarah changed jobs and went to work for a business, who, because they had knowledge of these things, advised her to make a will, helped her with her insurance and so forth. In her will, Sarah left everything she owned to her husband. But it quickly became clear that Sarah had made a mistake. Not only was Johannes 'fast', he also slept around, drank too much and had a violent temper.

Life became intolerable for Sarah. By the time she had been beaten up for the fourth time, she decided to move out. She approached her employers, and before long she was divorced from Johannes. Johannes threatened her with violence, harassed her at work and even threatened her boss. Sarah realized that she had to get out of Cape Town and move somewhere where her violent former husband could not find her.

Armed with the good reference, she found employment in the town of Petrusberg as manager of a supermarket. After two years, she met the marketing manager of a local farming co-operative and before long she was head over heels in love. She knew that she never wanted to risk marrying again and when Jantjie (her new boyfriend) asked her to move in with him, she accepted on the condition that they would never discuss the prospect of marriage.

The years passed and the new couple prospered. From their joint funds they were able to put down a substantial deposit for a house. They bought themselves a car and spent a lot of time and money beautifying and furnishing their new home.

And then it happened. One night on her way home from the supermarket, a farm truck pulled out in front of Sarah and she was killed instantly.

Jantjie was beside himself with grief – he had lost the most important person in his life. But he was in for another shock when a lawyer advised him that everything that Sarah had contributed to their home had to be given to Johannes, whom they had traced to a prison in Grahamstown. It was then that the tragic truth struck home: he and Sarah had never consulted an attorney on the legal consequences of being in a cohabitation relationship. Sarah's original will, insurance policies, etc had never been changed.

In Sarah's determination never to be hurt again, and in Jantjie's determination to ensure that the painful subject was never brought up, they had both neglected to pay adequate attention to the consequences of the law.

What could Sarah have done?

She could have:
- drafted a new will
- named new beneficiaries of her insurance policies
- drawn up a cohabitation contract with Jantjie.

CHAPTER TWO:
Financial inequality: husbands and wives

Introduction

During marriage most women are financially dependent on their husbands, who also control the money. In many cases, wives stay at home, earning no income. If they stay at home, they are usually so busy with their domestic duties and raising the children that they find no time to learn skills that can help them to earn an income outside the home. Those who do work outside the home often have lower-paid, part-time or temporary jobs as office helpers, shop workers, and so on. These jobs offer very little or no opportunity to acquire what is termed 'new property', that is, pension interests†, gratuities† and other job-related benefits. For many people, especially those who cannot afford to buy expensive assets such as houses, cars and shares, these job-related benefits form the biggest part of their estate†. But because of the jobs they have or because they are housewives, women do not have access to these benefits. Many women who work outside the home also earn much less than their husbands because of the types of jobs they have.

As a result of these problems, women in this position do not usually have the money to acquire assets. If the marriage ends, the wife who has stayed at home usually finds that she is left with no assets, no money and very few skills that she can use to earn an income. She may also discover that there is little help to be found from the State, because South Africa does not have a properly developed social security system.

Another problem for working women is the unequal distribution of domestic burdens. Even though these women work outside the home, they must often still perform all or most of the household chores. This places a double burden on them: they are economically active, meaning that they must work in order to make money *and* they must also bear the full burden of domestic duties.

The problems referred to above are not unique to married women. In many cases, single mothers experience these problems even more acutely, whether they were never married or are divorced or widowed; but in this chapter we focus only on the position of women who were or are in a civil marriage. In it we set out the rules regarding the financial aspects of a civil marriage and divorce. We also explain how a husband and wife can deal with the assets that they possess at the time of entering into the marriage and those that they acquire during the existence of the marriage. We further explain how the spouses' assets are divided when the civil marriage comes to an end. In the chapter that follows (Chapter 3: Support of the household, below) we explain how a woman can claim support from her husband, both during the marriage and after the marriage has ended.(For a discussion of cohabitation relationships, see Chapter 1, above.)

It is very important for a woman to know these rules, particularly the rules regarding divorce, even before entering into marriage, because the type of marital arrangement she agrees to will affect her for the rest of her life. In particular, if a woman knows what the law says she should get, then she is better prepared to demand from her husband what is rightfully hers. Also, in this situation, she will not – as so often happens – accept a divorce settlement that leaves her with nothing or very little when she is clearly entitled to more.

When two people decide to marry, they make some very important choices, in some cases without even being aware of the far-reaching consequences of those choices. One example is the choice of what we call the matrimonial property system.[†] This determines exactly how the marriage affects the financial position of each marriage partner.

Matrimonial property systems

The choice of a matrimonial property system is one of the most important financial decisions a wife-to-be makes in her life. It is therefore essential to inform a woman about the different matrimonial property systems available and their consequences – *prior* to marriage.

When we speak of matrimonial property systems, we mean the set of legal rules regulating the financial position of a married couple. Different matrimonial property systems exist in our law. Each leads to a different type of marriage. Couples getting married are free to choose the system that they want to apply to their marriage. While the marriage exists, the rules of the chosen system will apply and determine the financial position of both husband and wife. The rules of the system also determine how the property of the spouses will be divided between them when the marriage ends through death or divorce. This has a major (and potentially ruinous) influence on the financial position of each spouse after the dissolution of the marriage.

In legal parlance, matrimonial property refers to property in its broadest sense, including the following:
1. All the possessions or assets of economic value such as:
    (a) money, investments, goods and fixed property, and

(b) debts owed to each of the spouses.
2. All debts† owed by each of the spouses.

The rules of a matrimonial property system therefore deal with the assets (what you own) and liabilities (what you owe) of the two people in the marriage. These rules determine the following:
- who the assets belong to during the marriage;
- how and by whom assets can be dealt with while the marriage exists;
- who is entitled to the assets when the marriage comes to an end;
- who can incur debts while the marriage exists (and how one incurs those debts);
- who is liable† and can be sued for such debts, both during and after a marriage.

There are three basic matrimonial property systems:
1. community of property: in South African law, the natural consequence of a marriage (for which no antenuptial contract is necessary);
2. the accrual system: a marriage 'out of community of property' but subject to accrual sharing; and
3. complete separation of property (sometimes called the exclusionary system): where the antenuptial contract specifically excludes community of property and the accrual system.

The main implications of each of these matrimonial property systems for the financial position of the spouses, both during the existence of the marriage and when the marriage ends, are explained in more detail below.

COMMUNITY OF PROPERTY

Community of property is the natural consequence of a marriage. That is, all marriages are in community of property unless the spouses enter into a valid antenuptial contract. An antenuptial contract is an agreement between parties getting married in which they make financial arrangements for their marriage. In this contract, community of property can specifically be excluded from the future marriage.

The phrase 'antenuptial' means 'before the marriage'. An antenuptial contract is therefore one that has to be made prior to the marriage, and it has to be executed and registered by an attorney who is also required to be a registered notary. (Not all attorneys are notaries.) When spouses conclude such a contract, they exclude community of property and opt for either the accrual system or complete separation of property, both of which are called marriages 'out of community of property'.

During the marriage

When two people marry in community of property, all the assets and liabilities that either has when they marry, as well as all the assets and liabilities that either acquires during the marriage, become their joint property for as long as the marriage lasts.

The joint property of the spouses is known as a common or joint estate and is made up of their joint assets and liabilities. The joint estate belongs to both spouses during the marriage: jointly and in equal shares. The same applies to all liabilities: all debts incurred by either party have to be paid from the joint estate. As a consequence, when the debts of the estate are greater than the sum total of the assets, the joint estate is bankrupt and both parties to the marriage are declared insolvent.

While the marriage lasts, the joint estate is seen as a single entity and is not divided between the marriage partners. It is only when the marriage is ended by either death or divorce that the estate is divided between them.

The rule that all assets and liabilities of either spouse form part of the joint estate does not always apply, however. Exceptions apply to certain types of assets that remain or become the property of only the person who acquires them and which therefore do not form part of the joint estate. Such assets are referred to as separate property and include the following:

- assets which the spouses, in an antenuptial contract, agree to exclude from the joint estate;
- property donated to or inherited by one of the spouses and expressly excluded from the joint estate by the donor or testator[†];
- certain assets excluded from any joint estate by various laws of Parliament, such as amounts which are excluded from the joint estate by the Matrimonial Property Act 88 of 1984.

Separate property belongs to one spouse only and can be dealt with by that spouse alone in any way seen fit during and after the marriage. For example, the wife can decide what to do with her separate assets, to buy, sell, lease, save, invest, use them for security, or dispose of them in any manner.

Exceptions apply similarly to certain debts incurred by either of the parties to a marriage which do not fall into the joint estate but which have to be paid for from the separate property of that spouse. Such debts include:

1. debts incurred by a spouse in regard to her own separate property; and
2. damages that have to be paid to a third party by a spouse as result of a wrongful act (that is, an act causing loss to another) committed by him or her.

The following example illustrates what falls into the joint estate:

Anne and Bruce get married in community of property. At the time when they marry, Anne has no debts and she owns a car worth R30 000. Bruce, on the other hand, has debts of R15 000 and has no assets. During their (very short) marriage, Anne inherits a house from her father. Her father stated in his will that the house must not become part of the joint estate. During the marriage, Bruce buys a hi-fi set on credit for R8 000. The hi-fi is stolen from the couple's home. They are not insured. When the couple divorce five months after their wedding, the following items form part of their joint estate:
- Anne's car;
- Bruce's premarital debt of R15 000 which he still has not paid; and
- the debt for the hi-fi set.

The house Anne inherited does not fall into the joint estate as it is her separate property.

General rules regarding the administration of the joint estate
Specific statutory rules apply to the administration of the joint estate, that is, the control over the estate in the full sense of the word, including both decision-making about and actual dealings with the assets and liabilities of the estate.

Until 1 December 1993 the main drawback of a marriage in community of property was that, in marriages entered into before 1 November 1984 (in the case of whites, coloureds and Asians) or before 2 December 1988 (in the case of Africans), the husband had the marital power.[†] Only he therefore had the power to administer the joint estate. As far as the wife's ability to deal with joint property or to make financial decisions was concerned, she was in the same position as a minor child, needing her husband's consent for most transactions and legal acts. However, on 1 December 1988, in another Act (the General Law Fourth Amendment Act 132 of 1993), the marital power was completely abolished in regard to all existing and future marriages. The same rules now apply in all marriages in community of property.

Now, the starting point is that both spouses have equal powers to administer the joint estate independently of each other. However, neither spouse can effect certain types of transaction (named in the Matrimonial Property Act) without the consent, in some form or other, of the other spouse.

There are three different types of consent. The type of transaction determines which type of consent is needed:
1. Transactions requiring witnessed, written consent:
   (a) selling, acquiring, mortgaging (that is, using as security) or burdening fixed property;
   (b) standing surety for the debts of another; and
   (c) credit transactions such as hire-purchase agreements;

2. Transactions requiring written consent:
   (a) selling or pledging (that is, using as security) investments, for example insurance policies or investments in things such as jewels or art works;
   (b) instituting or defending legal proceedings;
   (c) withdrawing the other spouse's money from his or her bank account or post office savings account; and
   (d) selling, ceding or pledging the other spouse's shares, insurance policies, mortgage bonds, fixed deposits or similar assets.
3. Transactions requiring oral or tacit consent[†] (which can be deduced from conduct):
   (a) selling or pledging household goods;
   (b) the receipt of money due to the other spouse, such as salary, interest payments or dividends; and
   (c) donations made to other parties if the donation would unreasonably prejudice the other spouse's interest in the joint estate.

All other transactions require no consent from the other spouse.

If the consent required for a particular transaction is not obtained, is the transaction valid? The answer to this question depends on whether the person with whom the transaction was entered into knew that the other spouse's consent was required and was not obtained. If he or she knew this, the transaction is invalid. This means that the transaction will not have the legal consequences intended by the parties. If, however, he or she did not know and could not reasonably have known that consent was required and not obtained, the transaction is valid.

Where the transaction is valid, there is little that can be done by the spouse whose consent was not obtained. All he or she can do is to ask to be compensated when the joint estate comes to an end. He or she will, however, be compensated only if the other spouse knew that he or she would not have consented to the particular transaction and the joint estate had suffered a loss as a result of the transaction. This protection is not very effective: it will only make good a loss suffered as a result of the transaction if there are sufficient assets in the joint estate when the marriage is dissolved. The following example illustrates this:

At the beginning of 1997, the joint estate of Mr and Mrs Smith is worth R10 000. Mr Smith buys a hi-fi set on hire-purchase for R8 000 without obtaining Mrs Smith's consent. The hi-fi set is actually only worth R2 000. Because the person from whom Mr Smith bought the hi-fi set did not know that Mr Smith was married and therefore did not know that there was a Mrs Smith whose consent was necessary, the contract is valid. When Mrs Smith finds out about the transaction, she is so cross that she divorces Mr Smith. But by that time there is only R2 000 left in the joint estate. All Mrs Smith will get is half of that. There is not enough left in the estate to compensate her for the loss of her half of the R8 000 that Mr Smith spent on the hi-fi set.

A spouse can also suffer a loss as a result of a transaction for which consent is not required. Because the consent requirement does not apply to all transactions involving the joint estate, it is possible that a spouse may be financially prejudiced† by unwise or careless transactions or dealings with the joint estate by the other spouse. For example, if the husband gambles and loses money, the wife will be losing money from her part of the joint estate. In such a case, she can approach the Court to order an immediate division of the joint estate. Such a division will ensure that she receives her share of the joint estate before the estate diminishes further because of her husband's actions. Her share will then become her separate property over which only she will have control.

An immediate division of the joint estate does not, however, provide a spouse with any protection against transactions already completed – in such cases there is very little a spouse can do. The following example illustrates this:

At the beginning of 1994, the joint estate of Mr and Mrs Van der Merwe is worth R500 000. Mr Van der Merwe goes on a gambling spree and loses heavily. Soon Mrs Van der Merwe realizes that all their money is disappearing and applies to the Court for a division of the joint estate. But there is only R50 000 left in it – all she will get is R25 000.

In this case, the immediate division of the joint estate does not really help the wife.

What happens if one spouse needs the other's consent and the other spouse spitefully refuses to give consent or can for some reason not give consent, for example because he or she is too ill to consent? In such a case the Court can consent in the place of the other spouse.

Finally, it should be noted that one spouse can ask the Court to suspend any power of the other spouse over the joint estate. This suspension means that the other spouse loses his or her power to deal with the joint estate. But the Court will do this only if it is essential for the protection of the interests of the spouse who asks for the suspension.

At the dissolution of the marriage

A marriage comes to an end through either death or divorce. This is called dissolution of the marriage. When a marriage in community of property is dissolved, the general rule is that any outstanding debts of the joint estate are paid first and what remains is divided in equal shares either between the spouses or between the surviving spouse and the deceased spouse's estate.

When a spouse dies, an executor is appointed to administer the estate of the deceased, that is, to oversee the disposal of the deceased's property.

Where the deceased was married in community of property, the executor must do the following:
1. pay all outstanding debts of the joint estate and the separate debts of the deceased spouse;
2. divide the joint estate equally between the surviving spouse and the estate of the deceased spouse;
3. deal with the deceased's portion of the joint estate, and any separate property belonging to the deceased, as directed in the deceased's will (if there is one), or in accordance with general legal rules where there is no valid will (ie the person died intestate).

Apart from getting his or her half-share of the joint estate, a spouse may inherit from the deceased's portion of the joint estate if this is written in the will. There is, however, nothing that forces one spouse to will anything to the other. If there is no will, the surviving spouse is always entitled to a portion of the deceased's property in terms of general legal rules regulating inheritance.

Since 1990, a surviving spouse has also had a right to claim maintenance from the deceased's estate under the Maintenance of Surviving Spouses Act 27 of 1990. For example, when the husband dies, the wife can claim maintenance, whether she has inherited from the spouse or not. This is the case if she does not have enough property or income to support herself. This rule applies to all marriages under any matrimonial property system.

Where the marriage is ended by divorce, the joint estate is in principle divided equally between the two spouses (after payment of outstanding debts). There are, however, certain provisions of the Divorce Act 70 of 1979 which can affect the general rules and change the way in which the joint estate is divided between the spouses. These provisions relate to the following:
- forfeiture of benefits;
- pension; and
- settlement agreements.

These are very important factors, which are explained below.

Forfeiture of benefits
When a divorce is granted[†] on the grounds of irretrievable breakdown of the marriage,[†] the Court can under certain circumstances order the forfeiture of benefits against a spouse. The term *benefits* refers mainly to those financial benefits a spouse is entitled to at a divorce flowing from the type of matrimonial system applying to that marriage. In a marriage in community of property, this refers to the half-share of those assets of the joint estate that become part of the joint estate as a result of the other spouse's efforts.

Upon divorce, either spouse can ask for a forfeiture order against the other. A forfeiture order can be made against a husband or a wife. The idea behind this rule is that a spouse should not benefit financially from a marriage which he or she has caused to fail. For example, a wife can ask for this order if her husband left her and she believes he does not deserve his share of the benefits she brought into the marriage. The Court has to decide whether not granting such an order will result in one spouse getting too much in relation to the other. In arriving at its decision, the Court takes into consideration the following:
- how long the marriage lasted;
- the circumstances which led to the breakdown of the marriage; and
- any substantial misconduct of either party.

The Court therefore has to decide whether it is fair to divide the estate equally between the spouses. If not, an order will be granted that one spouse should forfeit either all (total forfeiture) or some (partial forfeiture) of the benefits. For example, if partial forfeiture is ordered against the husband, he receives only the assets he brought into the joint estate, and a half-share of some of the assets brought in by his wife. He does not receive

> **SINGH V SINGH 1983 (1) SA 781 (C)**
>
> The husband and wife had been married in community of property for 20 years when the husband sued his wife for divorce and forfeiture of benefits. He proved that the marriage had broken down because of his wife's adultery and because she had neglected her duties as a wife and mother.
>
> The Court granted the husband a divorce and ordered that the wife forfeit some of the financial benefits of the marriage. The Court awarded her only 20% of the joint estate and the husband received the balance of 80%.

the full half-share of the joint estate that he would normally have been entitled to.

Pension benefits
It is important to note that the Divorce Act states that pension interests are also assets. So, for example, the pension interests of a man are regarded as part of his assets for the purpose of dividing assets at divorce. The value of future pension benefits of a spouse will therefore be taken into account as part of the assets available for division and also in respect of an order for forfeiture of benefits.

Settlement

Spouses do not have to ask the Court to divide the assets between them because they are free to agree between themselves on how the assets of the joint estate should be divided. They can do this in a divorce settlement. If such a settlement is reached, the Court will normally not interfere and will order that the provisions of the settlement be carried out.

In a settlement, spouses do not have to follow the legal rules which normally regulate the division of the estate. Yet such rules will usually form the basis of the agreement between the parties. That is why it is so important that a spouse knows these rules. It should also be remembered that the settlement usually provides not only for the division of the estate but also for other financial matters, such as maintenance (see Chapter 3: Support of the household, below). The legal rules regulating the maintenance of spouses and children after divorce thus also influence the agreement eventually reached in a settlement. It is also important to realize that a spouse is not obliged to accept a settlement if she or he is not happy with it. In that case, the Court will order a division as explained above.

Advantages and disadvantages of community of property

The main advantage of a marriage in community of property has to do with the nature of the joint estate. Because all the assets acquired by both parties during the marriage become part of the joint estate which belongs to both spouses equally, this form of marriage provides the best option for a woman in what we call a '*traditional marriage*'. This means a marriage where the husband earns a living outside the home while the woman either has no job at all or works only part-time. When she does work outside the home, it is usually in a lower-paid occupation without significant job-related benefits, such as a pension. In this case, the system of community of property ensures that the woman owns half of the estate. She is legally entitled to half of what the husband earns and builds up during the marriage to compensate her for her contributions in the household, including child care and taking care of the home.

There are, however several disadvantages to a marriage in community of property:
1. The debts of both spouses also form part of the joint estate, with two consequences:
    - a debt incurred by either spouse normally has to be paid from the assets of the joint estate;
    - when the liabilities of the joint estate exceed the assets, both spouses are declared insolvent and even their separate property can be used to pay the creditors.

A marriage in community of property therefore gives virtually no financial security to the woman if her husband has many debts.
2. The protective measures that can be taken against a spouse who deals irresponsibly with the assets of the joint estate do not help when this irresponsible behaviour has already taken place; they only prevent future problems.
3. The manner in which the joint estate is administered is fairly complicated; in particular, this can make ordinary commercial dealings difficult because of the requirement of consent.

THE ACCRUAL SYSTEM

Another type of matrimonial property system is called the accrual system. A marriage subject to this system is a marriage out of community of property but subject to accrual sharing. By law, the accrual system applies to all marriages out of community of property concluded after 1 November 1984 by white, Coloured or Asian spouses or after 2 December 1988 by African spouses unless the antenuptial contract specifically states that accrual sharing will not apply.

The accrual system means that for the duration of the marriage the couple is married out of community of property – accrual sharing takes effect only at the end of the marriage. We shall first explain the position during the marriage and then turn to the consequences of death or divorce.

During the marriage

While a marriage subject to the accrual system lasts, each spouse remains financially independent of the other. This means that each is the owner of all the assets and property he or she owned when they married, and each one becomes the owner of any property and assets independently acquired during the marriage. The same applies to debts or liabilities: if the husband incurs debts before or during the marriage, only he must pay for them from his own assets and vice versa.

The financial independence of the spouses during a marriage out of community of property also has a further consequence. During the marriage, each spouse has complete control over his or her separate property and he or she alone can make decisions regarding it. This means that a wife does not need her husband's permission to buy, sell, mortgage or otherwise deal with money, property or other assets belonging to her or to incur any debts or liabilities whatsoever.

The financial independence of the spouses during the marriage is qualified by the duty of support that exists between all spouses while the marriage lasts: each spouse is obliged to contribute to the maintenance of the other (see Chapter 3: Support of the household, below).

© JUTA & CO, LTD

There is an important exception to the rule that debts incurred by a spouse are personal debts, however: a creditor can claim payment for debts for household necessaries from either party (even the one who did not incur them), or from both spouses jointly. This issue is discussed below.

CLARK & CO V LYNCH 1963 (1) SA 183 (N)

A wife bought household necessaries, including groceries and soap, on credit. The storekeeper sent the account to her husband, but he refused to pay. He said that he had written a letter to the storekeeper to tell him that he would no longer pay his wife's debts.

The Court decided that the husband could not escape having to pay for household necessaries and ordered him to pay the storekeeper.

Liability for household necessaries
Both spouses are liable for any debt for necessaries acquired for the joint household.

In establishing liability for necessaries, the financial means of the spouses are compared and this determines the proportion of each spouse's contribution in relation to the other. Where one spouse is in debt for household goods, payment of the debt can be claimed from either individually or from them jointly.

Where a spouse has contributed more than his or her share to household necessaries, he or she can claim the excess amount back from the other party, but only if the couple were married before 1 November 1984.

If they married after this date, a spouse can claim back excess contributions only if the spouses expressly agreed (preferably in their antenuptial contract) that this should happen. Such a right to reclaim excess contributions (called a 'right of recourse') could amount to a claim for a large amount of money against the other spouse. Such a claim is usually instituted only when the marriage is ended by death or divorce. The amount of the claim will, however, have to be substantiated and therefore the keeping of detailed records is necessary (eg till slips, cheque stubs, etc). Where the antenuptial contract does not provide for a right of recourse, spouses will have to be careful *not* to pay more than they have to towards the household expenses. Otherwise they will have no claim for excess contributions at a later stage.

At the dissolution of the marriage

The system of accrual sharing really comes into effect only when the marriage is ended by death or divorce. The termination of the marriage automatically brings about an equal sharing of the accruals of the marriage.

The crucial question now is: what does accrual mean? Accrual is the amount by which the separate estate of each spouse has grown (or accrued) during the marriage. The effect of the accrual system is to share equally between the spouses the property that each spouse acquired during the marriage; each spouse keeps the assets and the property he or she had when marrying, as this does not from part of the accrual. The underlying philosophy is that in marriage both spouses contribute equally to the growth of each other's separate estates, even if the one spouse in actual fact amasses more than the other.

The actual sharing in the total accrual is postponed until the end of the marriage. Therefore the accrual system is sometimes described as a system of postponed community of gains: both partners gain from the marriage, but not until it ends.

Accrual sharing, which is regulated in the Matrimonial Property Act, is put into effect in the following manner when the marriage ends through death or divorce: the accrual of the estate of each spouse is determined by subtracting the net value of the estate when the marriage was entered into (the 'commencement value'), from its net value when the marriage is dissolved (the 'end value'). Net value is the amount remaining after the settlement of all outstanding liabilities and debts.

The following are some of the most important rules that apply to the determination of the accrual:

- the commencement or beginning value of an estate is adapted according to the consumer price index to reflect the changing value of money over the duration of the marriage (ie to allow for inflation);
- when the marriage ends because of the death of a spouse, the end value is determined before the payment of any inheritances from his or her estate;
- the commencement value of a spouse's estate is said to be nil if the spouse had more debts than assets at the time of the marriage;
- certain assets are excluded from the accrual. They are subtracted from the end value of a spouse's estate even though they were acquired during the term of the marriage. These assets are:
    (a) anything excluded by the spouses in their antenuptial contract;
    (b) inheritances or gifts received by either spouse during the marriage from third parties;

(c) damages for non-financial loss (eg damages awarded to you because you were slandered by someone, or because someone inflicted pain and injury on you);
(d) gifts by one spouse to the other.

- Future pension benefits are included in the assets that form part of the accrual in the case of divorce (this was explained earlier with regard to marriages in community of property – see above).
- The result of subtracting the commencement value and the excluded assets from the end value of a spouse's estate is the accrual of that estate.

Once the accruals of the estates of the two spouses have been determined, the smaller amount is subtracted from the larger. Equal sharing of the accruals is brought about by giving the spouse whose estate has the smaller accrual the right to claim half of the difference between the two accruals from the spouse with the larger accrual.

For example, when John and Mary marry, John has saved R10 000 through working for a few years. Mary has just finished her studies and has nothing. When they divorce five years later, the consumer price index is taken into account so that the commencement value of John's estate is now deemed to be R14 000. During the marriage John has run a successful business and at the end of the marriage his estate is worth R100 000. Mary, who has only worked part-time, has an estate of R4 000.

To calculate the accrual, the adapted commencement value of John's estate is subtracted from the end value:

R100 000 – R14 000 = R86 000

A similar sum is done to find out what Mary's accrual is:
R4 000 – R0 000 = R4 000

Now the smaller accrual is subtracted from the larger to find out the difference between the accruals:
R86 000 – R4 000 = R82 000

Half of R82 000 goes to Mary because she has the smaller accrual. She, therefore, is awarded R41 000 and this added to her R4 000 gives her a total of R45 000.

This system has flexibility to provide for the exact needs of an individual couple since spouses are free to agree in their antenuptial contract to any other basis of sharing, such as a 70:30 division, if it would better suit their circumstances and requirements.

The manner of dissolution of the marriage – that is, whether it is dissolved by death or divorce – has no influence on accrual sharing at dissolution. When the marriage is dissolved by death, an executor is appointed to do the following:
- determine and divide the accrual between the spouses in the manner explained above;
- see to the disposal of the estate of the deceased spouse in exactly the same manner as explained in regard to marriages in community of property (see above);
- to apply the same rules that apply to spouses who are married in community of property in regard to the surviving spouse's inheriting from the deceased and the possibility of his or her claiming maintenance from the deceased estate.

When there is a divorce, the determination and division of the accrual takes place as explained above. In addition, two things must be kept in mind:
1. In the case of divorce, the right to share in the accrual is a benefit of the marriage. This benefit can be forfeited under an order of forfeiture of benefits granted against the spouse entitled to claim a share in the accrual. Forfeiture of benefits here works in exactly the same way as explained in regard to marriages in community of property (see above).
2. As in the case of marriage in community, the spouses' future pension benefits are also included as part of their assets (see above).
3. The position concerning divorce settlements which was explained in regard to the marriage in community of property applies in the same way under the accrual system (see above).

Advantages and disadvantages of the accrual system

The accrual system holds several advantages for spouses during and after the marriage:
1. The automatic sharing of accrual effectively protects the financial interests of the spouse who cannot obtain, or does not have the chance to increase, her own separate estate during the marriage – a wife who has no outside income has the legal right to a share in her husband's assets. Accrual recognizes her contribution to the growth of his estate. (Similarly, where the traditional roles are reversed, accrual recognizes his contribution to the growth of her estate.)
2. The fact that the couple are married out of community of property has several benefits when it comes to administration. Because there is no sharing of accrual during the marriage, administration is uncomplicated, unlike joint administration. Each spouse is in full

control of his or her property and does not need the consent or co-operation of the other for financial dealings.
3. The accrual system ensures financial independence during the marriage and allows each spouse the maximum financial freedom. The one spouse is not in danger of becoming liable for the debts of the other – a problem in the marriage in community of property.
4. The insolvency of the one spouse does not affect the other – the separate assets of the one party are protected from the other's creditors.

The financial independence of each spouse during the marriage under this system can, however, have one very important drawback: neither spouse has any say over the way in which the other deals with his or her own assets, even if this takes place in a reckless manner. A woman who is married with the accrual system can do very little to stop her husband from mismanaging his assets.

The Matrimonial Property Act does provide some protection for a spouse whose right to share in the accrual of the other spouse's estate at dissolution is being endangered by that spouse's conduct. A prejudiced spouse can request the Court to order an immediate division of the accrual. Such an order will prevent a husband, for example, from reducing his wife's share in the accrual any further. Where such an order is granted, the accrual is immediately determined and divided according to the rules explained above. The amounts paid out to the spouses become their own separate property over which they have sole control. However, this measure once again protects only against possible problems in the future; nothing can be done about assets already squandered by a spouse.

COMPLETE SEPARATION OF PROPERTY

The last main type of matrimonial property system is a marriage out of community of property in which the accrual system is also excluded. Because both community of property and accrual sharing are excluded, this system is called complete separation of property.

In marriages with complete separation of property the spouses are treated exactly as if they were not married from a financial point of view, and they are completely independent legally. This applies both while the marriage exists and when it ends.

During the marriage

During the marriage, each spouse is independent in regard to the following:
- the ownership of property;

- control over that property;
- the power to incur debts.

You will notice that this corresponds to the position under the accrual system. As in the case of accrual, the independence of the spouses is qualified by their duty of support and liability for household necessaries – as discussed above.

At the dissolution of the marriage

The main differences between a marriage subject to complete separation of property and one subject to accrual sharing relate to what happens when the marriage comes to an end.

In a marriage with complete separation of property, the one spouse has no right to share in any of the assets belonging to the other when the marriage is ended. The wife is therefore entitled only to her own assets and is alone responsible for her own debts, as is the husband.

If the spouses made special provision in their antenuptial contract for marriage settlements† in favour of one of them, then the specified assets have to be given by one of them to the other. If the promised transfer of assets has not been made when the marriage ends, the spouse to whom they were promised can claim them from the other spouse or from his or her estate.

Where a marriage comes to an end through the death of one of the spouses, the role of the executor is the same as explained previously (see above). The executor has to settle the spouse's estate according to the applicable matrimonial property system and, furthermore, deal with the deceased's estate. In a marriage out of community of property, the spouses have no general claims, based on the matrimonial property system, to each other's assets.

As we have said before, where persons marry out of community of property, they are regarded as unmarried for financial purposes, and it is possible for them to enter into ordinary transactions with each other. Such transactions are dealt with exactly like any other transaction between a spouse and any third party. It is possible that one spouse may be indebted to the other for money or goods as the result of ordinary legal transactions that took place between the two of them during the marriage. When such debts are settled at the end of the marriage, it is not due to the matrimonial property system applicable to the marriage – the creditor spouse, being an independent person, is treated like any other creditor.

Where the marriage is dissolved by divorce, the position in regard to marriage settlements and possible claims for contributions to household necessaries is similar to the case of a marriage dissolved by death. One difference, however, is that the marriage settlements are regarded as benefits of the marriage, which can be forfeited under the circumstances explained earlier (see above).

Redistribution of assets

One very important measure which applies only to certain marriages with complete separation of property which end in divorce, needs to be highlighted: the redistribution order.† This can have a major influence on the financial position of the spouses after the divorce.

Where a marriage out of community of property and without any form of accrual sharing (ie the complete separation of property system) was entered into prior to 1 November 1984 in the case of white, coloured or Asian spouses, or before 2 December 1988 in the case of African spouses, a provision of the Divorce Act allows the Court granting a divorce to order a redistribution of assets at the request of one or other of the spouses. In terms of the order, certain assets or a portion of assets is transferred to the applicant.

The Court will issue such an order if it decides that it will be fair in the light of the direct or indirect contribution made by the applicant to the growth or maintenance of the other spouse's estate. Such a contribution can consist of the following:

- the rendering of services, which includes services in the common household or with regard to the care of the children;
- the saving of expenses which would otherwise have been incurred;

> **BEAUMONT V BEAUMONT 1987 (1) SA 967 (A)**
>
> Mr and Mrs Beaumont were married with complete separation of property in 1964. At the time of their marriage, the couple had no assets. During the marriage the husband started and ran a very successful business. His wife kept house, cared for the children and helped him run the business without ever being paid for her contribution. Twenty years later, Mr Beaumont sued for divorce. At this time he had accumulated R450 000 in assets while she had only R10 000 of her own.
>
> The Court made a redistribution order in favour of Mrs Beaumont and ordered her husband to transfer R150 000 of his assets to her.

- any other kind of contribution.

The redistribution cases are most commonly instances where the wife worked without payment in the husband's business and/or in the home, and acquired very few or no assets in her own name during the marriage, whereas the husband built up a substantial estate.

A redistribution order usually states that a certain portion of the other spouse's assets must be transferred to the applicant. In most cases that have come before the Court, the portion has amounted to approximately one-third of the opposing spouse's estate, but this is not a fixed rule in our law. In fact, there is no fixed rule or even guideline concerning the size of the portion, and the individual merits of each case are considered by the Court.

A redistribution order will be made only where the divorcing spouses have not, in the divorce settlement, agreed on how their assets are to be distributed. Obviously the fact that such an order can be applied for – as with other legal rules that regulate the division of assets at divorce – will be an important bargaining factor in reaching a settlement.

The redistribution of assets is a flexible tool that can be used to make sure that each spouse is dealt with fairly. In the majority of cases, though, it is the wife who needs this protection.

It is to be noted that this measure applies only to marriages with complete separation of property which were entered into either before 1 November 1984 or before 2 December 1988 (whichever is applicable), where the spouses have not reached an agreement about the final division of their assets.

Advantages and disadvantages of complete separation of property

There are several advantages to complete separation of property:
1. The complete legal and financial independence of the spouses during the marriage allows both spouses maximum freedom to deal with their own property as they see fit.
2. If a spouse becomes insolvent during the marriage, this does not directly affect the financial position of the other party.
3. One spouse's property cannot be used to pay the other spouse's creditors.
4. Even marriage settlements received from an insolvent spouse are protected against his or her creditors under certain circumstances.

On the other hand, there are also disadvantages:
1. The financial independence of the spouses means that one spouse is without any protection where the other deals recklessly or unwisely with his or her estate. This applies even when the recklessness prejudices the other spouse's or the children's right to claim maintenance from that spouse.
2. The main disadvantage of this type of marriage is that there is no provision for any form of automatic sharing of assets. A spouse is therefore completely dependent on possible marriage settlements

or voluntary donations from the other spouse in order to obtain any kind of share in the assets built up by the other. The problem with donations and marriage settlements (made during or at the end of the marriage) is that they can be made only if the donor spouse co-operates and agrees. The disadvantages for a wife who is unable to build up her own assets during the marriage are obvious – she will have no financial security, and no financial recognition is given to her non-income earning contributions such as traditional household and child-rearing duties.

THE CHOICE OF A MATRIMONIAL PROPERTY SYSTEM

Prior to marriage, spouses should consider carefully which of the above systems best suits their individual needs. It is especially the woman, who is usually in the weaker financial position, who should ensure that she receives the maximum financial recognition and protection that a particular matrimonial property system can provide.

It is an unfortunate, but undeniable, fact that financial hardship is often suffered by women simply because neither spouse has adequate financial means. No matrimonial property system – or any legal rule, for that matter – can overcome this problem. But spouses can and should choose the best possible option, and use it in the manner fairest to them both.

Changing the matrimonial property system

Spouses often find after marrying that they made the wrong choice regarding a suitable matrimonial property system. This can happen because they were unaware of the options, because they had the wrong information or misunderstood the legal position, because their actual circumstances after the marriage were different from what they had anticipated, or because of unforeseen changes in their circumstances during the marriage. Before 1984 very little could be done about this once the marriage had been concluded, because it was not possible to change the system.

The Matrimonial Property Act brought about an important change in this respect. It provides that, during the marriage, both spouses jointly can approach the Court for permission to change the system applicable to their marriage.

The Court will grant such a request and order that a notarial contract be drawn up to regulate their future matrimonial property system if the following requirements are met:

1. There is good reason for the change.

> ### EX PARTE KRÖS 1986 (1) SA 642 (NC)
>
> The husband and wife had married in community of property. Three years after their wedding they applied for the system to be changed to complete separation of property. Their reasons for wanting the change were:
> - that the husband wanted to start a business and did not want his wife to run any financial risk because of his business dealings;
> - that the wife had been married before and she wanted to be sure that her children from the previous marriage would get the benefit of the assets she had brought into the marriage.
>
> The Court gave the couple permission to change to the system of complete separation of property.

2. Creditors of the spouses have been given notice.
3. No person will be prejudiced (disadvantaged) by the change.

This measure provided some much-needed flexibility and relief for spouses who have previously entered into a matrimonial property system that is actually unsuitable for their circumstances. Since it applies only where the spouses agree to the proposed change, it cannot solve the situation where one of the spouses resists the change.

Spouses should therefore still choose their original system with extreme care and circumspection in the light of the far-reaching consequences their choice will have on their present and future financial positions.

Summary: the correct choice

Community of property
Tends to be most suited to the average traditional marriage, where both parties have few assets when they marry and the husband will be the main breadwinner, working in a salaried occupation. It ensures that the wife will share equally in the assets built up during the marriage. It could, however, lead to problems:
- it does not provide good protection against a spendthrift or reckless spouse and should be avoided where there is evidence of this;
- because of the consent requirement and the general financial dependence of the spouses on each other in this kind of marriage, it is also not well suited to a marriage where one of the spouses is in business on his or her own account.

Accrual system

A good choice where one or both of the spouses enter into the marriage with considerable assets that they do not wish to share, or where both partners work during the marriage. The reasons why the accrual system works well in these instances are:

- accrual has the advantage of sharing what was built up during the marriage through joint effort;
- it does not have the disadvantage of making one spouse liable for the other's debts or share in other spouse's financial problems during the marriage;
- it also avoids the problems of complicated administration and is well suited to cases where one or both spouses earn their living in the business or professional world.

Complete separation of property

Suitable where both spouses are wealthy or have large incomes and where there is no need or desire to view the marriage as a joint financial venture. The main advantage of this form of marriage is the almost complete financial independence of the spouses. It tends to be an unsuitable choice for young couples marrying because:

- there is no sharing of assets, even at the dissolution of the marriage;
- there is no financial protection for the young spouse who does not have many assets or who has a low level of income.

CHAPTER THREE:
Support of the household

INTRODUCTION

The family has traditionally been regarded as the primary support system in society. Because of the increasing rate of family breakdowns, and because of changing roles inside the family itself, new problems have arisen concerning the duty of support.[‡] A strong trend is the increase of single-parent families, headed mostly by women. Studies reveal that, in the United States, this family type is the fastest growing of all – South Africa seems to be following this trend too. Studies have also indicated that divorced women tend to have lower incomes than their male counterparts. This highlights the critical issue of maintenance[†](financial support) for the family, during the marriage and after divorce.

FINANCIAL SUPPORT IN MARRIAGE

In a marriage a duty of support exists if one spouse needs maintenance and the other spouse has the ability to provide support. A duty of support also exists between parents and children and, in certain circumstances, between grandparents and grandchildren. In South African law, blood relationship, adoption and marriage create a duty of support. This duty is reciprocal: that is, the husband and wife and parents and children are supposed to support each other. Whereas the husband and wife owe a duty of support to each other, this duty does not extend to their other relations by marriage, for example to mothers-in-law, sisters-in-law or stepchildren.

Duty of support between spouses

One of the invariable consequences of marriage is that the spouses owe each other a reciprocal duty of support according to their means[†]. This duty takes precedence over[†] the duties of support which stem from blood

---

[‡] The terms 'support', 'alimony' and 'maintenance', having virtually the same meaning, are used interchangeably in South African law.

relationship, which means that if a woman's husband can support her, she cannot claim support from her parents or adult children.

The duty of support includes the duty to provide the other spouse with accommodation, food, clothes, medical and dental attention, and other reasonable requirements. The scale of the support depends upon the couple's financial means, their lifestyle and their social position.

In practice the heavier duty often rests on the husband because he is the main, or sometimes the only, money earner in the family.

The manner in which support is provided is left to the discretion of the one who provides the support; but it should never be humiliating or unreasonable.

A separate issue from the duty of support is the wife's capacity to buy household necessaries such as groceries. As with the duty of support, the capacity to buy household necessaries stems from the marriage. It exists only if there is a joint household – that is, if the couple live together. If there no longer is a joint household, the wife can continue to claim from her husband if he still owes her a duty of support. He does not owe her a duty of support if she is to blame for the fact that there is no longer a joint household. (On household necessaries, see Chapter Two, above.)

The duty of support normally comes to an end on the death of one of the spouses and on divorce. Death or divorce does not always mean the end of the provision of maintenance, however. The Court may order one spouse to pay maintenance to the other after divorce. After death, the widow or widower can sometimes claim maintenance from the deceased spouse's estate. (See Chapter Two, above.)

Duty of support between parents and children

The duty of parents to support their children exists if:
1. the parents are capable of supporting the children, and
2. the child is not capable of supporting itself.

Both parents must support their children according to their means (or financial ability). The fact that the father is more often the parent with the main or only income, does not mean that the mother is exempted[†] from her duty of support.

The ordinary rules governing the duty of parents to support their children apply in respect of illegitimate children also. Even though the father of an illegitimate child may have no right of access or custody to the child, he is legally obliged to contribute to the child's financial support.

The duty of support continues even if the parents live apart from their children and ends only when the children can support themselves. This means that a parent can have this duty in respect of a child who is older than 21.

> **GLIKSMAN V TALEKINSKY 1955 (4) SA 468 (W)**
>
> A widow with six young children claimed maintenance from her father. He was wealthy whereas she had assets of her own and her husband had died insolvent.
>
> The Court decided that her father must support her and her children.

The duty includes the provision of food, clothing, accommodation, health care, education and everything that may be necessary for the proper upbringing of the child. The scope of the duty depends on the needs of the child, on the social standing of the family and on their financial position.

The parents' duty of support is not affected by divorce or remarriage. Although divorce ends the husband–wife relationship, it does not end the parent–child relationship or the duty of support which flows from that relationship. A Court granting an order of divorce may make any order it chooses for the support of a minor child. But a step-parent does not have to support a stepchild. It is, however, true that if a second marriage is in community of property, the maintenance which a parent has to pay for a child of the first marriage will be paid out of the joint estate. This places an indirect burden on second spouses, who, by virtue of the matrimonial property system, may find themselves supporting the children of their spouses' first marriages.

When a parent dies, maintenance for a child (or children) can be claimed from the estate of the deceased parent.

Where a non-custodian parent (ie the parent who does not have custody of the children) applies for a reduction in maintenance because of other financial responsibilities, the Court will determine whether those other responsibilities stem from factors beyond the non-custodian parent's control. Our Courts are not inclined to be sympathetic if the non-custodian parent cites financial obligations arising out of a second marriage as the reason why maintenance should be reduced.

As we have said already, the duty of support between parents and children is reciprocal: just as parents are obliged to support their children, so are children supposed to support their parents, if this becomes necessary. The requirements for the duty of support are the same in both cases.

Family ties and support have declined in South Africa as a result of various factors such as the migrant labour system, urbanization and the high divorce rate among middle- and upper-income families. Child support is inadequate partially because claims are not properly assessed[†], maintenance orders are not properly enforced and defaulters[†] are not always prosecuted as they should be. On the other hand, it is also true that many defaulting parents are unable to meet their support obligations towards their children. Many children are born to very poor mothers who are unmarried or whose husbands are part of the migrant labour system. Women are also often greatly discriminated against and exploited in the marketplace, which makes it hard for mothers to provide for their children. Their only source of support is their own income from a job which may often require absence from home for up to 12 hours a day. There is also a total lack of adequate child-minding or pre-school facilities for the offspring of working mothers.

Maintenance and divorce

Divorce has an immediate effect on the spouses' duty of support. It is usually after divorce that most of the problems concerning maintenance arise.

Interim relief

Rule 43 of the Uniform Rules of the High Court regulates how difficulties can be resolved in the interim period, when divorce proceedings have been started but the divorce has not yet gone through. If a spouse wants to divorce, he or she can claim certain help even before the divorce order is made. This is called 'interim relief'. For example, a wife can approach the High Court to get this relief from her husband while she is waiting for the final divorce order to be made. This is explained in more detail in Chapter 5: Divorce law, below, but is summarized briefly below, since rule 43 is very important at the time when divorce proceedings start.

Rule 43 sets out the interim relief which can be claimed. The Court can be asked for the following:
1. maintenance in the form of weekly or monthly amounts to help support the spouse and/or the couple's children;
2. a contribution towards the costs of the divorce;
3. interim custody of the couple's children until the divorce is granted, when another arrangement may be made;
4. interim access, permitting the other spouse to have access to the children until the divorce is granted.

Note that rule 43 will apply irrespective of whether it is a wife or a husband who requires interim relief. This rule applies only during the waiting period until the divorce is finalized.

Maintenance of former spouse after divorce

Divorce brings to an end the reciprocal duty of support which exists between the spouses during marriage, but maintenance can continue in some circumstances, which are explained below.

Where there is a written agreement between the spouses, the Court granting a decree of divorce can order the payment of maintenance by the one spouse to the other in terms of that agreement. The Court may, however, refuse to make an order if it disapproves of the agreement. Spouses who fail to have their agreement recognized by the Court at the time of divorce cannot return to Court later to have their agreement made an order of Court. Read the story below. It will give you some idea of the complications that can arise.

Case study: Mr and Mrs Ayyad

Mr and Mrs Ayyad were married in community of property. They lived in a small but comfortable home in Chatsworth. They had three children, all of whom went to the local school. Unfortunately, their marriage was not a happy one, and after 13 years they decided to divorce and go their separate ways. It was a sad decision, but both realized that perhaps it was the only way to reduce the terrible stress in their relationship. In terms of the laws governing their joint assets, Mr Ayyad was entitled to half of the total value of their joint estate. However, he let his wife keep the house and agreed, in a letter he sent to her from Durban, to pay her R1 500 a month to maintain herself and the children. Mr Ayyad was a man of his word, so neither of them thought it necessary to mention the existence of the letter to the lawyers who handled their case, and the payment of maintenance was not made part of the divorce order. Mrs Ayyad and the children in Chatsworth, and Mr Ayyad in Durban, settled down to start a new life apart.

But, as we all know, things never remain the same for long. It wasn't three years later that Mr Ayyad met Miss Rugunanan, who came to work in the credit department at his company. It was love at first sight and they decided to marry.

Suddenly, the generous allowances that he had made for his former wife became a major obstacle in the way of Mr Ayyad's attempt to make provision for his new relationship. He phoned Mrs Ayyad to ask her whether she would agree to sell the house and pay over his half so that he could put down a deposit on a small flat. He also told her that he would now be paying her only R1 000 a month, especially since he was earning only about R2 500 a month.

Mrs Ayyad panicked and rushed off to see her attorney. What do you think he told her?

What should Mrs Ayyad have done?
She should have had the arrangements which were set out in the letter written down in a formal agreement between the spouses, and she should have asked the Court to make this agreement part of its order.

What can she do now?

She cannot now ask the Court to recognize the arrangements made in the letter. She cannot claim any maintenance from her husband because the divorce court did not order him to pay maintenance (see the discussion below this case study). Mr Ayyad will, however, have to continue paying maintenance for the children (see below). Because marriage entitles him to half of the assets of the spouses, the house will have to be sold and half of its value will have to be given to him, unless Mrs Ayyad can prove that he donated his half of the house to her – not an easy thing to prove.

Sometimes there is no written agreement between the divorcing couple. If they have not reached agreement about the payment of maintenance, the Court will make the decision for them. This decision will take into account the following issues:
- the present and future means of both parties;
- the age of the man and the woman;
- how many years they had been married;
- the couple's standard of living prior to the divorce;
- the conduct of the man or the woman, if this contributed to the breakdown of the marriage;
- the couple's separate earning capacities, financial needs and obligations; and
- any other factors which should, in the opinion of the Court, be taken into account.

The Court then makes an order which it considers fair for the payment of maintenance to the one by the other for any period or until the death or remarriage of the person who is to receive maintenance. For example, the man can be ordered to pay maintenance to the woman until she remarries.

If the Court does not make an order for the maintenance of one former spouse by the other, neither one may later claim maintenance. Therefore, if a wife does not get a maintenance order in her favour at the time of the divorce, she can never claim maintenance from her former husband.

A maintenance order made in terms of the Divorce Act may be ended, changed or suspended at any time by the Court if it finds a good reason to do so.

Types of maintenance

Usually, in the past, women received maintenance from their husbands after a divorce. However, because an increasing number of women are entering the marketplace, the Courts are today less likely to award women maintenance. The idea that marriage ought to provide a woman with a 'meal ticket for life' has changed. Also, an increasing number of men are awarded maintenance in cases where all the circumstances indicate that such an order would be just and fair.

However, many women still need to receive maintenance from their former husbands in order to live. A middle-aged woman, for example, who has for many years devoted herself full-time to her household, husband and children, may be awarded maintenance for herself as well as for the children dependent on her. The maintenance for herself may be for a certain period to enable her to be trained or retrained for a job. This maintenance is called rehabilitative maintenance. An elderly woman, who is too old to earn her own living and who is unlikely to remarry, may be awarded permanent maintenance. On the other hand, the young working woman who is able to support herself will seldom be awarded maintenance. She will usually, of course, still be paid maintenance for the children if she has custody.

Important considerations which the Court may take into account are the woman's age, how long she has been absent from the marketplace, her responsibilities towards her children, the duration of the marriage, etc. The behaviour of the man and the woman, which is not relevant in the granting of a divorce order, may become relevant when the Court has to decide whether to grant maintenance. The Court will evaluate and examine all the facts and circumstances of each case on its own before making its decision. As to the amount to be awarded, no rule can be formulated: the same factors which are taken into account when deciding whether an award of maintenance should be made will apply.

Kroon v Kroon 1986 (4) SA 616 (EC)

The Court had to decide whether rehabilitative maintenance should be awarded to a middle-aged woman who had been a housewife during her marriage.

The Court decided that, because the woman had not worked outside the home for 20 years, she would not be able to be trained or retrained for a job. Therefore the Court awarded her permanent maintenance.

A woman who is not in need of support at the time of the divorce may need it at some time in the future. If this seems a possibility, the Court will award her a small amount of nominal or token maintenance. It may be as little as R5 monthly, which can be increased when this becomes necessary. Thus, for example, if she becomes unable to work because of serious illness, an application can be made for this token maintenance to be increased to meet her needs. Sometimes no provision is made for the husband to pay the woman even token maintenance; if she later becomes unable to support herself, her former husband cannot in any way be forced to support her.

Nowadays, there is a tendency to regard marriage as a partnership between two economically independent individuals which lasts only as long as it suits the two people. This has led to the so-called 'clean break principle' regarding divorce and maintenance. This principle is of special interest to well-off couples. 'Clean break' means that the couple will have a quick separation, with as little trouble as possible. It lets the man and the woman become economically independent of each other as soon as possible after the divorce. In practice, though, it often takes the form of the two people agreeing on a certain settlement sum to be paid once, instead of periodic maintenance payments. For example, the husband may pay his former wife an amount of R500 000 upon divorce.

This concept has been accepted by our courts, but only in those rare cases where the spouses' financial position permits such a distribution. Note that, although the 'clean break' allows and encourages the couple to become economically independent of each other as soon as possible after the divorce, it cannot apply to the children involved, as the parents' duty to support a child is unaffected by divorce.

KATZ V KATZ 1989 (3) SA 1 (A)

The husband had assets of R7,5 million, whereas his wife had R26 000. On divorce the wife claimed maintenance and asked the Court to order that a share of her husband's estate be transferred to her, in terms of a redistribution order.

The Court applied the 'clean break' principle. It awarded her R1,5 million of her husband's estate, but awarded her no maintenance.

The question arises whether such a lump sum is regarded as a maintenance payment in terms of the divorce laws. The Maintenance Act 23 of 1963 defines a maintenance order as 'any order for the periodic payment of sums of money towards the maintenance of any person made by any Court in the Republic', so the answer to this question would appear to be *no*.

The 'clean break' principle does not take account of all the disadvantages still suffered by many women, such as the lack of equality in the marketplace, the fact that the role of custodial parent hinders career advancement, etc. Another problem seems to be that it is difficult, and sometimes impossible, to keep separate the amounts needed to support a child and those needed by its custodial parent, especially with regard to the provision of housing, food, electricity, etc.

Another issue which has been addressed by our courts is whether the award of maintenance should be considered separately from the issue of division of the couple's property in terms of our divorce laws. In our view, the correct approach for the Court to take is to adopt an overall view of how justice can best be achieved between the two parties, taking into account their means, obligations and needs.

Maintenance of children after divorce

A Court granting a divorce may make whatever order it deems fit for the maintenance of a dependent child of the marriage. A maintenance order in respect of children may include provision for any unborn children of the marriage.

For 'sufficient reason' the maintenance order may be ended, suspended or changed by the Court which made it or by any other Court. Although reference is made to the 'Court granting the divorce', this does not mean that if a maintenance award with regard to a dependent child has not been made at the time of the divorce, no order may be made subsequently. A maintenance order in favour of a child may be made or changed at any time.

Since both parents are obliged to maintain their children, the Court will distribute the burden between them according to their means, taking into account the needs of the child and the financial circumstances and social position of the parents. But the parents themselves may enter into an agreement about the maintenance of their minor children after the divorce. This agreement may be made an order of court. However, a clause in an agreement between the two parents which stipulates that one of the child's parents will not be responsible for the maintenance of the child is against public policy and therefore unenforceable.

A maintenance order may provide that maintenance is to be paid (monthly, weekly) until the child reaches a certain age, such as 18, 20 or 21 years. In certain circumstances the payment of maintenance may continue after children reach the age of majority – for example, while they attend college or university.

When the spouse who has custody of the children dies, custody may pass to the other spouse; but if custody passes to a third person such as a grandparent, a new order for maintenance must be made.

The insolvency of the spouse who has to pay maintenance does not end his or her obligations under a maintenance order. Also, a parent cannot stop paying maintenance just because he or she has lost his or her job or has resigned from employment.

Enforcement of maintenance

There are several different ways in which the payment of maintenance can be enforced. This is a very important aspect because many women in South Africa suffer when they become single parents and cannot take care of themselves or their children, even though they have been granted maintenance by the Court. Sometimes the other spouse is simply not able to pay the required maintenance. But in many other cases, spouses do not pay maintenance because of bad feelings left over from the divorce, or out of spite, or because of the lack of a sense of responsibility towards the children.

Enforcement under the Maintenance Act and the Child Care Act

Two laws which regulate maintenance liability and enforcement are the Child Care Act 74 of 1983 and the Maintenance Act. The Child Care Act provides that any person who is legally liable to maintain a child, and who can do so is guilty of an offence[†] if he or she fails to provide the child with adequate food, clothing, lodging and medical aid. The difference between this offence and an offence under the Maintenance Act is that a maintenance order need not have been made against the parent in order for that parent to be charged under the Child Care Act. The penalties under this Act are much more severe than those under the Maintenance Act.

The Maintenance Act provides that every magistrate's court is deemed to be a maintenance court within its area of jurisdiction[†]. The maintenance court can start an investigation or enquiry when a complaint is made under oath to a maintenance officer that a person who is legally liable to maintain another person has failed to do so.

The maintenance officer must investigate the complaint and, if necessary, start an enquiry into the matter in the maintenance court. For the purposes of the enquiry, the maintenance officer may summon any person to appear before the Court to give evidence or produce any book, document or statement to the Court. The 'statement' may include proof of the earnings of the liable person, signed by his or her employer. After considering the evidence, the Court may order the payment of sums of money towards maintenance if no maintenance order is in force, and may determine the period and times of payment. If there is an existing maintenance order, the Court may replace this with a new order.

The first question the Court must determine is whether the accused person is truly legally responsible to maintain the other person. During a maintenance enquiry there should be full disclosure of the financial position of both parties. When it is decided that someone must pay maintenance, he or she can be forced to give evidence about his or her financial situation in order to establish the amount of maintenance that must be paid to the former spouse or child.

The Maintenance Act contains penalties for failure to obey a maintenance order, namely a maximum fine of R4 000 or imprisonment for one year, or both such fine and imprisonment. The Court may also order that photographs be taken of that person, and the maintenance officer may furnish particulars to businesses which give credit or are involved in giving credit ratings, so that the defaulter will no longer be allowed to buy on credit.

Types of enforcement

There are several other ways to enforce maintenance orders. A Court which has convicted a person of the offence of not paying maintenance may make an order authorizing the convicted person's employer to make the required maintenance payments out of that person's salary. This is known as a garnishee order and can provide some relief to someone who experiences difficulty in receiving maintenance. For example, if Mr Smith does not pay maintenance for his children, the Court can order money to be deducted from his regular salary cheque. In these circumstances, the maintenance officer serves notice on Mr Smith's employer, stating the amount and the manner in which the deductions in lieu of maintenance payments must be made.

The parties often agree that the maintenance payments will be paid in at the local magistrate's court. They can also be paid directly into the bank account of the person who is entitled to the money. This has its advantages, because a record is kept of what maintenance has been paid, and when, which may be very useful if there is a disagreement at a later stage over whether maintenance payments were made regularly.

It is regrettable that the Maintenance Act does not provide for garnishee orders to be placed on the liable spouse automatically or for those orders to follow a person from one place of employment to another. In terms of the Act, if a person who has to pay maintenance under a garnishee order quits his or her job and moves to another place, the new employer is not forced to deduct the maintenance from his or her salary. For this to happen, a new garnishee order has to be made and notice served on the new employer. Consequently, it often happens that, after a garnishee order has been granted, the person simply leaves that job and moves to another place, or simply disappears, leaving the former spouse without maintenance.

Another problem with enforcement is that it is difficult to deal with arrears[†] in payment. For example, one of the reasons why women entitled to maintenance do not report non-payment when their former husbands default is the lengthy and troublesome procedure that reporting involves.

And once the person who has to pay maintenance falls into arrears, it becomes virtually impossible to catch up with the payments. For example, a person may be given a suspended sentence on condition that he or she complies with a maintenance order of R55 a month, and pays an extra R5 per month in order to pay off the past debt. If the person is in arrears to the amount of R985, it will take 197 months (more than 16 years) to complete the payment of arrears.

The only defence available to persons charged with failure to make payment in terms of a maintenance order is a lack of means – that is, they simply do not have the money. But this lack of means must not be the result of unwillingness to work or misconduct.

The ordinary methods of enforcement are also available to a maintenance creditor†. Arrears may be recovered either by contempt of court† proceedings or by a writ of execution†. Either of these options should be embarked upon only with the assistance of an attorney.

If the parent who has to pay maintenance decides to go and live in another country, the parent who has custody does not need to go to that country to enforce payment of the maintenance order. If the country is one of those mentioned in the Reciprocal Enforcement of Maintenance Orders Act 8 of 1963, the maintenance officer in South Africa, acting through the Department of Foreign Affairs, can enforce the order in that country. Examples of signatory countries are: England, Northern Ireland, Germany, Botswana, Kenya, Lesotho, Malawi, Nigeria, Swaziland, Zambia and Zimbabwe. For example, if a South African man has been paying maintenance for his children in South Africa but then decides to move to Malawi, his wife does not have to travel to that country in order to enforce the payment of maintenance. All she has to do is ask the South African Department of Foreign Affairs to arrange for the enforcement of the maintenance order.

Conclusion

It should by now be clear that one of the biggest problems relating to maintenance is that of effective enforcement. The main problem, as we have seen, is that some people cannot provide the necessary support for their families. Factors which play a role here are poor education, unemployment and poverty. It has often been suggested that the problem could be more effectively addressed if part of the burden of maintenance were carried by the State. Clearly, the State alone cannot carry the full burden. The most effective solution would appear to be a combination of public and private support.

No matter what solution is found, it will probably be a long time coming. Even so, it is important for South African women to be aware of the problems of maintaining a household and a family, especially in the case of divorce. Under current circumstances, women who are left alone, either by the death of a spouse or by divorce, are likely to be faced with the necessity of surviving largely or entirely on their own.

CHAPTER FOUR:
Child law

INTRODUCTION

This chapter deals with the legal position of children in South African law. The following questions are examined:
1. When does a child become a legal subject and when does it stop being one?
2. What is the law on legitimacy and illegitimacy in South Africa?
3. What is meant by parental authority and who has such authority over children?

THE LEGAL SUBJECT

A legal subject is a person who can have rights and duties. A child becomes a legal subject at birth if the following requirements have been met:
1. There must have been complete separation between mother and the foetus.†
2. The child must have lived after such separation, even if only for a second.

South African law does not award rights to an unborn child, because it has not yet become a person in the eyes of the law (in other words, it has not yet become a legal subject). The unborn child will therefore not generally be protected by the law. There are, however, certain exceptions to this general rule. Protection of the potential interests of the unborn child will, for example, be given in the following cases:
- If X leaves his property to 'A's children' and X dies while A is pregnant, the property will not be divided until A's child has been born.
- If a pregnant woman divorces the child's father, the child will be entitled to maintenance from the father once it is born, .
- If a person causes an unborn child physical injury before birth, the child may, after its birth, claim damages from the person who caused the injury.

JUTA & CO, LTD 75

The legal position of the child in the above instances will be held in abeyance† until the child is born alive.

The child ceases to be a legal subject when it dies.

LEGITIMACY AND ILLEGITIMACY

A child is legitimate in the following cases:
1. If the parents of the child were married to each other at the time of the child's conception† or birth, or at any time between conception and birth. It is important to note that, as a result of a recent amendment to the Births and Deaths Registration Act, the parents of the child are deemed to be 'married' even if the marriage is a customary, Muslim or Hindu marriage. Children born of such marriages are now also registered as legitimate.
2. If the child's natural parents† marry each other after the date of birth of the child (this is termed legitimizing illegitimate children).
3. If the child is adopted.
4. If the child was conceived by means of artificial insemination† and the mother's husband agreed to this.

All children who do not fall into one of these categories are illegitimate. For example, a child born to a woman who is not married is illegitimate. If a child is born to a married woman but is not fathered by her husband, there is a 'presumption of paternity'†, which means that the child will be regarded as the child of the mother's husband. There is a legal saying that 'the father is the one to whom the marriage points'. If the husband rejects the presumption of paternity and is able to prove that he is not the father, however, the child will be regarded as illegitimate.

The rights and duties of legitimate and illegitimate children differ considerably, as is explained below.

There is a world-wide trend to abolish the legal distinction between legitimate and illegitimate children, and South Africa seems now to be following this trend. Various laws have been introduced to remove these differences. The elimination of the negative consequences of the distinction follows the spirit of the Constitution, which places a high premium on equality.

PARENTAL AUTHORITY

'Parental authority' is the term used to describe the extent to which parents may control the lives of their children. It is the sum of the rights and duties that parents have in respect of their minor children.

Parental authority can be acquired on the birth of a child, upon legitimization† or by adoption. This authority is made up of two elements, namely:
1. custody, which refers to the daily care of children, including their education, physical care, protection and physical and mental development, and
2. guardianship, which refers to the administration of a child's estate and the rendering of assistance in legal transactions and proceedings.

Which parent exercises the powers outlined above? This is answered in the next two sections.

Legitimate children

During a marriage both parents have custody and guardianship over any legitimate child of the marriage and of any adopted child.

When the parents separate, that is, stop living together, the children generally live with one parent. The parents can, if they are seeking a divorce, apply to the Court for an order to determine where the children will live until the divorce is heard. (On such interim applications see further Chapter 5: Divorce law, below.) At that time, the questions of custody and guardianship will be decided. Otherwise, the parents may arrange between themselves where the children will live until the divorce is granted.

The High Court is the upper guardian of all minor children. The Court will determine which aspects of the parental authority will be exercised by each of the parents. This means that the Court will decide which rights belong to each parent:

- The Court may award guardianship and custody to either parent.
- It may award custody to one and guardianship to the other.
- It may award custody and/or guardianship to both parents – this is known as joint custody and/or guardianship.

Custody and/or guardianship will be awarded to a person who is not a parent of a child only in exceptional circumstances. For example, if both parents are killed in an accident, custody and/or guardianship may be given to the grandparents or to a friend of the family.

In principle, custody is awarded to the parent who is best able to promote the interests of the child in its day-to-day life. This parent becomes the custodian and the other parent is the non-custodian. It is most important to decide what is in the best interests of the child. Often the parents are able to agree upon the arrangement to be made for the children and, if there is no problem with this, the Court will simply make this agreement an order of the Court. The Court will also generally order that a non-custodian parent be permitted certain rights of access to the child –

allowing reasonable opportunities for visiting and even taking the child to his or her own home.

Custody and guardianship orders may be changed after the divorce. Application must be made to the Court to show that the previous arrangement is no longer in the best interests of the child.

If one parent dies, the other parent acquires full custody and guardianship of the (legitimate) children, unless the Court had appointed the parent who dies as the child's only guardian.

Illegitimate children

The mother of illegitimate children exercises both custody and guardianship, unless she herself is a minor. In that case, her guardian has guardianship of the children.

For the purposes of parental authority, the law virtually regards an illegitimate child as not having a father. The father must nevertheless support the child according to his means, even though he has no automatic right of reasonable access to his child. If he wishes to have access, he has to approach the High Court for permission. In his application the father will have to persuade the Court that it is in the best interests of the child that he be granted access. The same is true if the father wats custody or guardianship of his child. In deciding whether to give him access, custody or guardianship the court will look at things like the relationship between the father and the mother, any history of violence or abuse between the parents or of the child, the child's relationsip with the parents, the probable effect the separation from the mother of father would have on the child, the child's attitude to the father, the father's degree of commitment to the child including whether he has been paying maintenance for the child, and whether the child has been born of a customary or religious marriage. The family advocate may be asked to investigate the position and submit a report on what will be in the best interests of the child.

When the Natural Fathers of Children Born out of Wedlock Act 86 of 1997 comes into operation the father will enjoy some protection if the mother gives the child up for adoption. In the past the adoption could take place without the father's consent or knowledge. In 1997 the Constitutional Court[‡] decided that it is unconstitutional never to require the father's consent to his illegitimate child's adoption. The Natural Fathers of Children born out of Wedlock Act still does not require the father's consent to the adoption but it at least says that he must be given written notice of the planned adoption. The only cases where the father would not get notice would be in he could not be identified, if the child was born from incest or rape, or if it would be in the child's best interests theat the father not be informed of the planned adoption.

---

‡ *Fraser v Children's Court, Pretoria and others* 1997 (2) SA 261 (CC)

Termination of parental authority

Parents cannot give up their parental authority and it ends only in the following circumstances:
1. on the death of both parents;
2. on the death of the child;
3. on the minor's attainment of majority at the age of 21;
4. on the adoption of the child;
5. by an order of the High Court.

DUTY OF SUPPORT

For more information on the legal duties regarding the support of children, see Chapter Three: Support of the household, above.

CHILDREN AND DIVORCE PROCEDURE

There has long been criticism of the divorce procedure used in this country. It is time-consuming and expensive. It is also said that because the procedure is adversarial†, it encourages hostility between the man and the woman. Sometimes the children are drawn willy nilly into the parental battlefield.

Many people question whether divorce serves the best interests of the children. Much research has been done about the effects of divorce on children. This research has shown that the divorce itself and the stress within the family both before and after the divorce affect many children adversely. In some instances, the effects are long-lasting. One must, however, beware of blaming the divorce procedure itself for the adverse effects on the child. Often children blame themselves for the conflict between their parents. In other cases, their loyalties under threat, they become confused, afraid and withdrawn.

Alternative dispute resolution

Because of the problems mentioned above, many people are seeking new ways of resolving divorce disputes. In particular, efforts are being made to keep the children of divorcing parents out of their parents' battles. Also, some people argue that alternative forms of dispute resolution such as arbitration† and mediation,† are preferable to the normal divorce procedure.

Alternative dispute resolution is, however, not an accurate description of these procedures, for any agreements reached by these means still have to take account of the existing law. Divorce bargaining takes place 'in the shadow of the law', which means that the parents are not entirely free to make any arrangements they wish; they have to obey the legal rules. A better phrase would therefore be 'informal dispute resolution', since the agreements are only informal.

In South Africa arbitration is not permitted as a means of resolving divorce disputes. Mediation has, however, become a popular means of dealing with divorce disputes. In divorce mediation, the couple meet to try to reach an agreement which is acceptable to both. They try to reach agreement on all issues that are in dispute; or, if that is not possible, they try at least to reduce the level of conflict. A mediator is also present during their deliberations. He or she must try to take a neutral stance and takes part in the discussions in order to reduce the level of hostility and anger between the two people. The mediator may act as the facilitator[†] and even guide and control the discussions, but the two parties themselves are supposed to be in control of the process – the mediator is not there to make decisions for them.

Divorce mediation is not always voluntary, but it should be. Mediators believe that if parents can reach agreement in mediation, then they will probably co-operate in the future when, for example, the needs of the children change. As yet this belief has not been confirmed by research.

Some mediators prefer the children of divorcing parents to attend at least one mediation session, at which they are encouraged to express their feelings. Attending a mediation session helps the children to realize that both their parents care about them and wish to make the best possible arrangements for them.

Apart from divorce, mediation may be used to try to resolve a wide range of other family problems, such as maintenance or access disputes, whether fathers of illegitimate children should have access, disputes over property when cohabiting couples break up, etc.

Does divorce mediation provide all the answers? Divorce mediation is seen by many people today as the solution to all the difficulties of the divorce process. Some people believe that informal procedures should be welcomed in South Africa because they have been the preferred way of resolving disputes in traditional African society. Over the last 10 or 20 years, however, some writers have pointed to problems with mediation and indicated that it holds dangers for women in particular. These researchers argue that many of the claimed advantages of mediation are unfounded. Since nobody can ever be completely neutral, how can a mediator claim to be? If the mediator is not neutral, the two people cannot be in control of the process. Claims that mediation saves time and money have also not yet been tested.

Particular disadvantages of mediation from the woman's point of view are the following:

- Unless the mediator has a thorough knowledge of the law, the woman may not benefit as much as she might by consulting an attorney.
- By encouraging the two people to adopt a conciliatory approach and come to an agreement, mediation may deprive a woman of the opportunity to express legitimate anger.
- Mediation cannot succeed where the disputing people have unequal power in marriage, and in South Africa the husband usually has more power than the wife.
- Divorce cases involving child or spousal abuse should not be mediated because marriages involving violence represent the most extreme form of power imbalance in a family. The abused woman may not have the courage or strength to defend herself in a mediation situation.

It is clear that although the traditional adversarial divorce procedure presents many problems for the two parties and their children, divorce mediation does not provide all the easy answers. We must therefore continue to search for further solutions to the problems inherent in the current divorce procedure.

The family advocate

During the early 1990's family advocate offices were introduced in all the main centres in South Africa. Family advocates are equivalent to the officers of the courts who in other countries are sometimes known as 'the children's friend'. Their specific task is to protect the interests of the children of divorcing parents. So, for instance, family advocates may conduct enquiries into the arrangements being made for children when a divorce is pending. They may do so on their own if, after they have read the divorce papers, they think it is necessary. They may also be asked to do so by one of the divorcing parties or by the Court itself.

The appointment of family advocates represents the most important step yet taken by our law to protect the interests of the children affected by divorce. The family advocates' offices are like the family court in small form. It would be good news if the government were to take the further step of introducing full family courts throughout the country, where an even wider range of divorce issues could be handled. Whether this will happen soon is in doubt, however, because the family advocates' offices are experiencing problems of insufficient staff and funding, even now.

Although it was an Act called the Mediation in Certain Divorce Matters Act 24 of 1987 which created the family advocates' offices, what the family advocates do cannot really be called mediation. The most important reasons for this are as follows:

- Family advocates are permitted, in theory at any rate, to force the parents to attend meetings, while mediation is said to work best if it is voluntary.
- The family advocate acts as the child's representative and therefore cannot be called neutral – a prerequisite for a mediator.
- The family advocate actively participates in the process of reaching an agreement, something a mediator should not do.

Conclusion

This chapter has discussed how the law deals with children, especially in the areas of parental power and divorce procedure. While there have been several changes recently regarding children, more reform is needed. For example, the distinctions between the legitimate and illegitimate status of children need to be reconsidered in the light of world-wide trends, the Constitution of the Republic of South Africa Act 108 of 1996 and the fact that African customary law does not draw the same distinction between legitimate and illegitimate children.

CHAPTER FIVE:
Divorce law

INTRODUCTION

Since the new Divorce Act was passed, the number of divorces in South Africa has increased dramatically. In 1976, 12 329 whites, coloureds and Asians were divorced. (No statistics were available on the number of Africans who were divorced in 1976.) By 1993 the number of divorces granted had more than doubled to 26 616 white, coloured and Asian couples. The figures for African couples are calculated from 1 July every year to 30 June of the following year. During the 1992–93 year, 6 789 divorces were granted to African couples in Johannesburg, Durban and King William's Town alone.

GROUNDS FOR DIVORCE

Since the passage of the Act, there have been only two grounds for divorce in our law:
1. irretrievable breakdown, and
2. mental illness or continuous† unconsciousness.

These two grounds are discussed below.

Irretrievable breakdown

A divorce will be granted if one of the spouses proves that the marriage has broken down irretrievably. This means that the husband or wife must prove that the spouse's relationship has deteriorated to the point that the marriage no longer exists as a marriage in the true sense of the word, and that it cannot be foreseen that a real marital relationship will be restored in the future. In other words, it has to be shown that:
1. the marital relationship is no longer normal, and
2. there is no reasonable prospect of a return to a normal marital relationship.

Anything can lead to this state of affairs, and the husband or wife can rely on any facts to show that there has been an irretrievable breakdown. The Court will then decide whether those facts prove that the marriage has indeed broken down irretrievably.

There are, however, three factors that the Court will usually accept as proof of irretrievable breakdown. These are:
1. The fact that the spouses have not lived together for at least one year immediately before the divorce action was started.
2. The fact that the other spouse has committed adultery and the spouse who wants the divorce finds this irreconcilable† with a continued marriage.
3. The fact that the other spouse has been declared by the Court to be a habitual† criminal and as a result has been imprisoned.

It is important to note that these three factors are not the only ones to prove that a marriage has broken down irretrievably – any facts can be used.

Mental illness or continuous unconsciousness

If your spouse is mentally ill, you can obtain a divorce if you can prove that:
- your spouse is in an institution or is being held in a place for mentally ill prisoners, and
- he or she has not been released from there for at least two years immediately before the start of the divorce action, and
- there is no reasonable prospect that he or she will be cured of the mental illness. This must be proved by the evidence of two psychiatrists, one of whom will be appointed by the Court.

If your spouse is unconscious for a continuous period, you will be granted a divorce if it can be proved that:
- your spouse is unconscious because of illness or injury to his or her body, and
- he or she has been unconscious for at least six months immediately before the start of the divorce action, and
- there is no reasonable prospect that he or she will recover consciousness. This must be supported by the evidence of two doctors, one of whom must be a neurologist or neurosurgeon appointed by the Court.

Divorce and religious marriages

It can happen that a couple enters into a marriage which is valid both in terms of South African law and in accordance with their particular religious faith. Most Jewish marriages, for example, are valid in terms of both South

African common law and Jewish religious law. If the couple obtain a divorce in terms of South African law but not in terms of Jewish religious law, they are considered still to be married in the eyes of Jewish religious law. Thus, Jewish religious law ignores their civil divorce. Furthermore, in Jewish religious law, only a husband can arrange for a divorce (*get*[†]): a wife has no power to start the procedures for a *get* (although in certain circumstances she can approach the rabbinical court to complain about the conditions in the marriage). It sometimes happens that the husband refuses to grant the wife a *get* after the divorce under South African common law. The result is that the wife cannot marry again under Jewish religious law because, if she were to, Jewish religious law would view this second marriage as adulterous and the children born of it as illegitimate.

In order to avoid this situation, our law (in s 5A of the Divorce Act) provides that a South African divorce court which is asked to make a civil divorce order can refuse to do so if the religion of either or both of the parties requires that the couple must also divorce under the religious sytem before they can marry somebody else. The Court may also make any other order it deems fit, for example, an order forcing the man to make the necessary arrangements to obtain the *get*. The Court may do these things even if the person who wants the divorce has proved that the marriage has broken down irretrievably. In this situation proof of one of the grounds for divorce will therefore not entitle one to a divorce under South African law until a *get* has been granted or all the steps have been taken to arrange for this.

Consequences of divorce

The main consequences of divorce relate to property, maintenance and children.

Property

How the divorcing couple's property will be divided depends on which matrimonial property system their marriage is based on. This was discussed in detail in Chapter 2: Financial inequality: husband and wives, above.

Maintenance

Post-divorce maintenance was discussed in Chapter 3: Support of the household, above.

Children

The consequences of divorce for the couple's children were dealt with in Chapter 4: Child law, above.

INTERIM RELIEF: RULE 43 OF THE UNIFORM RULES OF COURT

Rule 43 of the Uniform Rules of the High Court deals with how a wife or a husband can seek financial support during the time between the effective end of the marriage and the final granting of the divorce – that is, during the 'interim period'. During this time, a spouse can seek some help known as interim relief.

In terms of rule 43 a spouse who is waiting for his or her divorce to be finalized can claim the following:

1. Maintenance: if the spouse cannot support herself or himself, she or he can apply for an order forcing the other spouse to give an amount of money weekly, monthly or on some other basis. The maintenance can be for the spouse alone, or for the spouse and the couple's children. (See further the paragraph on Maintenance and divorce, in Chapter 3: Support of the household, above.)
2. A contribution towards the costs of the divorce. For example, if the wife does not have enough money to pay for the divorce and her husband has the means to do so, she can ask the Court to force him to pay some of her legal expenses.
3. Interim custody: the husband or wife can ask the Court for an order permitting him or her to have interim custody of the couple's children until the divorce is granted and the Court decides who must have final custody of the children. The Court will look at the best interests of the children in deciding whether the application should be granted.
4. Interim access: if one spouse has custody of the couple's children, the other can ask the Court for an order permitting him or her access to the children (in other words, to have contact with the children) until the divorce is granted and the Court decides who must have final custody. The best interests of the children will here also determine whether the application is granted or not. (On the question of access to children, see Chapter 4: Child law, above.)

WHAT WILL HAPPEN WHEN YOU DECIDE TO DIVORCE?

Once you know the rules which determine on what grounds divorce is possible and you are fully informed of the financial and other consequences that will flow from divorce, you must carefully weigh up the situation. If you still want to proceed with the divorce, you have to proceed as follows:

1. First of all, you have to make an appointment to see an attorney. Choose someone you are comfortable with and who you think will look after your interests.
2. At that first appointment, explain to him or her why you want a divorce. You will also have to give the following information: your financial affairs, whether you work, whether you need maintenance, what you want for the children, etc. Ask the attorney to start divorce proceedings for you. You can also ask him or her to claim interim relief for you in terms of rule 43 if you need it.

    Once you have instructed the attorney to start divorce proceedings, the following will happen:

3. A summons will be issued and will be delivered to your spouse by the sheriff of the Court.
4. Once your spouse has received the summons, he or she has ten working days in which to decide whether to defend the divorce action or not. If your spouse wants to defend the action, he or she must inform the Court within the prescribed period and must file a notice of intention to defend the action with the Court.
5. If your spouse does not file a notice of intention to defend, a date will be arranged for the case to be heard by the Court.
6. If your spouse does file a notice of intention to defend, your attorney and your spouse's attorney will try to get you and your spouse to reach a settlement regarding the consequences of your divorce. This is where disagreements often arise about maintenance, the division of property, and the children. (See the next section below on what you must consider when you are asked to enter into a divorce settlement.)
7. If you and your spouse have children, the family advocate will consider your case and decide whether or not to become involved. Alternatively, you or your spouse could ask the family advocate to look into the position of the children. If the family advocate becomes involved, he or she will have to meet you, your spouse and the children, and may also ask to speak to other people who have information about your children.

    Once the family advocate has carefully looked at the position of

your children, he or she will write a report which will be handed in to the Court.
8. If you and your spouse succeed in coming to an agreement that the marriage has broken down irretrievably and about the consequences of the divorce, only you have to appear in Court on the date on which the case is heard. The case will then be heard in Court as an unopposed divorce and the divorce will usually be granted on that date. Such a divorce is normally not as expensive as one in which the spouses cannot reach agreement and do not enter into a divorce settlement.
9. If you and your spouse cannot come to an agreement and you do not want mediation, the case will go to Court as an opposed divorce. In Court, evidence must be produced about all the aspects over which you and your spouse cannot agree. The Court will then decide the outcome of the disputes. Such a divorce is normally expensive and takes longer than an unopposed divorce to reach finality.

Entering into a divorce settlement

When you are asked to enter into a divorce settlement you must remember what your rights are. Do not simply accept whatever is offered to you and do not just sign any settlement agreement that is put in front of you. The following case study will show you some of the dangers of entering into a settlement without thinking carefully about your rights and about what the future might hold.

Case study

Sarah, a teacher, married David, a clerk. Sarah stopped working when they had their first child, John. The couple also had a daughter, Milly. David was promoted regularly and by the time of the divorce had a senior position, whereas Sarah had not worked outside the home for ten years and found it difficult to obtain work.

They entered into a divorce settlement and in it David appeared to be generous: he offered to pay R400 maintenance per month per child and to keep the children on his medical aid. Sarah received most of the couple's furniture, their second car, which was paid for but was already ten years old, and half the proceeds of the sale of the house, after the payment of the bond. This turned out to be less than Sarah had expected, and after the motor car broke down and was repaired, she had hardly any money left. She was forced to take a job as a clerk, which did not pay much. Her salary was hardly enough to pay the rent, water, electricity and telephone accounts each month. The maintenance money was used to buy food and clothes for the children. When the new school year started, Sarah realized that she did not have any money to pay the children's school fees or to buy them school clothes. Nor could she afford Milly's piano lessons or the karate lessons John wanted.

Sarah asked David to increase the maintenance for the children, or to help pay for the children's school fees and clothing. David was, however, only willing to increase the maintenance by 5% per year, leaving Sarah still unable to pay the children's school fees, and for clothing and extracurricular activities. The next year, David remarried and refused to pay more maintenance. Sarah applied to the maintenance court for an increase in maintenance, and after a couple of postponements, the case was eventually placed on the roll and Sarah had to give evidence about all her expenses and income. Luckily, she was granted a small increase in maintenance. However, the following year, dreading doing through all the trauma of a Court appearance again, she gladly accepted David's offer of R100 towards school clothes instead of again applying for an increase in maintenance for the children.

If she had negotiated the payment of expenses such as the children's school fees, clothing and extra lessons in the divorce settlement, as well as an annual increase in the maintenance, Sarah would not have had to contend with these difficulties.

Divorce settlement: checklist

When you have to decide whether to accept a divorce settlement, do not fall into the same trap as Sarah did. You must think carefully about your own and your children's future. Make sure that you make the best possible arrangements – especially in respect of finances and the children. When deciding whether to accept a settlement offered to you, you must remember in particular:

- to make provision for an annual increase of the maintenance for yourself and the children – otherwise you may need to go to the maintenance court every year to ask for an increase;
- that, if you do not qualify for permanent maintenance, you may ask for rehabilitative maintenance for yourself to enable you to get back on your feet, especially if you did not work prior to the divorce;
- to specify who will be responsible for the children's school fees, school clothing, school books, stationery and fees, and clothing and equipment for their extracurricular activities such as sport;
- to specify who will be responsible for the children's medical and dental expenses and on whose medical scheme they will be;
- to ask for a study policy or other kind of insurance policy to be taken out on the life of your former spouse with either yourself or the children as the beneficiaries; remember also to include a clause in the settlement that your former spouse may not cede the policy to someone else;

- to specify when and where and how often the non-custodial parent may have the children for school holidays, public holidays and weekends;
- to state with whom children will spend birthdays;
- to state that the non-custodial parent may not take the children away on holiday while he or she has access without first informing the custodial parent;
- to state whether the parents will continue to share guardianship of the children – this is important to avoid disputes over consent to the children's contracts, etc;
- to state that the parent who has custody may not change their surname without the non-custodial parent's consent.

To ask for the insurance policies mentioned above, for example, may be a good negotiating strategy as well as being important for your children's future needs. Taking into account the enormous cost of schooling, clothing and fees for other activities your children might be interested in, the sharing of these payments, specified in the settlement, may be better than just accepting a fixed amount of maintenance.

When negotiating a settlement, it is often a question of give and take, but make sure that you understand every last detail of that settlement, because once it is signed and made a Court order, it is very difficult to change the contents.

PART THREE:
Women and violence

INTRODUCTION

One of the basic principles that applies in our society is that every person has a right to be protected from violence or bodily injury by another. This principle is also included in our new Constitution, which states in s 12(1):

> *Everyone has the right to freedom and security of the person, which includes the right –* …
> *(c) to be free from all forms of violence from both public and private sources;*
> *(d) not to be tortured in any way; and*
> *(e) not to be treated or punished in a cruel, inhuman or degrading way.*

We can see that it is a function of the law to protect people from any form of violence. However, if we wish to make use of this protection, it is important that we know two things:

1. we must have some basic knowledge of the different forms of violence, so that we can recognize them when we come across them, and
2. we must be aware of the different types of protection offered by the law and how this protection can be obtained.

These are the aspects discussed in Part Three: Women and violence. First, we explain what is meant by 'violence'. Then we discuss the commoner forms of violence which women and female children normally encounter: assault,[†] rape[†] and incest. We also consider the possibility that a woman may defend herself when she is attacked, and suggest how far she can go in her defence. The special protection offered by the law is also discussed, as well as the help that can be obtained from the community. We hope that this part will give women more information about the laws that are meant to protect them from violence so that they will be able to avoid violence. And if they cannot avoid violence altogether, by acquiring knowledge and

© JUTA & CO, LTD

by using the laws which are there to protect them, at least women can know how and where to find help and justice from the law.

What 'violence' means

Violence is not a legal term with a precise legal meaning. It appears as part of the definition of several crimes and it therefore has to be explained. By 'violence' we mean the use of physical force to the body of another person which causes injury or is intended to cause injury.

When people use physical violence against other persons, they normally intend to harm those persons. The law is not concerned with the form the violence takes. The violence does not even have to be excessive or very strong. The slightest use of force, such as a blow, or grabbing hold of the victim's arm, will normally be regarded as violence. The violence can be applied directly, as with a punch or a kick, but it can also be applied indirectly, as for example when a vicious dog is urged to attack someone.

Apart from physical violence, people can also be subjected to mental violence, as when one person locks another up in a dark room or threatens that a witch doctor will cast a spell on the victim. Threats of violence are therefore also regarded as violence. Yet other violence can have a sexual component where force is applied in the sexual act.

No person should be subjected to torture. This merely means that no persons, including women and children, should be the victims of any form of violence. For this reason, our law says that the use of violence against another person should be regarded as a crime and that those who inflict violence should be punished by the State.

> **TO THINK ABOUT**
>
> Before reading further, think about what you know about women and violence, consider the stories, movies, television shows or reports of women who have been abused, attacked or raped.
> - Do you know any women who have been victims of violence?
> - Think about the women in your life. Have any of these women or female children experienced violence?
>
> Now, think about what you know of the law and the legal systems available to help these women. As you read further, keep these stories, reports and women in mind.

It is as well to remind ourselves that it is no longer acceptable to regard women as inferior to men merely because they are female. This is the view of the State and it is clearly set out in two sections of the 1996 Constitution. First, s 187 makes provision for the institution of a Commission for Gender

Equality. This commission is intended to promote equality between the sexes and to advise Parliament on laws which affect the status of women. Secondly, s 9 of the Constitution provides as follows:

- *every person is equal before the law and has the right to equal protection and benefit of the law;*
- *no person shall be unfairly discriminated against, directly or indirectly ... on one or more of the following grounds ...: race, gender, sex, sexual orientation, pregnancy, marital status, age ... birth.*

The view of the State is in step with the world-wide trend towards taking steps to eliminate violence against women. The Commission on Crime Prevention and Criminal Justice of the United Nations has for many years been involved in a crime prevention and criminal justice program. The Economic and Social Council of the United Nations, in its resolution 1991/18, recognized that 'violence against women in the family and society was pervasive and crossed lines of income, class and culture', and urged member states to take all appropriate administrative, social and educational measures to protect women from all forms of physical or mental violence. This Council also adopted resolution 1995/27 in terms of which the Secretary-General was requested to prepare a draft plan of action, in the context of crime prevention and criminal justice, on the elimination of violence. This plan would provide practical and action-orientated suggestions on how to address this issue by means of, inter alia, legislative action, technical co-operation and training.

In 1994 the United Nations General Assembly adopted the Declaration on the Elimination of Violence against Women, expressing concern that violence against women is an obstacle to the achievement of equality, development and peace, and affirmed that it constitutes a violation of women's rights and fundamental freedoms. The Declaration gives a detailed definition of violence against women and then calls on states to condemn it and to pursue without delay a policy of eliminating violence against women. How they should do it is explained in detail.

South Africa ratified the United Nations Convention on the Elimination of All Forms of Discrimination Against Women on 15 December 1995. Although this Convention does not specifically deal with violence against women, the Committee on the Elimination of Discrimination against Women has subsequently made certain recommendations in this regard. It has also defined gender-based violence and requires State Parties to the Convention to act to protect women against violence of any kind occurring within the family, in the workplace or in any other area of social life, and, amongst other things, to report back on measures they have taken in this regard.

CHAPTER SIX:
Common forms of violence encountered by women

Violence can take any of the different forms mentioned above: physical, mental, sexual.

Therefore it is important to distinguish different crimes in which violence of any kind plays a role. We discuss two of the most common types of violence against women, namely assault and rape.

In the case of assault, any person can be the victim of the violence: man, woman or child. In the case of rape, on the other hand, the victim always has to be a woman or a girl. In South Africa, where one man forces another man to have sex with him, we do not call it rape, but it is referred to as sodomy, a specific crime. (Sodomy is no longer considered a crime by the Western Cape High Court.) Lay persons sometimes refer to it as 'indecent assault'.

In the discussion that follows, we always refer to the victim as a woman, but it must be kept in mind that a man or a child can also be the victim of assault. The person who applies the violence – the culprit or the accused – may be either male or female and may be either a complete stranger to the victim or a relative.

VIOLENCE THROUGH ASSAULT

Violence through assault is, unfortunately, very common. Assault occurs when someone violently attacks another person, or even threatens to attack that person. It could take place in a bar, in the street, in a dark alley, or even in the home. In law, assault is generally defined as:

> *The crime which occurs when one person* unlawfully *and* intentionally uses force *against the body of another person, or when one person threatens another person with violence in such a way that the threatened person believes that the threat can be carried out.*

Various aspects of this definition might be unfamiliar to the reader. If a suspect is to be found guilty of having committed assault, the State must prove in a court of law that all of these aspects (or elements) are present.

We shall therefore explain some of these in more detail. The three key aspects are:
- (a) use of force or violence,
- (b) unlawfully, and
- (c) intentionally.

Use of force or violence

The violence or physical abuse can take any form, including beating, hitting, punching, slapping, biting, burning or cutting. Injuries may be inflicted by hands, feet, teeth, knives or other sharp objects, hot liquids or hot objects (such as burning cigarette ends), sticks, pipes, ropes, hosepipes and so on.

> ### S v MARX 1962 (1) SA 848 (N)
>
> A certain Mr Marx gave two children aged five and seven years some wine to drink. After drinking the wine, the children became ill. The younger child could not even walk and was in a semi-conscious condition.
>
> Mr Marx was found guilty of assault.

Assault can even be committed without physical contact, though the victim is threatened. It is not important to know whether the culprit intends carrying out his threat or whether he is capable of doing so. What is important is whether the victim believes him. Here violence exists in the fear that the victim feels.

Unlawfully

The use of violence is not always unlawful or contrary to the law. In a number of everyday circumstances violence does occur, but it is not regarded as a crime. How do we know whether violence is lawful or unlawful? In other words, when is violence a crime and when is it not? Here we have to consider the views of our society. Where the community regards violence as unacceptable, then it is unlawful.

In practice, the community has already indicated that it finds the use of violence acceptable in certain situations, and if it occurs within certain limits. It should be reasonable and moderate and should not cause serious injuries. Some of these situations are:
- where a person has agreed that violence may be applied to the body (for example, when a person consents to take part in a boxing match);
- where parents discipline their children;

- where there is a state of emergency (for example, where a building is on fire and the people trying to escape trample on others);
- where people have to use violence in an effort to protect themselves (discussed in more detail in Chapter Seven: Private defence, below).

Intentionally

Intentionally, when used as a legal term, means that the attacker must know that his or her conduct is prohibited but nevertheless act deliberately to harm victims in spite of this knowledge. Now you will understand why babies who bite their mothers while being suckled cannot be punished, although they apply violence to her body. Since they don't know what they are doing, they do not act 'intentionally'.

Only when all three elements mentioned above are present – violence, unlawfulness and intention – can an assailant be found guilty of the crime of assault and be punished by a court of law.

There are certain forms of assault which occur so often that they have been given special names to distinguish them from the common assault described above. Three of these forms of assault are explained below:
- assault with intent to do grievous bodily harm,
- indecent assault, and
- domestic violence.

Assault with intent to do grievous bodily harm

Assault with intent to do grievous bodily harm is common assault where the attacker also intends to cause serious injury to the victim. In other words, it is a more serious form of common assault. For example, the culprit who merely twists someone's arm does not normally want to cause serious harm. But if someone who is already lying flat on the ground is kicked in the face with a hard boot, we assume that the culprit wants to cause grievous or serious injury.

Indecent assault

Indecent assault can be defined as the unlawful and intentional assault of another person with the aim of committing an indecency.

Indecent assault occurs where the culprit directs the violence at the victim's private parts or sexual organs. Examples would be where a man puts his hand under a woman's dress, even if he does not succeed in touching her private parts. (Remember, it is not necessary that a woman's private parts are actually touched for the act to be indecent assault.) Anal intercourse with a woman without her consent is also considered to be indecent assault.

The amount of violence used in this form of assault can be minimal. The law does not require the victim to be injured: a mere touching of the body in a private area would often be enough to break the law. For example, a culprit may touch a woman's breasts without her consent. A husband can also commit indecent assault against his wife.

As indicated above, a man can also be a victim of indecent assault.

Assault within the family circle (domestic violence)

There are certain forms of assault which occur most often within the family circle. These include:
- assault on a wife or a husband by the other spouse;
- assault on the children by the parents or other relatives, or
- assault on the elderly by their children or grandchildren.

In this type of assault the victim often cannot escape being hurt because of family ties to the attacker. Unfortunately, one frequently comes across this form of assault today and it is often covered up. However, everything that has been said with regard to assault applies equally within the family. One should therefore preferably refer to 'assault' and not to 'battery', as some people tend to regard 'battery' as a somewhat lesser crime because it occurs within the family. This is a misperception as they are one and the same crime. Others consider it a more serious crime because it is generally considered that a relationship of trust exists within a family circle, and assault within this circle amounts, in addition, to a violation of that trust.

Therefore, although the same victim is continuously assaulted by the same person, and it has become customary to refer to the assault as 'battery', 'battery' remains common assault which takes place over a period of time. The various forms of this type of assault that you will encounter include child abuse and even abuse of the elderly, so-called 'granny battery'.

Bear in mind that people often use the term 'abuse' when indicating that harm, hurt or injury is inflicted on a person or that a person is maltreated. As is the case with the term 'violence' (see above), abuse is not a legal term, but has more or less the same meaning.

Family violence not only affects the members of a particular family: the community at large is also negatively affected. For instance, information released by the Harriet Tubman Women's Shelter in Minneapolis indicates that an estimated 25% of workplace problems in the United States of America – such as absenteeism, low productivity, high staff turnover and excessive use of medical benefits – are due to family violence. This means that not only do medical expenses resulting from family violence total billions of dollars annually, but businesses forfeit even more in lost wages, sick leave, absenteeism and non-productivity. One can expect this to apply equally to South Africa.

Various myths surround family violence – these are widespread and often accepted as the truth. This has led to a situation in our society where family violence is still largely a hidden occurrence and often regarded as a private matter. Because many people are unaware of family violence in their own communities and because information about it is limited, they tend to deny its existence. Others do not want to know about it and choose to ignore signs of it because they do not want to become involved. Only recognition of the tremendously negative effect of violence on families and the community at large, coupled with a determined effort on the part of the community and the government to combat it, will lead to the effective control (and ultimate eradication) of this crime.

For society to tolerate violence in the home ('in private') but to denounce it in public is to espouse double standards. Society should then not be shocked when children who grow up in violent homes in turn become violent and abusive adults themselves. It is often at home where young boys, especially, are taught by example that violence is a means of resolving conflict. Sexual stereotyping plays a great role in upholding this notion: men are supposed to be strong, aggressive, in control, assertive and able to fight for what they want, while women are supposed to be 'feminine', submissive, pleasing and appeasing.

Sexual stereotyping poses a number of problems. First, it is artificial and arbitrary. For example, in Western society men have traditionally been thought to be biologically suited to hard physical work and thus to being the 'breadwinners' and providers to wives and families, while women have been seen to be most suited to nurturing roles. However, in many African countries it is primarily the women who perform manual labour. Also, notions of what is suitable or appropriate change over time: in Victorian times it was generally accepted that studying was beyond the intellectual capabilities of women and that, because they were 'delicate', they should be 'protected' from the realities of such matters as politics and finance. Today, by contrast, many women are educated at tertiary institutions and they are to be found in practically all the professions.

Secondly, sexual stereotyping is very common and widely accepted despite being distorted. We find that it starts at birth (for example, baby girls are dressed in 'feminine' pink, baby boys in blue), and continues through all stages of life. For example, girls are generally given toys such as dolls and tea sets, while boys are given cars and chemistry sets. Unfortunately this stereotyping is often reinforced by schools, community organizations and churches. At school, girls are taught domestic science and boys are taught woodwork. In churches men are the spiritual leaders while women serve tea and do fundraising but are excluded from important decision making. The media are also at fault. Newspapers with so-called women's pages give the impression that women are interested only in the superficial matters covered in these sections and not in serious news. Moreover, advertisements portray women as more interested in the whiteness of their washing than in anything else; 'soaps' and other television productions portray women as prone to hysterics, concerned only with their outward appearance, having dubious driving skills, etc. Unfortunately, many women stereotyping as a standard for 'good' or 'womanly' behavior: failure to measure up often leads to guilt or feelings of worthlessness.

Thirdly, sexual stereotyping lowers women's status. Certain jobs are considered less important and not so much status is attached to these jobs. Women are often seen as automatic candidates for such jobs. They are usually employed in service-type work such as office cleaning, not in production. (Even in the clothing industry, women are employed as machinists rather than cutters, who are better paid.) Women often work as secretaries, 'girl Fridays' or administration personnel and not as managers, or executives. Because of the perceived lowly status of these jobs, they are badly paid and carry fewer benefits.

The preceding discussion highlights the most important need in the fight to rid society of family violence, namely education. We need a public education campaign which is aimed at changing peoples' attitudes and values in order to create a culture of non-violence and to provide the notion of gender equality.

We now discuss the first two forms of domestic (or family) violence separately.

Wife beating or spouse abuse

This form of assault occurs when a woman is assaulted by her husband or partner. In the past, wife-beating was considered an appropriate way of correcting a woman's behaviour. It was not regarded as wrong or unlawful, but was compared to the disciplining or correcting of a child. If a wife was disobedient or neglected her duties, it was argued, her husband could punish her by assaulting her. This view probably originated from the general belief that a wife belonged to her husband. As head of the family, the husband was expected to control his wife and children. If a wife was beaten by her husband, the State would not intervene because this was regarded both as acceptable and as a private matter.

The present legal position, however, is that violence against a wife is just as criminal as any other form of assault. It is no longer a matter for the family alone to deal with, but should be dealt with by the police and the formal legal system. If women themselves do not indicate that violent behaviour perpetrated against them is unacceptable, it will never stop. It is important, therefore, that women take legal action to prevent their husbands or partners from beating them. One of the ways of preventing further violence is to make use of the remedies offered by the legal system, which are discussed later. (See Chapter Eight: Remedies in law, below.)

However, if a woman feels herself unable to make use of the legal system, she does have a number of alternative courses of action at her disposal – see Chapter Nine: Support systems in the community, below.

Let us look at some of the myths surrounding the abuse of women.

Only certain types of men abuse women. Untrue: the abuse of women crosses all cultural, educational and economic boundaries – men from all walks of society abuse women, not only, for example, those who are unemployed or uneducated. There is no typical abuser. However, what is clear is that the abuser generally needs to be in control at all times. Abuse is about power and control. This often manifests itself in monitoring the movements, telephone calls and other social contact of the spouse or partner, the questioning of her decisions, even the screening of TV viewing and generally in behaviour that seeks to isolate the woman from friends, colleagues, family, etc who form part of her support group.

It is a private family matter. Untrue: the fact is that the home is the least safe place in the world for many women (female children included). This is where abuse, incest and rape occur, and here family members are mostly the culprits. These crimes must not be hidden.

Stress causes abuse. Untrue: stress may trigger violent behaviour, but is not the cause of it. Consider a parallel situation: stress is also present in the workplace, but most men who abuse women do not also abuse their colleagues at work, where violent outbursts can usually be controlled. There is no reason why they cannot be controlled in the home, too.

Abused women are uneducated and/or working class women. Untrue: as is the case with the abuser, women from all cultural, educational and economic levels of society are liable to be subjected to abuse.

Women who are abused ask for it. Untrue: nobody asks to be abused. Blaming a woman for deserving or 'asking for' abuse because she is 'cheeky' or 'nags' or 'does not know her place' is merely to provide an excuse for a man's wilful and unbridled behaviour. The reality is that people choose to abuse or not to abuse.

Women enjoy being abused: 'if it's so bad, why doesn't she leave?' Untrue: nobody enjoys, for example, being hit or being burned by a cigarette stub or sustaining bruised limbs or broken bones – and women are no exception. There is a huge difference between a woman's staying because she sees no way out and staying because she enjoys abuse. It is important to understand that there are often complex reasons for staying, ranging from the purely practical to sheer terror.

The reason why women stay has been the focus of much academic research: this in itself indicates how complex the matter is.

Some of the reasons why women stay in abusive relationships are:
- for financial reasons;
- out of fear that they will not be believed by their families, the police, the community;
- because society puts pressure on women to stay 'for the sake of the children';
- because family members feel that if a woman leaves her husband or partner, this will 'stigmatize' the family;
- for emotional reasons: constant abuse may have destroyed the woman's self-confidence or even her inner strength so that she cannot cope on her own.

Alcohol and drugs cause abuse. Untrue: these substances often play a role in abusive relationships, but many men abuse women when they are sober or not on drugs. Also, not all men who use alcohol (and even get drunk) or drugs abuse women. Clearly, this is simply a lame excuse or justification for abusive behaviour.

These myths should be exposed for what they are: fiction. If we allow them to go unchallenged, abusive behaviour will continue. In South Africa today it is estimated that one in four women (some estimate it as high as one in three) is abused by a person with whom she is involved in an intimate relationship; and that at least once every six days a woman is killed by her male partner. In the United States of America, where more information on domestic violence is available, recent findings by the Surgeon-General reveal that domestic violence is the leading cause of injury to women between the ages of 15 and 44. Indeed, it occurs more commonly than car accidents, muggings and cancer deaths combined.

Finally, domestic violence is perhaps best explained by the so-called 'cycle of violence' theory put forward by psychologist, Dr Lenore Walker of Dobash. This theory is based on her interviews with and research among abused women. Walker came to the conclusion that abusive relationships are usually cyclical and that a complete cycle consists of three stages (note that this cycle is not necessarily present in all violent relationships):

Phase 1: Tension building During this phase, stress builds up. Women who have been abused several times report that during this stage they expect violence. They try to stay out of the abuser's way and to avoid violence by 'correct' behaviour. This phase may last a long time and it is impossible to predict exactly when the violent outburst will occur. Verbal abuse is common during this phase.

Phase 2: The violent outburst When the major abusive incident occurs, it can take the form of psychological cruelty. Verbal abuse also occurs. Although the woman is traumatized, the abuser may appear calm and rational. The abuser may even accompany the woman to a doctor or the casualty department of a hospital after the outburst.

Phase 3: Reconciliation or honeymoon An abuser frequently expresses remorse, even cries and often promises that it will never happen again. He brings home gifts and takes the woman out as he did during courtship, offering the hope of better behaviour. The woman is often blamed for the violence and she usually accepts responsibility for it, is made to feel guilty for having 'provoked' him, and often feels worthless. (See the discussion of sexual stereotyping above) If she left her abuser after the violent outburst, she usually returns during this phase, often out of dependence and/or remorse or guilt.

The conflict remains unresolved, though, and the cycle begins again. Walker has noted that over time phase 3 becomes shorter and shorter, whilst phases 1 and 2 become longer and the abuse grows more severe.

Child abuse

This type of assault occurs when weak and defenceless babies or children are assaulted. The culprit is often the father or mother or another authority figure in the family. Normally there are a series of assaults, until one day the assaulter goes too far and the victim's injuries are so serious that the crime is detected by a friend, neighbour, teacher, etc.

The legal situation with regard to child abuse is precisely the same as that in respect of assault of a wife. Where the father beats his children, the mother can summon help by making use of the procedures described in Chapters Eight and Nine, below. If the mother beats the children, she can be punished in the same way as any other perpetrator of assault. In this case, her husband can make use of the same legal procedures to prevent her from beating the children.

TO THINK ABOUT

Think about the stories you have heard on the radio or programmes you may have seen on TV about cases of wife-beating or child abuse. Or think about a situation you may know about where a woman or a child has been beaten by members of the family.

- How do these stories make you feel?
- What do you think the community can do to help prevent these cases from recurring?

By law, anyone who reasonably suspects that a child is being ill-treated has a duty immediately to report the circumstances to a police officer, a commissioner of child welfare or a social worker. Therefore, many child abuse cases are brought to Court by watchful teachers, doctors, nurses or neighbours who care about the children.

From the above paragraphs it is obvious that no female of any age may be assaulted by anybody – neither by her husband nor by her father nor by a friend. That the culprit or assailant is related to the female is completely irrelevant for the purposes of the law.

VIOLENCE THROUGH RAPE

In South Africa, rape is legally defined as sexual intercourse with a woman where she has not agreed to it. In law, this means that the victim has not given her consent to sexual intercourse. A woman can be raped by a stranger or by someone she knows. Some rapes happen when a man wielding a gun or a knife threatens a woman with death unless she has sex with him. Sometimes a woman is raped by her employer under threat of losing her position if she says no. Sometimes a young girl is raped by a teacher under threat that she will fail if she doesn't have sex with him. Rape is not just a matter of sexual interest: it is a crime of power. The man attacks the woman sexually to demonstrate his power over her (or over women generally).

Rape is probably one of the oldest crimes known to humanity. It differs from other crimes in that the victims can only be women. Our forefathers regarded rape as a crime, not because they wanted to protect women, but because they wanted to protect the interests of men. In those days, a woman was regarded as the possession of her father if she was unmarried, or as the possession of her husband if she was married. To rape a woman was to tarnish or debase the father's or the husband's possession. In modern times, however, rape is made a punishable offence in order to protect the woman herself from sexual abuse.

If one looks at the definition of rape more closely, three important aspects become clear:
  (a) sexual intercourse must take place,
  (b) with a woman, and
  (c) without her consent.

Each of these aspects is discussed below.

Sexual intercourse
According to our law, the man's penis must enter the female's vagina for the act to be rape. How deeply it enters is irrelevant, because the slightest

penetration is enough. It is not necessary that the woman should be injured or that the man should have emitted semen. It is also not essential that the woman should become pregnant.

If a man tries to penetrate the woman with his penis and cannot – because she fights him off or he is caught in the act, for instance – he is then guilty of *attempted rape*. He has committed a crime and can be punished. If he has sexual intercourse with a female in any way which does not involve his penis entering her vagina (for example, by making use of a stick or a bottle), the act is not rape, but it is the crime of indecent assault. In any of these cases where the woman has not consented to sexual intercourse, the man can be punished.

With a woman

In terms of the definition, rape can occur only between a man (the assailant/rapist) and a woman (the victim). From this it follows that a man cannot be raped and a woman cannot commit rape. However, a woman can help the rapist – this means that she can act as an accomplice and she will also be punished for doing so.

Furthermore, any female can be the victim of rape – it doesn't matter what age she is. And it makes no difference whether she is a prostitute or a promiscuous woman. As long as she has not consented to sexual intercourse, it is rape. The only potential problem is that the victim's version of the alleged rape may not be believed, especially where she is a woman of questionable morals.

Until now, South African judges have not had much understanding of how women experience rape, as this newspaper report shows:

> *Rape victims 'traumatised' by judges' rulings – report*
> *Johannesburg – South African judges were often biased and sexist in rape case rulings. This further traumatised victims and shook their faith in the law, a report by the New York-based Human Rights Watch reports today.*
>
> *As an example, the report refers to the case of a convicted rapist who was sentenced to five years' imprisonment, whose term was cut in half by Mr Justice Michael Corbett, now South Africa's Chief Justice, who viewed the rape as a 'non-serious injury'.*
>
> *'In my opinion the lack of any serious injury to the complainant and the fact that she was obviously a woman of experience from a sexual point of view, justice would be served by a suspension of half the sentence imposed,' Mr Justice Corbett ruled in 1987.*
>
> *The human rights report, entitled 'Violence Against Women in South Africa, details the escalating problem and is packed with testimonies of women, police officers and judges.*
>
> *The report cites the 1993 case of a Port Elizabeth policeman, Anton Weitz, who was convicted on four charges of sexual assault –*

one involving a teenage girl. The magistrate ruled that the policeman should not be fired as his victims had 'overreacted'.

The report says magistrate Peter Campbell commented: 'We men must learn to keep our hands to ourselves.'

Sexual gratification

In March 1994, Mr Justice Pierre Olivier delayed a seven-year jail sentence for two rapists – George Biggs and Gavin Adriaanse – because the rape was 'not based on violence but on sexual gratification; the woman raped had suffered no serious injury or psychological harm and the woman knew one of the rapists.

Another judge, named only in the report as Marais, sentenced a man who raped a prostitute at gunpoint to two years' in prison and an R8 000 fine but said: 'If the complainant was an innocent young woman, I would not have hesitated to send you (the rapist) to jail for a very long time.'

Reported rape cases in South Africa have doubled in the past 10 years with a 1994 total of 32 107, and the number of child rapes have almost doubled from 1993's 4 736 cases to 7 559 in 1994. For every rape reported in South Africa, 35 more go unreported, the report says. Human Rights Watch called for a revamp of the police, judicial and medical system when dealing with abuse victims.

It suggests abolishing the 'cautionary rule' that gives judges the right to analyse testimonies of 'questionable' victims such as prostitutes. (Pretoria News 24 November 1995)

Finally, it should be borne in mind that, in terms of s 1 of the Law of Evidence and the Criminal Procedure Amendment Act 103 of 1987, it is possible for a boy under the age of 14 years to be convicted of rape. (Prior to 1987 it was irrebuttably presumed that a boy under the age of 14 years was incapable of sexual intercourse.)

Without consent

Whenever a man has sexual intercourse with a woman when she doesn't agree to the act, it is rape. It is rape even if
- the man does not use physical violence to force himself on the woman;
- the man has no weapon;
- the woman does not suffer cuts and bruises;
- the woman does not fight her attacker off as long as it is clear that she does not agree to have sexual intercourse with him.

A woman may be afraid to fight off a man because she is afraid he will hurt her or kill her. She may also fail to do so if she is afraid of losing her job or failing at school. Whatever the underlying motivation, if she has not given her consent to sexual intercourse, she has been the victim of rape.

Moreover, a woman may at first agree to have sexual intercourse but then say *no* at any time before the intercourse actually begins. If the man then forces her to have sex, it is rape.

It is important to note that in terms of s 5 of the Prevention of Family Violence Act, it is possible for a woman to be raped by her husband, and he may be convicted of rape. From the reply by the Minister of Justice to Question No 71 (written) in the National Assembly during 1996, it would appear that since 1993 eight convictions had followed prosecution and that imprisonment had been imposed in four of such cases.

The main distinction between rape and normal sexual intercourse lies in the fact that, in rape, a woman does not consent. Therefore, it has become customary in the legal system to look for some form of proof that the woman did not consent. In the past there was always the belief that a virtuous or good woman would fight back as hard as she could to prevent someone from raping her, even if this meant risking her life. Clearly, this is to apply the wrong criterion. We now know that many rape victims submit to being raped in an effort to save their lives. They allow the rapist to do what he wants in the same way that many victims of theft allow the robber to take their money so that they may live. Therefore, mere submission does not amount to consent.

The law takes this fact into consideration. If a woman agrees to sex simply because she is afraid, then she has not truly agreed or consented. This means she has been raped. It also does not matter why the woman is afraid. It could be because the rapist has threatened her with a knife or a gun. It could also be because he is her employer and threatens her with the loss of her job. In such instances, she merely chooses the lesser of two evils, allowing the rape to happen so that she can go on living or working.

Unfortunately, some police and magistrates still seem to look for proof of resistance before they will believe that a woman has been raped. While rape is difficult to prove if the victim is considered untrustworthy, lack of resistance should not be misinterpreted as evidence of an untrusworthy victim.

If a woman agrees to have sex with a man and then after sexual intercourse has begun she protests, her protest is of no effect. For example, Mr X and Mrs Y had already begun having sex when Mrs Y heard her employer approaching. She changed her mind and tried to withdraw her consent. In this case, Mr X's conduct will not be regarded as rape.

When a woman consents to sexual intercourse, she must do it freely and voluntarily – having sex by her own choice – otherwise there is no consent. Consent must also be consciously given, in other words, she must also know what she is consenting to. If she was tricked into consenting, she has nevertheless consented and the man will not be guilty of rape. For example, in one case, a woman went to a witchdoctor to find out why she could not have children. As part of the treatment, she had sexual intercourse with him. She knew that the witch doctor was having sexual intercourse with her, but believed his story that it would cure her of her barrenness. In this case, the witchdoctor's act was not considered rape as she had consented.

Consent must be based on a true knowledge of the facts relating to intercourse and therefore consent is absent where someone has intercourse with a sleeping woman (because she has no knowledge of what is taking place). Neither can consent be given by a woman who is in a state of intoxication or whose senses are deadened as a result of drug-taking.

A woman must have the mental ability to understand what she is consenting to. If she suffers from a mental defect which makes her incapable of giving or withholding consent, she cannot be said to have consented to sexual intercourse.

Anybody who is concerned about rape victims should know what the law says about rape. This can help considerably in ensuring that a rapist gets the punishment he deserves. When a rapist is punished or sentenced, the victim also feels less humiliated. Moreover, punishment may also play a role in preventing rape from occurring: if would-be rapists know that a severe punishment is waiting for them, they may be less inclined to attempt rape.

S v K 1966 (1) SA 366 (RA)

K represented to X that intercourse would cure her of her infertility problem. K was not found guilty of rape: the representation related to the outcome of the act, and not to the act itself.

The position of girls below the age of 16 years

Sexual intercourse with a girl below the age of 16 years is, of course, also a statutory crime in terms of s 14 of the Sexual Offences Act 23 of 1957. If the girl is a willing party, the man will be guilty only of contravening s 14 of this Act. However, a girl under the age of 12 years is, by law, incapable of

S v CHAPMAN 1998 (3) SA 345 (SCA)

The Supreme Court of Appeal confirmed a 14-year sentence for a convicted rapist by a Cape magistrate, and said the following in delivering its judgment:

The Courts are under a duty to send a clear message to the accused, to other potential rapists and to the community: we are determined to protect the equality, dignity and freedom of all women, and we shall show no mercy to those who seek to invade those rights.

consenting. In this way, the law protects young girls, even if they seemed to have consented to sexual intercourse.

Proving rape in Court

Due to a rule of ancient origin (the continued application of which is currently under review by the Supreme Court of Appeal) and general rules of evidence, our Courts apply certain precautionary measures when a rape case is heard. Every woman should have at least a basic knowledge of these measures so that she will be prepared if she takes a rapist to court.

Whenever it is alleged that a crime has been committed, it is the State's responsibility to prove the accused's guilt – the accused is, in our law, always presumed innocent until proven otherwise – the State prosecutor has to prove the accused's guilt.

To succeed in proving the accused's guilt, the State will subpoena different witnesses to appear in Court, to take the oath[†] and to give evidence. Depending on how reliable these witnesses are, the State may or may not be successful. In the case of rape, the victim will most probably be the only witness and whatever she has to say will be most important in proving the accused's guilt.

We therefore have two opposing sides in the case. On the one hand, there is the accused, fighting for his freedom, because rape is regarded as such a serious crime that, in South Africa, a sentence of life-long imprisonment can be imposed. On the other hand, we have the victim who wants recompense and who wants justice to be done. It is the word of one against the other. In such a situation we refer to the victim as a single witness and the court must be satisfied that the testimony of the victim is credible before the accused can be convicted. This cautionary approach by the Court applies to all single witness cases.

Unfortunately, in sexual assault cases a further rule, the so-called cautionary rule, is also applied. This rule requires the Court to treat the victim's testimony (usually that of a women) with caution as the complaint may be false.[‡]

To overcome this problem, our Courts have decided to look for corroborative evidence of the rape – evidence which confirms the victim's story and supports her report. Such evidence can be obtained in the form of the following:
- medical evidence such as blood, semen, skin from fingernail scrapings, cuts, bruises, or internal injuries;

[‡] As mentioned above, the possible abolition of this rule is currently being considered by the Supreme Court of Appeal. The abolition will be in keeping with decisions in other countries, as this rule is inherently discriminatory against women and is indefensible in the light of the Constitution.

- clothing analyses: blood or semen stains, hairs or thread or merely torn clothing itself;
- proof of resistance, such as signs that the man broke into the victim's home or signs of a struggle;
- evidence that the man had a weapon;
- positive identification of the accused in an identification parade or line-up;
- evidence which shows that the rapist did have the opportunity to rape the woman;
- the lack of an alibi on the part of the rapist. For example, he may be unable to produce any people to swear in Court that they saw him somewhere else at the time of the rape.

This is one of the reasons why it is so important that a rape victim receive medical attention as soon as possible after the rape. The medical report can help provide some of the corroborative evidence mentioned above and can therefore support the woman's story during the trial.

The mere fact that a witness repeats his or her statement does not necessarily make a false statement truthful: a lie can be repeated just as often as the truth. If a witness therefore makes a second or third statement, these further statements cannot be used to prove that the first one was true.

In the case of rape, however, we have a strange exception to this rule. Where a rape victim has related her experience to another person soon after the rape, this other person may give evidence during the trial. This evidence does not prove that the victim's story is true, but it indicates that she repeated her story that she did not agree to sexual intercourse.

When a woman has been raped, it is therefore important that she tells somebody else about the experience as soon as possible. This person can then confirm her statement, among other things, that she did not consent.

During a trial, it is normally not permissible to refer to a witness's character in order to support or undermine his or her testimony. It may be mentioned only when it is directly related to the case. However, in rape cases the rules are somewhat different: the victim is a witness and the Court has to determine whether she is speaking the truth when she says that she did not consent to sexual intercourse. Whether the victim can be believed will depend on her general credibility. In other words, is she the type of person who normally tells the truth, who is respectable and honest and of good morals?

> **TO THINK ABOUT**
>
> Think about what you have just read about women and rape.
> - Do you know of any woman who has been raped?
> - How do you think this woman felt after the attack?
> - How could you help a victim of rape, if she approached you?
> - What steps should a rape victim take immediately after the attack?
> - What does a rape victim need to do when she reports the rape to the police?
>
> See also Chapter Seven: Private defence (self-defence), below.

If the victim has had a sexual relationship with the rapist before the alleged rape, the chances are that she may be lying for some reason or other. Therefore she can expect to be questioned about her honesty and morality and about her sexual relationship with the rapist, and even with other men.

One reason a woman may lie is that she is too embarrassed to tell her family the truth. She may say that she has never had boyfriends and that she has never had sex before the rape. If she is caught telling this one lie, the Court is unlikely to believe the rest of her story, even though the rape may really have occcurred. Therefore it is essential for the rape victim to be completely honest with the Court when she is telling her side of the story.

There are many common ideas about sexual assault or rape that are untrue or that are distortions of the truth. One example is the widely held belief that most rapists are strangers to their victims. Experience shows that, in most cases, a woman is raped by someone she knows or even by someone who is related to her. And the fact that there is a relationship between the victim and the rapist does not make the rape less of a crime.

Because of the sensitivity of cases such as those mentioned above where the rapist is related to the victim, the Court arranges to protect the identity of these victims by hearing the case *in camera*.

In camera hearings

The normal rule in South African law is that all trials must be conducted in an 'open court', which means that the public can attend and the newspapers or media can usually publish information about cases. The reason for this is that the whole process of justice must be open and 'justice must be seen to be done' in the literal sense.

However, the law allows certain exceptions to this rule. One such exception is in the case where an indecent act has been committed against a complainant.

In such a case the complainant may ask that the case be held *in camera*. Where, for example, a charge of rape or indecent assault is heard, the complainant may make this request. In this way the identity of the victim will not be revealed, because the public will not be permitted into the Court during the trial and newspaper reporters will not be allowed to print names in the paper when reporting the case. If the trial is held behind closed doors, the public will be allowed into the Court only when judgment is handed down and sentence is passed. This assists rape victims.

When the hearing is held in camera, the magistrate asks members of the public to leave the courtroom. Then only the people who are actively involved in the trial may stay, although the victim may request that a friend or relative be allowed to stay behind. The members of the public will be allowed to return when the victim has finished giving her evidence. Information which may reveal the identity of the victim may be published only if a magistrate permits this. Such permission is given only if the victim gives her consent. This makes the trial less stressful for victims, particularly since they know that the embarrassing details of the crime will not become public knowledge.

The Criminal Procedure Amendment Act 86 of 1996 provides that a court may, amoung other things, order a witness to give evidence by means of closed circuit television or similar electronic media if such facilities are readily available or obtainable. This provision should help victims against intimidation by the accused in Court.

VIOLENCE THROUGH INCEST

Incest is defined as unlawful and intentional sexual intercourse between male and female persons who are prohibited from marrying each other because they are related within the prohibited degrees of consanguinity, affinity or adoptive relationship.

People related to each other by reason of such relationships are incompetent to marry each other.

'Consanguinity' refers to the blood relationship that exists between all persons who have a common ancestor, for example, mother and son, brother and sister. 'Affinity' exists between a husband and the blood relations of his wife or between a wife and the blood relations of her husband.

The prohibited degrees of consanguinity are:
(a) ascendants (ancestors) and descendants (offspring) in the direct line in eternity, for example a mother and her son, or a grandfather and his granddaughter, and

(a) collaterals (people not related in the direct line) if either of them is related to their common ancestor in the first degree (ie one generation) of descent, for example a brother and a sister, an uncle and a niece.

As we have seen previously, affinity is established only by a legally recognized marriage and therefore a polygynous marriage or a customary union is excluded. The prohibited degrees of affinity refer to the relations by marriage in ascending and descending line in eternity, for example a man and his former mother-in-law or daughter-in-law.

The Child Care Act prevents an adoptive parent from marrying his or her adoptive child. Sexual intercourse between such persons would therefore constitute incest.

Women (including girls) are, as we have seen above, often victims of sexual violence within their family circle. When a female child is raped by someone in the family, the same principles apply as when an adult is raped. If the rapist is directly related to the girl – if he is her father, grandfather, brother or uncle – he will further be charged with incest. Where the girl is older than 12 and has consented to the sexual intercourse, the man will not be guilty of rape but only of incest, and the girl will also have committed the crime of incest.

CHAPTER SEVEN:
Private defence (self-defence)

One of the ways in which a woman can protect herself against assault or rape is to use violence herself in order to ward off or foil her attacker. Whereas violence is normally a means of attack, in these exceptional circumstances the woman now uses it as a defence. When using violence in this way as a form of self-defence, the woman is actually taking the law into her own hands in order to protect herself. This is known as private defence (or self-defence): it is permissible and will not be regarded as a form of counter-assault. There are, however, certain requirements that should be met. These are discussed briefly below:

Private defence may be used only where an attack has already begun or where it is obvious that an attack is definitely going to take place. There should be no time left for the attacked person to try any other way out or for the attacker to change his mind. Any measure taken once the attack is over is no longer defensive but is considered to be revenge (which is not permissible). Private defence is not a means of revenge, nor is it a form of punishment. If violence is used when there is no threatening attack, then the defender herself becomes an attacker and may be found guilty of assault.

Normally, private defence is used to ward off a life-threatening attack. It can, however, also be used to protect weaker persons who cannot themselves ward off an attacker singlehandedly. This means that a woman who physically defends her children, when they are assaulted by, for example, her husband, is making use of private defence and is therefore not guilty of a crime.

A person's own life doesn't have to be threatened for private defence to be used. It can also be used as a defence when a woman's reputation or good name is at stake, or in protecting property.

The defence must be directed against the attacker and should not injure another innocent person.

The defence should be necessary to avert the attack. There should be no possible way in which the threatened person can escape harm other than the use of violence. The basic concept underlying private defence is that a person is allowed 'to take the law into his own hands' only if the normal legal remedies cannot at that moment give adequate protection.

The defence should not be more harmful than the attack itself. When a fistfight takes place, the person who is attacked cannot use a firearm to shoot the attacker unless he or she is physically too weak to use fists. Everything depends on the relationship of the two people. If the person attacked is a woman, she can use the most extreme means of warding off the attack, even if it amounts to killing the attacker. The same applies when she has to defend her chastity against a would-be rapist. A man, on the other hand, who is perfectly able to deal with an attacker may not kill his attacker unless *not* doing so would place his own life in danger.

CHAPTER EIGHT:
Remedies in law

However difficult it may be to do so, women must start speaking out against violence, otherwise it will not stop. If women remain silent, men and the rest of society may get the impression that such treatment is acceptable to women. Taking action in this manner may be the only way that women can persuade both men *and* the legal system that they will not tolerate physical abuse.

There are many places where women may go to find help and safety from attackers, both in and outside the legal system of this country. In this section we first concentrate on the types of help available through the law, then we deal with help available from other sources outside the legal system.

Currently, there are several remedies available in law to women who are the victims of assault, but many women find it difficult to decide whether or not to take legal action against their violent attackers. There are many reasons for this, including any and all of the following:

- They may feel that being a victim is shameful and may worry about what other people might think of them should their situation be divulged.
- Some women worry that, if action is taken, they will not be believed, whereas others may even feel that the law will not take the incident seriously because of the relationship which exists between themselves and their attacker.
- Some women believe that what has happened to them is their own fault. (Some women have been brought up to believe that the man is 'the boss' and that therefore they have to endure whatever they are subjected to.)
- Sadly, some women believe that what has happened to them is 'normal' or their 'lot in life' because they grew up in violent homes or because violence is commonplace in their community.

It may be very difficult for a victim to report a violent crime, such as assault or rape for a number of reasons. Many women do not want to think about the incident any more; they just want it to 'go away' so that they can get on with their lives. This is a very common response to any kind of attack. But if we want to make our society healthier and safer for women, children and all of us, we must make use of the remedies available through the legal system.

Within the legal system, it is important to know the difference between criminal and civil proceedings. These two types of proceedings entail different procedures and different ways of dealing with the victim and the attacker. These are explained in some detail below.

CRIMINAL PROCEEDINGS

Criminal proceedings are launched when a criminal charge is laid with the South African Police Services, and the Attorney-General as representative of the State decides to prosecute the accused. One may say that the State acts on behalf of the victim, called the complainant. At the end of the proceedings, the Court will decide whether the accused is guilty or not guilty. If found guilty, the accused is normally sentenced either to a jail term or a fine, or both. The fine is paid to the State and not to the complainant. When a case is referred to as 'the State versus (the name of a person)', one knows that this is a criminal case. For example, in 'the State versus Y' a criminal charge has been laid against Y. If he is found guilty of assault, he may have to pay a fine to the State.

The type of violence committed against a victim will determine the type of charge that will be brought against the culprit. If a woman or a man has been assaulted, a charge of assault will be investigated by the South African Police Services. In the case of rape, a charge of rape will be investigated. In this section we use the example of a woman (the victim) being attacked by a male attacker (the accused), but the same will apply if a man is attacked.

When a woman is attacked, first she must report to the police station closest to the place where the attack took place. It is important to report the attack and lay a charge with the police as soon as possible after the event. If a woman waits too long, in the first instance certain crucial evidence may be lost and, secondly, questions may be raised at the trial about her credibility. (Either way, she runs the risk of weakening her case.) At the trial, she will be asked to explain why she waited so long and her explanation will have to be believable. If it is not, the Court may feel that the victim is not being completely honest about the reason for the charge.

There have been instances where a woman has laid a false charge of rape against a man in order to get back at him for some personal reason or out of revenge. By doing this, she not only abuses the law but also makes it more difficult for women who actually are attacked to be believed. This kind of behaviour is not fair towards other victims: indeed, it makes their task of convincing the Court of their credibility that much tougher.

When a person is attacked and there are no witnesses to the incident, it is always a good idea for the victim to tell the first person she meets after the incident. She should explain what has happened and take the name and address of the person to whom she speaks. This person could be a helpful witness at the trial. This is especially true when rape has been committed.

In a rape case, the woman should not wash, bath or shower before she has had a medical examination. The district surgeon who examines her will collect any evidence from her body which may help the police in their investigations. This evidence may include blood, semen, hairs and fingernail scrapings. The victim should also preferably not change her clothes; if she has to change for any reason, she should put these clothes in a paper bag and take them to the examination with her. (A plastic bag must never be used since the chemical reactions inside a plastic bag may destroy the evidence of blood and semen.)

When a criminal charge is laid at the police station, the victim will be asked to make a statement under oath which will be taken down by the police officer on duty in the charge office. (This person should preferably be a female.) The victim will be asked to describe exactly what happened, and to state the place and the time of the attack. The victim must also give particulars of any witnesses so that the police can take statements from them too. The police will also visit the scene of the alleged crime to see whether they can get any clues that will help them in their investigation. At this stage one can talk only of 'an alleged crime' because it has not yet been decided if a crime has been committed. Remember that, under our law, the accused is presumed innocent until proven guilty.

After the investigation has been completed, the police compile a file on the case known as a docket. This docket contains all the relevant statements, medical reports and other information. It is sent to the Attorney-General who, after reviewing the contents, must decide whether or not there is the likelihood of a successful prosecution. Once the Attorney-General has decided to prosecute, the accused is brought before the Court. In some instances the accused is arrested and in other cases the accused is not arrested but warned to appear in Court. The accused could also be granted bail† thereby avoiding being remanded in custody until the date of the trial.

On the date set for the trial, the accused will be asked to plead guilty or not guilty to the accusation (if a plea has not been entered at an earlier appearance in Court) – indicating whether or not he is guilty of committing the crime with which he is charged. If he pleads 'not guilty', the Public Prosecutor will then call the complainant (the victim) to give evidence. She will have to tell the Court exactly what happened and she will have to ensure that her version of events is the same as that in the statement she made to the police.

If the victim changes her story, she will be asked to explain why the two versions are not the same. This may show that she is not telling the truth, or it could mean that she changed her story because someone has intimidated or threatened her. If the complainant is not able to give a satisfactory explanation for the differing statements, the Court could find that her testimony cannot be believed and the case will be dismissed.

For this reason, it is important when she makes a statement to the police upon reporting the crime that she should sit down and write out a copy of her statement to the police. Another reason for doing this is that her case may come before the Court only some time after the incident took place. It is only natural that some aspects of the incident may fade from a person's mind and this written statement will help refresh her memory. It is also a good idea to discuss the matter with the prosecutor before the trial so that the two of them can go through the victim's statement to clear up any problems there may be. At this time, also, the whole procedure of the trial can be explained to the victim. The legal process and the procedures of the trial are explained below.

Outline of the legal process

Trials are held either in a magistrate's court or in a provincial or local division of the High Court, depending on the seriousness of the case. On the date of the hearing there will be a number of people present in the Court besides the victim. The most important people are the following:

- The magistrate or judge – the former presides in a magistrate's court, whereas the latter presides in a High Court. He or she decides whether or not the accused is guilty. If the accused is found guilty, then the magistrate or judge has to pass sentence (ie the form of punishment).
- The public prosecutor – the lawyer who represents the State in the trial and who is on the side of the complainant against the accused. In the High Court this official is known as a State Advocate.
- The accused – the person against whom the charge has been laid by the complainant. The prosecutor will attack the evidence given by the accused in an attempt to convince the magistrate or judge that he is guilty. This is done by cross-examining the accused.
- The defence lawyer – the lawyer on the accused's side who will try to show that the accused is not guilty by attacking the evidence presented by the State. This is done by cross-examining the complainant and other witnesses. Witnesses who can help to prove the innocence of the accused may be called by the defence lawyer. (Sometimes the accused is not represented by a defence lawyer because it is not compulsory to be represented. In such an instance, the accused conducts his own defence. In some areas such an accused can be represented by a Public Defender. At present this service does not exist in all areas.)
- The interpreter – where anybody giving evidence in Court does not feel comfortable speaking in a language that is not his or her mother tongue, she or he may speak through an interpreter. The interpreter

will also assist this person to follow everything that is said in Court by any other person.

The trial procedure

The police will notify the victim (complainant) of the trial date. If all the witnesses and the accused are present at the Court, the hearing will start; if not, the case will be postponed to a later date. Below we go through a criminal trial for assault or rape step by step. In our example the complainant is a woman and the accused is a man (though the trial resulting from an assault on a man would follow the same steps).

Step 1
The trial starts with the case being 'called'. The prosecutor/State Advocate calls out the case number and the name of the case (for instance 'Case No 12345, the State versus N').

Step 2
The accused is then asked whether he pleads guilty or not guilty to the charge (if his plea has not previously been noted). If he pleads guilty, he will be sentenced after the magistrate or the State Advocate has been satisfied that the accused understands the charge against him and that he means to plead guilty in legal terms. If he pleads not guilty, he will be asked to explain why, and to indicate the grounds for his defence.

Step 3
If the accused pleads not guilty, the next step is for the prosecutor to call the complainant as the first witness. The complainant is first asked to take the oath. The prosecutor asks the complainant to tell the Court exactly what happened and asks questions to try to give the Court the best possible idea of what happened.

Step 4
When the complainant has finished telling her side of what happened, the accused or the defence attorney then cross-examines her. The cross-examination tests the truth of what she has said in an attempt to prove the accused's innocence.

Step 5
If there are further witnesses for the State, they will be called and the same procedure will be followed in respect of each one.

Step 6
Once the State has called all its witnesses, it declares its case 'closed', indicating that no further witnesses will be called to testify in favour of the complainant.

Step 7
The accused then gives evidence in the same way as the complainant did. Thereafter, the State cross-examines him. The accused will be able to call witnesses to give evidence in his favour (repeating steps 3 through 6 above, but now for the accused).

Step 8
The accused or his lawyer then declares the case for the defence 'closed'.

Step 9
The Court then gives the State and the accused the opportunity to make closing statements to the Court, indicating why they think the accused is guilty or not guilty of the crime as charged.

Step 10
The Court then gives a summary of the evidence put before it. It will indicate whether it accepts the evidence given by the complainant or the accused.

Step 11
The Court then announces its decision based on the evidence. (This may happen only after the magistrate or judge has had time to consider all the evidence again, which could take minutes, hours or even days.)

Step 12
If the accused is found guilty, he will be sentenced by the Court.

In the case of rape or indecent assault, there may be one difference from this trial for assault: the public will not know the identity of the victim.

In Chapter Six: Common forms of violence encountered by women, we explained that the law now allows for the identity of the victim in a trial for indecent assault or rape to remain withheld from the public. Therefore a rape victim may ask that her trial be held behind closed doors (*in camera*). In such a case, her identity will be kept from the public and the reporters will not be permitted to publish her name.

Criminal proceedings are very serious and should not be entered into lightly. If the accused is found guilty, he may have to serve a sentence and will then have a permanent criminal record. This is one way that the attacker will be brought to justice and will be forced to think about the violent acts he committed. Another way for victims to seek justice is by means of civil proceedings.

CIVIL REMEDIES

In civil proceedings, two or more private individuals (also referred to as 'parties') litigate against one another. The State does not play a role in the proceedings and the people in these proceedings are called either the plaintiffs or the defendants (if a summons[†] has been issued) or applicants and respondents (if a notice of motion[†] has been issued). Case names indicate the names of the people involved in the case – *A versus B or XYZ (Pty) Ltd versus Q.* In this type of case, no fine is imposed and the Court does not pass sentence. Instead, the Court issues an order and the wrongdoer must do whatever the order instructs him to do. This may include payment of an amount of money to the other party or it may be that the wrongdoer is forbidden to do something, for instance to talk to the other party or to come near the other party again.

Remember that there are certain differences between criminal and civil proceedings. In criminal proceedings an accused is convicted and sentenced. However, in civil proceedings one person may be ordered by the Court to do something or to pay something to the other party. There are no sentences and no criminal records. For example, a person found guilty of assault may be ordered to pay the victim a specific sum of money, or damages,[†] for the pain and suffering and medical expenses caused by the attack.

Interdicts

In our legal system, another type of civil remedy[†] is called an interdict. An interdict is a specific remedy in law and is used to protect a person against the wrongful actions of another. Where a person makes a threat, an interdict is used to stop that person from carrying out the threat (eg a person threatening to evict members of the family from the family home). Also, where there has already been an act, an interdict is used to stop a person from continuing that act (eg beating a spouse, or withholding maintenance payments).

The Prevention of Family Violence Act No 133 of 1993

A specific type of interdict is provided for in the Prevention of Family Violence Act. This Act came into effect on 1 December 1993. Although an interdict can be obtained in terms of normal legal procedures, this Act has made a simpler, quicker and cheaper interdict available in cases of family violence. (See also Chapter Six, above.) As the title of the Act suggests, its purpose is to provide a method for abused family members to stop an abuser from causing them more, or further, harm.

When dealing with this Act, it must be remembered that it applies to married people and also to a man and a woman who ordinarily live together as husband and wife, although they are not married. Also, the remedy available in this Act is available to a man as well as a woman. However, for the purposes of this work, we focus only on the woman. Unfortunately, the Act, at this stage, does not provide relief to same-sex partners, to people in dating relationships or members of the extended family.

The Act helps victims of family violence to handle their problems without going to a criminal court. A victim may approach a judge or a magistrate in his or her chambers or offices. (Family or friends or 'third parties' may also approach the judge or magistrate on a victim's behalf.) Judges or magistrates who are appointed to hear these applications are available 24 hours a day. Victims should contact their local magistrate's court if they want to make use of this remedy, or, if there are no magistrate's courts in their particular area, they should contact their nearest police station. The police will then set the process in motion.

The victim is called an applicant because that party 'applies' (or asks) for an interdict. The interdict can do any of the following:

- forbid the respondent (the person who has been violent or has threatened violence) to assault or threaten the applicant or a child who lives with her.
- forbid the respondent to enter the family home or any other place where the applicant lives;
- make sure that the respondent cannot stop the applicant or child who lives in the family home from entering the family home or from living there;
- forbid the respondent to do anything else which has been set out in the specific interdict.

When issuing the interdict, the magistrate or judge will also issue an order authorizing the arrest of the respondent, but the execution of such an order will be suspended on certain conditions. This means that the respondent (or violent person) will not be arrested if he obeys the conditions of the interdict.

After the interdict has been granted it must be served on the respondent personally either by the Clerk of the Court (or the Registrar of a High Court) or by the sheriff. Service[†] should be either at his home or at his place of work; however, if he keeps these places closed, a copy of the interdict may be affixed to the door of such places. Remember, the interdict has force and effect on the respondent only after it has been properly served.

If the applicant cannot afford the fee for the service of the interdict, financial assistance from the State may be considered.

If the respondent does not comply with the conditions for suspending the order for arrest, the order will be executed and carried out when the affidavit is handed over to a peace officer. According to the law, this officer may be a magistrate, a justice of the peace or a police officer. A certified copy of the interdict and the original warrant of arrest must also be handed over. After an affidavit is made, the respondent is arrested, taken into custody and brought before a magistrate or judge, who will then investigate the alleged breach of the conditions. If it is found that there was a breach of the conditions, the respondent will be found guilty of contravening the Act.

This conviction may lead to the imprisonment of the respondent for a period not exceeding 12 months, or the respondent may be fined an amount not exceeding R20 000. Alternatively, the respondent may be given a jail sentence and a fine.

There are several ways in which this Act helps the victim. The Act has made a simple interdict a possibility in the case of family violence. In the case of a woman who is assaulted, the interdict makes it easier for her to get help, because:

- she need not take the man she is living with to the criminal court and face the trauma of a trial and possible negative reactions from the other people in her community.
- the whole process can be put into operation in only a few hours. She can get help from her nearest police station at all times. The police will get the whole legal process going. Not only is this help available during office hours at her nearest magistrate's court, but magistrates will also be available after hours to help her;
- the remedy under the Prevention of Family Violence Act is cheaper and quicker than the normal interdict procedure that is available in our law;
- the danger to her person and life can be removed quickly, since the man will have to stay away from her and her home.

Interdicts are a useful tool for women. For example, if a woman who suffers violence in her home wants to keep herself and her children safe but does not want to put her husband (their father) into prison, an interdict can be the solution. One would hope that men will learn that violent, threatening and intimidating acts towards the women they live with are unacceptable and that they will be punished if they continue to use violence against women.

Damages

'Damages' is the term that refers to the amount of money that is awarded to a victim as compensation for harm suffered. There is no fixed amount that is awarded and in every case the Court will look at all the facts and the circumstances of the violence before making a decision as to how much is to be paid by the one who committed the harm.

For purposes of this work, we refer to harm suffered through bodily injury. Where a woman has been assaulted, she may sue the attacker for damages. The damages will include an amount for her medical expenses and also for the pain and suffering that she experienced.

For a woman to be awarded damages, she will have to go to court and issue a summons against the person causing the harm in which she asks for the attacker to pay her an amount. The amount claimed will determine whether the claim will have to be heard in the magistrate's court or in the High Court (cases involving high damages claims are handled only in the High Court).

If a woman has enough knowledge of legal matters, she as plaintiff can conduct her own case against the defendant. Otherwise, she will have to make use of the services of an attorney (or an advocate and an attorney if the summons is issued out of the High Court).

Civil trials normally take months (in the High Court the trial may even take years) to come to an end. The reasons for this are that there is a specific legal procedure that has to be followed. There are also many cases that are waiting to be heard. These and other factors combine to make legal proceedings expensive. The plaintiff will be asked to pay a large deposit to her attorney for legal expenses (such as court fees, service fees, advocate's fees, etc) as well as some of the attorney's legal fees.

If the plaintiff wins her case, there is a strong possibility that the defendant will be ordered to pay her legal costs. However, it is important to remember that not all her legal costs will be paid by the defendant: the costs that she brought about before the summons was issued and certain other costs for services of a personal nature will not be covered in the order and she will have to pay those costs herself. If she loses her case, the Court may order her to pay the legal costs of the defendant.

Where the defendant (the attacker) fails to pay the amount awarded by the Court, the plaintiff can apply for an execution order to force him to pay. This is an order which authorizes a court official to go to the defendant's place of residence and to take possession of (or attach[†]) his property to pay the amount. This official may only take property to the value of the amount that has to be paid to the plaintiff. This property is then sold 'in execution' and the money received for the property is then paid to the plaintiff.

In both criminal and civil proceedings, the victim must have the courage to go to the authorities or to a lawyer and report the crime. This is often a very difficult thing to do, especially if the attacker is a member of the family or is known in the community. However, the only way that these violent crimes against women will stop is if the community becomes aware of them. Even after the trial is over, whether it entailed criminal or civil proceedings, the victim will still need a lot of support from family and friends. Also, the various support systems in the community should be contacted because they offer many services to victims. (See Chapter 9: Support systems in the community, below.)

Other legal options

Some alternative legal options are also available to victims of violence. These are:

Urgent court interdict:
This was the type of interdict used before the Act came into operation. Although it gives wider protection than the interdict in terms of the Act, it is more complicated and more expensive. Moreover, the services of a lawyer will be needed.

Divorce:
Here the services of a lawyer are generally required. (See also Part Two: Family law, above.)

CHAPTER NINE:
Support systems in the community

Some women do not want to make use of the legal system to help them in their situation. For them it is good enough to know that there are organizations which offer them help, counselling and advice. Moreover, even if a woman who is attacked decides to make use of the legal system, she can contact these organizations at any time.

As a first step, it is important for abused women to acknowledge that they are being abused (however painful that may be) and to seek help and support. They have to be honest about their circumstances and their bruises and injuries. If they are not, they can become more and more isolated and more and more vulnerable to further manipulation and abuse by their partners.

For these and other reasons, there is a need for lay support groups in the community to give assistance and support to abused women. Even if an abused woman is receiving counselling, she still needs someone, to accompany her to the doctor, for example, to lend a sympathetic ear or simply to show warmth and understanding of her situation, especially if she chooses not to leave the abusive relationship. One need not be professionally trained to provide this sort of help and to contribute to her healing.

It is not possible to list here all the support organizations available in South Africa that help people in trouble. Suffice to say that there are very many. What follows are examples of organizations that can be approached and the types of service they provide.

THE SOUTH AFRICAN POLICE SERVICES

Although the South African Police Services do not yet have a special unit to deal with rape cases, some of the police stations offer a very good specialized service to rape victims. Here they have staff who have been specifically trained to help in these cases. As soon as a woman lays a charge of rape at a police station, these trained officers take over and interview her in a private room at the station and then take her to the District Surgeon for a medical examination. Here she will also receive information on sexually transmittable diseases and other information to help her during this traumatic time.

Community-based support systems

Besides the South African Police Services, there are several organizations in the community that help people in trouble. These organizations provide information and advice about various problems which women and children experience. Some even provide safe shelters for women and children who suffer abuse at home, and who want to leave home but have nowhere to go. Other organizations specialize in counselling services for the victims of violence.

Information about these organizations listed below, and others in your local community, is available in your local telephone directory. You can look for these organizations by name. Also, you can contact your local publicity association or social welfare organizations to obtain a list of available services in your areas. Finally, in the appendix at the end of this chapter, we have included the names and addresses of several more organizations in regions throughout the country.

Rape Crisis Centres
These centres offer counselling to rape victims, and their services are available day and night. Besides their telephone couselling service, they will also go out to the victim after the incident if they are needed. They often also assist the victim during the trial. The police will be able to tell the victim if there is a Rape Crisis Centre in her particular area and they should be able to give her the telephone number of the centre.

Life Line
Life Line is an organization which also offers emergency counselling over the telephone. It has branches in most large urban areas, and its telephone number will be found in the telephone directory. The police should also be able to give the local telephone number to the victim. (See the appendix.)

FAMSA (Family and Marriage Council of South Africa)
FAMSA offers a counselling service for people who suffer from violence. Their telephone numbers and addresses are in all the local telephone directories. Their services are available not only to rape victims but to all victims of violence, especially as it affects the family.

The Salvation Army
The Salvation Army has an extensive social and caring ministry, and it operates in most areas throughout the country. In many areas, the Salvation Army has established homes where battered women and their chil-

dren can find shelter for a short period. Their telephone numbers can also be found in local telephone directories. A valuable part of their service to battered women is that they will even collect women from their homes and bring them to one of their shelters.

POWA (People Opposing Woman Abuse)
This organization is based in Johannesburg but also has an office at the Natalspruit Hospital. POWA offers counselling services, education and training workshops and para-legal assistance. It will also assist women during court appearances, if required to do so. POWA also runs a shelter for abused women in Johannesburg where they and their children can stay for a period of three to six months. A nominal fee is charged for counselling services.

WAWA (Women Against Women Abuse)
This is actually a project of the organization known as WILDD, the Women's Institute for Leadership, Development and Democracy. The aims of WAWA are similar to those of POWA, but it has support groups across the country. The work is largely done by field workers, who are all women working at the grassroots level. They offer counselling services and training for people who wish to become counsellors and also run self-development workshops for women who have been abused. WAWA has a shelter for abused women and their children in Eldorado Park, where shelter is provided for about two months. (See the Appendix.)

Legal aid organizations
Many institutions, non-governmental organizations, welfare organizations and universities have legal aid organizations available to help people who need legal advice. These institutions have been set up specifically to assist people who are unable to afford the costs of private attorneys and advocates. (See the Appendix.)

CONCLUSION

The use of violence in whatever form is unacceptable. In order to protect themselves, women should be aware of the different forms of violence and should also be aware of their rights when they find themselves in a violent situation. This chapter was designed to do that and more – it was also designed to dispel certain myths surrounding violence against women. Women can only be fully empowered through knowledge. However, knowledge brings responsibility and therefore women should also learn to take responsibility for their own lives and for the lives of their dependent children. Women should therefore make use of the help available to them through various organizations and also report abuse to the authorities. Change will occur only if we are prepared to work for it.

> **TO THINK ABOUT**
>
> If there is no support group or organization in your local area, you could start your own.
> - Think about the information you have to have about women and the law.
> - Think about the women in your area who need to know about their rights.
> - Think about the women and children who are violently assaulted or raped in your community.
>
> Now think about what you can do to help these people, as you are already a valuable member of your community.

> **SELECTED READING**
>
> Lee Anne de la Hunt. *Legal Aid Services in South Africa*. Social Justice Resource Project (SJRP), Cape Town and the Legal Education Action Project (LEAP), Institute of Criminology, University of Cape Town, 1992
>
> Jane de Sousa. *Behind Closed Doors* Catholic Welfare Bureau, Cape Town, 1991
>
> Derrick Fine. *Community Advice Services & Para-legals*. Social Justice Resource Project (SJRP), Cape Town and the Legal Education Action Project (LEAP), Institute of criminology, University of Cape Town, 1992
>
> Lorraine Glanz and Andrew Spiegel (eds). *Violence and Family Life in a contemporary South Africa: Research and Policy Issues*. HSRC Publishers, Pretoria, 1996
>
> Human Rights Watch/Africa. *Violence against women in South Africa: the State response to domestic violence and rape*. Human Rights Watch, 1995

PART FOUR:
Women and employment

INTRODUCTION

Part 4 briefly examines the legal position of women in employment. The first chapter examines the concept of sex discrimination. Chapter 2 gives a brief overview of sex discrimination in terms of the Constitution Act 108 of 1996 and the Labour Relations Act 66 of 1995. The remaining 7 chapters deal with specific issues such as affirmative action, equal pay for equal work, sexual harassment in employment and pregnancy rights.

CHAPTER TEN:
What is sex discrimination?

Women currently constitute over one-third of the world's labour market. Even though women are becoming more important in the workplace, and the number of women entering the market is growing steadily, research has shown that many working women have badly paid jobs or work in casual or part-time occupations which offer little or no stability.

One of the main reasons why women are often forced to accept these casual and part-time jobs is the fact that they still carry the bulk of domestic duties.[†] Besides doing their daily jobs, most women are responsible for taking care of the household. This makes it extremely difficult for them to cope with the hours and responsibilities of full-time work. The demands of the employment market (coupled with domestic and child-rearing demands and responsibilities) often leave women with no other option than to accept jobs with little security and virtually no career opportunities.

> ### CASE STUDY: NOMSA
>
> Nomsa is a good wife and mother. She takes care of the family home and her four children very well, doing all the cleaning and washing herself.
>
> She had a job as a secretary in the nearby city. Sometimes she arrived at work a little late because she missed the taxi. Other times she had to miss a day when one of the children was ill and home from school. Once she had to miss two days while she waited for the plumber to come to her house in order to repair the toilet.
>
> Her boss was not happy when Nomsa missed work, so she was dismissed from her job. Luckily she found another job soon, but this one was only as a clerk in a shop. The salary was less and she had to work longer hours, but what could she do? Her first responsibility was to take care of her home and her family.

Another feature of women's employment is this: statistics show the average pay for women is generally lower than and in some instances only a fraction of that earned by men. In some industrialized countries statistics show that, in real terms, women's wages may be between 55% and 80% of those of their male counterparts. For example, during the 1970s, statistics in the United States have shown that for every dollar earned by a man, a woman earned only 59 cents. This difference was even pronounced where men and women were doing exactly the same work. Although this margin has become smaller recently, many women still earn less than their male counterparts in the same jobs.

These statistics are equally true for South Africa, where women constitute 40% of the labour force. Women in South Africa tend to be poorer than, own less than and earn less than men. Statistics also confirm that South African women tend to be in jobs of a domestic nature (similar to household work) or in less skilled jobs with little or no prospect of advancement or opportunity. Women in South Africa have been marginalized from management and decision-making structures and are also more likely to be retrenched, underemployed or unemployed. In addition, they generally have less access to labour market opportunities than men.

South Africa (as elsewhere in the world) is also largely a patriarchal society[†] in which women are seen as the weaker sex. It is believed that women's main purpose in life is to be homemakers and to bear and raise children. This perception is further strengthened in our schools where girls are encouraged to take those subjects that prepare them for this homemaker role: needlework, home economics, and so on. There is nothing wrong in encouraging girls to take these subjects, but they should be made aware of the fact that they have other options and are not limited to these careers. In many societies young boys are also encouraged to assume a superior role over girls, which often results in women in employment having their career advancement frustrated or suppressed.

Another feature of a patriarchal society is that men are still regarded by society as the household 'providers' or 'breadwinners'. This belief ignores not only the important financial contribution made by women to the household, but also the fact that women are increasingly fulfilling the role of single parent and sole breadwinner. This may be the result of the soaring incidence of divorce worldwide or simply because many women are choosing to remain single. In at least one South African court case (Industrial Court, 1995), however, the Court rejected the notion that men (and not women) are primarily the breadwinners.

It does not come as a surprise therefore to learn that one of the areas in which women have felt the harsh effects of discrimination[†] most severely is in the workplace. Sex discrimination in employment relates to unequal employment practices such as:

- inequality with regard to recruitment and advancement opportunities;
- minimum job security;
- unequal pay structures between the sexes;
- practices whereby women are subjected to sexual harassment.

These discriminatory practices against women in the workplace often result in their being restricted to mediocre positions with no prospect of promotion or intellectual advancement or in being overlooked for well-deserved promotion in favour of their male colleagues. Undeniably, some women do rise to the top, but surveys have shown that, even in highly industrialized countries such as the United States, the proportion of women rising to the top is very small.

If it is accepted that women in employment still face discrimination, the next question should be what can be done to advance the position of women in the workplace? Some argue for legislation specifically addressing sex discrimination in employment. Such legislation should address existing inequalities and should actively promote a culture of equal treatment of the sexes in the workplace. There is such legislation in South Africa: The Labour Relations Act, 1995 deals specifically with sex discrimination in the workplace. If passed by Parliament, the Employment Equity Act (still in Bill form) will specifically outlaw discrimination against women in the workplace and encourage the implementation of affirmative action programmes as a method of redressing the disadvantages of past discrimination. Others however, are more cynical and argue that only a social revolution would bring about changes in society.

THE CONCEPT OF SEX DISCRIMINATION

What is meant by the concept sex discrimination? In simple terms, sex discrimination can be described as the less favourable, unequal or differential treatment of a woman or a man solely on the basis of his or her sex. The Convention on the Elimination of all Forms of Discrimination against Women (CEDAW, 1997 offers a more detailed definition) (see also Chapter 21)

> 'For the purpose of the present Convention, the term 'discrimination against women' shall mean any discrimination, exclusion or restriction made on the basis of sex which has the effect of or purpose of impairing or nullifying the recognition, enjoyment or exercise by women, irrespective of their marital status, on the basis of equality of men and women, of human rights and fundamental freedoms in the political, economic, social, cultural, civil or any other field.'

Two main approaches or models to sex equality can be identified:
- the liberal human rights model, and
- the radical human rights model.

Liberal human rights model

The liberal human rights model of equality is based on the belief that all human beings are equal. This model states that equality means 'equality of opportunity'[†] and it sees equality as 'equality before the law'.[†] In terms of this model, women must be treated equally and receive the same opportunities (in areas such as education and employment) as their male counterparts. Any discrimination against women for any reason would be prohibited by law.

This approach stresses that any intrinsic differences between men and women which may have an impact upon their employment are not recognized and cannot be taken into consideration by the law. A pregnant woman, for example, is treated in exactly the same manner as a man who is temporarily disabled.[†] Since men and women are regarded as equals, the fact that being pregnant is unique to women is ignored. Also ignored is the fact that a pregnant woman may need treatment that is different from that needed by the temporarily disabled man. Accordingly, special maternity benefits[†] for women are not envisaged by the equal-treatment proponents of the liberal human rights model. Disabilities related to maternity thus fall under the same model or policy as any other short-term disability (be it as a result of illness or as a result of injuries sustained during an accident).

Feminists who support this model are sometimes referred to as so-called equal-treatment feminists. Apart from treating women the same as other disabled workers, equal-treatment feminists are also in favour of a model which grants family leave or parental leave for the purposes of caring for newborn or sick children or even close relatives such as grandparents. Leave is granted on a sex-neutral basis: both parents are entitled to take leave to care for newborn babies, for example.

One of the reasons why equal-treatment feminists reject a special treatment model is that it can be argued that a model which grants special treatment to women is actually stressing the differences between men and women. This, they argue, may result in reinforcing the stereotyped notions about women as being different and the only ones responsible for caring for newborn babies and young children. Some feminists also argue that if employers are required to grant women special benefits some of them may well be tempted to hire men instead of women.

Another feature of the liberal human rights model is that affirmative action is viewed as a temporary measure only. The reason for this is that this model does not allow for one sex to be treated differently from or more favourably than the other. Affirmative action is, however, recognized as a temporary measure designed to remove the barriers which traditionally stood in the way of equal competition between men and women. Once these barriers have been removed and the playing fields have been levelled, women and men will be able to compete equally and, it is argued, affirmative action will no longer be necessary.

Radical human rights model

The radical theory of equality is different from the liberal human rights model explained above. It supports equality of outcome† or result. Proponents of this viewpoint require positive action from the government to ensure that the benefits that women and men receive under the law are in fact equal.

Supporters of the radical model criticize the liberal human rights view of equality. They argue that simply to grant women the same rights and opportunities as men will not necessarily result in equality between the sexes. They point out that merely to remove the barriers of competition by creating equal opportunities between the sexes will have the effect of actually placing women in an even weaker position. Louw (*Sex Discrimination in Employment*) illustrates this point as follows:

'Men have traditionally been dominant in the broader social field. If the law simply grants women identical rights to those enjoyed by men, that means that women would merely be admitted into the same environment. But this does not mean that women will have had any say in how the environment was structured. This does not mean that women will have the same power within the environment.'

According to this model, true equality between the sexes can be reached only if their differing needs are taken into consideration. Equal treatment of the sexes does not necessarily imply or mean identical treatment. This argument is succinctly summarized as follows by the well-known Judge Alice Reshick in the United States:

'The essence of gender fairness is to treat both men and women alike. But when one sex has added responsibilities that cannot be totally delegated, allowances must be made. If this is not done, women and men will never be on an equal playing field. After recognizing that difference, flexibility must be accorded women, since 85 percent of women become mothers. We have come a long way since maternity leave came into existence. Yet the myths and stereotypes concerning the roles of men and women must also be abolished.'

Feminists who support the radical model argue that society and the law should recognize the unique ability of women to bear children – an ability not shared by men. So special maternity benefits that only women enjoy must be put in place. These benefits may, due to the uniqueness of the condition of pregnancy, be quite different from the benefits which a man suffering from a temporary physical disability may receive. Proponents of special pregnancy benefits, however, warn that legislation which accommodates the differences between men and women should not entrench women's disadvantage, and it should not result in further stereotyping of women.

Maternity benefits for women should include granting a woman sufficient pregnancy leave (or time off from work) before the baby arrives, as well as after the baby is born. In addition, she must be protected so that she will not be dismissed from her job or replaced because she has had a baby. She must be allowed to return to the same job that she had before she fell pregnant.

Perhaps the strongest argument in favour of this model is the argument that differences between the sexes should not be emphasized, but should rather be recognized and accommodated in order to award women their rightful place in society. The following quotation summarizes this argument:

> 'As we approach the 21st century, society must recognize that the woman's dilemma is our problem and concern. Those in managerial positions must start to provide flexibility. By doing this, women will be retained during the childbearing years just as they become most skilled and useful to the firm or business. If these women are afforded flexibility in setting working hours, or the opportunity to work at home in this day of high technology, they will be productive. They will be able to remain in the work force and will serve as role models and mentors to women following in their footsteps.'

Evaluate this argument carefully. It is a fact that women have more responsibilities than men. Should this fact not be recognized by society? Can women ever attain their rightful place in the workplace if their added responsibilities are not accommodated? Equal-treatment feminists would probably argue no – men and women should be treated equally – stressing their differences will only reinforce the stereotyped notion that men can devote their full attention to their job whilst women cannot. Special-treatment feminists, on the other hand, would probably argue that the special needs of women, in particular in the case of pregnancy, should be accommodated. We cannot provide you with an answer – both models of equality have merit. You as the reader must decide which model will best advance the position of women.

Lastly, proponents of this model also view affirmative action as a more permanent way of accommodating the differences between men and women.

DIRECT AND INDIRECT DISCRIMINATION

Sex discrimination can be recognized in different ways. Although it is often reflected in the laws of a particular country, it is most noticeable in the social practices and attitudes of society. Moreover, sex discrimination can be either blatantly overt and direct or it can be more indirect and take more subtle forms. Both the radical and the liberal approaches to equality demand that both direct and indirect discrimination should be prohibited and prevented.

Direct discrimination is obvious. It is easily recognizable as it involves a direct differentiation between the sexes. For example, a financial institution which refuses to grant a loan to a woman simply because she is a woman is guilty of direct discrimination if it would have granted the loan to a man in similar circumstances.

Indirect discrimination is a more veiled form of discrimination and is not always easily recognizable. It occurs, on the surface, innocently, but it nevertheless results in differential treatment of the sexes.

An example of indirect discrimination would be where an employer sets a job requirement which is not relevant for the performance of a particular job but which would exclude women from qualifying for the position. For example, an advertisement specifically requires that only candidates taller than 1,75 m will be considered for employment. Although the height requirement in our example is not necessary to performing the particular job, women would be hesitant to apply for that position since most of them would not qualify. The height requirement appeared to be neutral, but in practice it had the effect of keeping most women out of the job.

Another example would be where an employer advertises a job, but with the express proviso that the applicant must be younger than 30. This requirement does not appear to exclude women from applying. However, the age limit has the effect of excluding many eligible females, since women under 30 are most often in their childbearing years. Their family and home responsibilities may make it difficult or impossible for some women to enter the job market before the age of 30. What seems to be a neutral requirement may, in practice, therefore, indirectly discriminate against women.

Indirect gender discrimination can, however, take even subtler forms, and it is often the result of existing discriminatory social practices and stereotyping. For instance, young women are steered into careers which require less training and skills. Often these careers are merely extensions of domestic tasks, such as nursing, teaching, child care, and work as a receptionist. Jobs of this nature are seen as intrinsic to womanhood. Many people feel that these 'female' skills do not have to be learned in the way that 'male' skills need to be learned. Women are accordingly discouraged from choosing careers which require a high degree of training and professionalism.

The distorted and deeply embedded social perceptions that view women as simply not equipped to perform certain jobs or to rise above a certain level of promotion need to be addressed. It is necessary to introduce policies and programmes aimed at eradicating these negative social attitudes.

Conclusion

Women in employment still face prejudice and stereotyping. Some of the following steps should be taken to reduce this prejudice:
- Anti-discriminatory legislation should be enacted to eliminate both direct and indirect discrimination in the workplace;
- Employers should be urged to accommodate women in the workplace and to help female employees attain their full potential. Whether this option would include providing women with special benefits in order to accommodate the family responsibilities they might have will depend upon whether a liberal or a radical human rights model is followed.

CHAPTER ELEVEN:
Enforcement of equality in the workplace: the Constitution and the Labour Relations Act

INTRODUCTION

One of the areas in which women are seeking equality is the workplace, and area in which discrimination is still widely practised against women. Discrimination on the basis of sex and gender is now specifically prohibited both in terms of South Africa's Constitution Act and in terms of the Labour Relations Act, 1995 which deals specifically with the law applicable to the workplace. These developments signal the beginning of a new era for the recognition of women's rights not only in society but, more specifically, also in the workplace.

In order for women to challenge sex discrimination in the workplace effectively, a basic knowledge of the law that outlaws discrimination on the basis of sex and gender is required. In the following paragraphs, the manner in which both the Constitution and the Labour Relations Act, 1995 outlaw sex and gender discrimination is explained briefly. The remedies available to women who have been discriminated against are also outlined.

THE CONSTITUTION OF THE REPUBLIC OF SOUTH AFRICA ACT 108 OF 1996

The date on which South Africa's first democratic elections were held, 27 April 1994, marks the birth of a free and democratic South Africa for all her citizens. The birth of our new nation was accompanied by the adoption of South Africa's first democratic Constitution (the so-called Interim Constitution). The final Constitution of 1996 came into force in February 1997. (see also Chapter 20)

Chapter 2 of the Constitution contains the Bill of Rights, which forms the cornerstone of our democracy and enshrines the various rights of all the people in our country. It also affirms the democratic values of human dignity, equality and freedom on which our new society is built. Although the Constitution (including the Bill of Rights) serves as a founding document of our society, other legislation may be enacted further to develop and regulate the rights recognized in the Constitution (see the discussion of the Labour Relations Act, 1995, below). Some of the fundamental human rights and freedoms which are recognized in the Bill of Rights are:

- the right to life;
- the right to equality;
- the right to human dignity;
- the right to personal privacy, and
- the right to freedom of conscience, religion, thought, belief and opinion (which includes academic freedom in institutions of higher learning).

All of the entrenched rights and freedoms are protected and enforced by the Constitutional Court, as well as the High Court. The Labour Court also enforces various rights and freedoms in terms of the Labour Relations Act, 1995 (see the discussion below).

A criticism that can be levelled against the Bill of Rights is that it does not go far enough to ensure equality between men and women. Some feminists argue that a separate chapter on Women's Rights in the Bill of Rights aimed at actual equality between men and women might have helped to clarify the content and extent of the rights and values pertaining to women in South Africa. They argue that such a chapter might have had an important impact on social attitudes and perceptions towards women. Although those who advocated the inclusion of such a chapter in the final Constitution may be disappointed by its omission, it is possible for other legislation to promote the equality of women both in society and in the workplace just as effectively. (See also the discussion of s 9(4) of the Constitution, in terms of which such legislation must be enacted, below.)

Of particular importance to women are the provisions of s 9 (also referred to as the 'equality clause') and, in particular, the provisions of s 9(3) of the Bill of Rights, which entrench the right to equality. Section 9 reads as follows:

'(1) *Everyone is equal before the law and has the right to equal protection and benefit of the law.*

(2) *Equality includes the full and equal enjoyment of all rights and freedoms. To promote the achievement of equality, legislative and other measures designed to protect or advance persons, or categories of persons, disadvantaged by unfair discrimination may be taken.*

(3) *The state may not unfairly discriminate directly or indirectly*

against anyone on one or more grounds, including race, gender, sex, pregnancy, marital status, ethnic or social origin, colour, sexual orientation, age, disability, religion, conscience, belief, culture, language, and birth.
(4) No person may unfairly discriminate directly or indirectly against anyone on one or more grounds in terms of subsection (3). National legislation must be enacted to prevent or prohibit unfair discrimination.
(5) Discrimination on one or more of the grounds listed in subsection (3) is unfair unless it is established that the discrimination is fair.'

The following important points flow from this section:
(a) Section 9(1) guarantees the right to equality before the law as well as to equal protection of the law. This right grants every individual the right of access to a court of law. Some writers interpret this section even more widely to encompass the duty of the State to grant protection to those groups (such as women) who in the past have found themselves in a particularly vulnerable position.
(b) Section 9(2) of the equality clause states that equality includes the full and equal enjoyment of all rights and freedoms. It is also stated that in order to promote the achievement of equality it is admissible to adopt legislative and other measures designed to protect or advance persons, or categories of persons, disadvantaged by unfair discrimination. This means that legislation and other programmes or policies may be adopted with the aim of advancing the position of persons or categories of persons (such as women or blacks as a group) who have been discriminated against in the past. In order to advance these individuals or groups of individuals, preferential treatment may be given to them. As will be discussed in Chapter 12 below, this practice of giving preferential treatment to historically disadvantaged individuals or groups of individuals is normally referred to as affirmative action. The process of affirmative action may involve treating women differently simply because they are women. This process may therefore involve discriminating against men, for example, in favour of women, purely on the basis of their sex.

Normally any measures which distinguish between individuals on the basis, for instance, of their race or gender, would be unconstitutional because they constitute a violation of the provisions of s 9(3) of the Constitution which expressly prohibits distinguishing or discriminating against individuals purely on the basis of their sex or gender. However, in an attempt to redress past discriminatory practices against certain individuals or groups of individuals, preferential treatment is deemed to be warranted in these circumstances.

It is important to note that affirmative action may be applied only to those groups which in the past have been 'disadvantaged by unfair discrimination'. In other words, only those persons or categories of persons who have been disadvantaged in the past by unfair discriminatory practices will be able to benefit from programmes aimed at securing their full and equal enjoyment of all rights and freedoms. Undoubtedly, it could be argued that women – and in particular black women – will be seen to qualify as one of the designated groups against whom past discriminatory practices have taken place. (Affirmative action is discussed in more detail in Chapter 12 below.)

(c) In terms of s 9(3), any unfair discrimination against any person, whether of a direct or indirect nature, on any one of the grounds listed in this section, would constitute a violation of the individual's constitutionally recognized right to equality. (See Chapter 10 above for a discussion of direct and indirect discrimination.)

Discrimination on the grounds of a person's sex or gender therefore constitutes a violation of the right to equality. Note also the use of the word 'unfairly' in s 9(3): it was included in this section to serve as a guideline to those interpreting the meaning and effect of the section. It is clear that what is required is not simply a differentiation between people on any of the listed grounds but that such differentiation should amount to unfair discrimination.

Section 9(3) prohibits discrimination on 'one or more' of the grounds listed in this section. A person complaining of discrimination is therefore not restricted to complaining of discrimination of one kind only. A woman may, for example, state that she was unfairly discriminated against because of her race as well as her sex. This fact is important, because black women particularly were traditionally in a vulnerable position, having often been discriminated against on the grounds not only of their sex but also of their race.

A further striking aspect of the factors listed in s 9(3) is the reference to both 'sex' and 'gender'. The term 'sex' refers to an individuals' biological features, whereas 'gender' has a more psychological connotation. Albertyn (*Introducting the Rights to Equality and the Interim Constitution*) argues that this distinction between 'sex' and 'gender' highlights the fact that not all of the distinctions between men and women are reducible to the biological differences between them.

(d) Section 9(4) requires the enactment of legislation to prevent or prohibit unfair discrimination. At the time of going to press, legislation outlawing unfair discrimination in the workplace is in the pipeline. (The Employment Equity Bill was published for comment in the *Government Gazette* on 1 December 1997.)

(e) Section 9(5) states that discrimination on one or more of the grounds listed in subsec (3) is unfair unless it is established that the discrimination is fair. It therefore places the burden of proof on the person who differentiates on these grounds to prove that the discrimination is not unfair.

It is notoriously difficult for women to prove the existence of a discriminatory practice, however. To overcome this problem to some extent, s 9(5) states that as soon as the victim of discrimination is able to establish proof of a discriminatory act or practice, it will be regarded as sufficient proof of the existence of unfair discrimination until the opposite is proved. In other words, it will then be up to the party who stands accused of discriminatory treatment to prove that his or her actions did not amount to discrimination in terms of s 9 of the Constitution.

EQUALITY IN THE WORKPLACE: THE LABOUR RELATIONS ACT 66 OF 1995

The Labour Relations Act, 1995 which came into operation on 11 November 1996, specifically sets out to combat sex discrimination in the workplace in accordance with the spirit of the Constitution. The following provisions of the Act are important to working women:

Automatically unfair dismissals

A dismissal will be automatically unfair in the following two instances:
- Dismissal on the basis of pregnancy: Where an employer dismisses a woman on the basis of her pregnancy, intended pregnancy or any reason related to her pregnancy, such a dismissal will be automatically unfair (s 187(1) *(e)* of the Labour Relations Act, 1995). She may refer the dispute to the Commission for Conciliation, Mediation and Arbitration (the CCMA) for conciliation. The CCMA will appoint a Commissioner, who will assist the parties (the woman who is complaining of the discrimination and her employer who allegedly discriminated against her) to resolve the dispute between them. The Commissioner's role is limited to assisting the parties to resolve the dispute between themselves. The Commissioner will not make any decision that will be binding on them. Proceedings at the CCMA are free of charge.

If conciliation fails to resolve a dispute, the complainant (ie the woman who was allegedly dismissed on the basis of her pregnancy) may refer the dispute to the Labour Court. Once the dispute has been referred to that Court, a court date will be arranged. At the hearing, a judge of the Labour Court will give both parties the opportunity to put forward their versions of what happened. After the Court has heard all the evidence, the judge will reach a decision. If the Labour Court concludes, after having heard evidence, that the woman was dismissed on the basis of her pregnancy, intended pregnancy or any reason related to her pregnancy, it may make an order that she be reinstated in the position she held prior to her dismissal. If the woman does not want to be reinstated or if there is any other reason why the Court should not order that the employer reinstate her, the Court may make an order for compensation.[†]

Section 194(3) of the Labour Relations Act, 1995 states that the Labour Court, in deciding the compensation to be awarded to a person whose dismissal was automatically unfair must be 'just and equitable in all the circumstances'. The Labour Court may, however, not order compensation which is more than the equivalent of 24 months' remuneration (salary) calculated at the (dismissed) employee's rate of remuneration at the date of her dismissal. This means that if the woman earned R800,00 per month at the time of her dismissal, that amount will be regarded as her rate of remuneration for the purposes of calculating the compensation which has to be paid over to her (ie R800,00 x number of months of award). (The dismissal of a women on the basis of pregnancy is discussed in more detail in Chapter 15, below.)

- **Dismissal on the basis of race, sex, gender or family responsibilities:** Where the reason for the dismissal of a woman (or any other employee) is the fact that the employer discriminated unfairly against an employee 'on any arbitrary ground, including, but not limited to, race, gender, sex, ethnic or social origin, colour, sexual orientation, age, disability, religion, conscience, belief, political opinion, culture, language, marital status or family responsibility', the dismissal will be automatically unfair (s 187(1)*(f)* of the Labour Relations Act, 1995.) An employer may therefore not dismiss a woman employee simply because she is a woman, black or married. If an employer dismisses a woman because she has family responsibilities (which may or may not hinder her job performance), such a dismissal will also be automatically unfair.

The only grounds on which an employer may dismiss an employee are: where such an employee is guilty of misconduct (eg if it is proved that the employee has stolen something), or if she is incapable of doing the work for which she has been hired (dismissal for incompetence), or if her employer is in financial difficulties and is no longer able to pay her salary (dismissal on the basis of operational requirements). Even in these instances, the dismissal must still be substantively fair (in other words, there must be a valid and fair reason for her dismissal) and procedurally fair (eg the employer must afford the employee the opportunity to respond to any allegations or charges against her – normally it is required that the employee be afforded a disciplinary hearing.) If the employer is no longer able to afford to pay the employee's salary, he or she must also discuss the possibility of retrenchment with her.

There are two exceptions to the rule that an employer may not discriminate against a woman employee when terminating her services:

- Age: where an employee has reached the normal or agreed retirement age for persons employed in that capacity, the employer may terminate the employee's services. This means that if the normal retirement age for a person is, for example, 65, it will not be automatically unfair if the employer terminates her services once that employee turns 65. Technically, one could argue that, in dismissing her, the employer is discriminating against that person on the basis of her age. But, because it is regarded as an acceptable practice for employees to retire once they have reached a certain age, terminating their services once they have reached that age will not be considered to be automatically unfair.

- Inherent requirements of the particular job: as we have seen above, if an employer dismisses a woman and the reason for the dismissal is her race, sex or gender (or any of the other listed grounds), the dismissal will normally be considered to be automatically unfair. This is so because employers are not allowed to discriminate against a woman on the basis of her race, sex or gender (or any of the other listed grounds). However, where an employer can prove that the inherent requirements of a particular job call for a person of a certain sex, the employer may dismiss a person who is not of the required sex, even if it means that the employer is discriminating against that person. (See also the discussion below, where some examples of inherent requirements of a job are given.)

Where a woman is dismissed and she believes that she was discriminated against, she may refer the dispute to the CCMA for conciliation. If conciliation fails to resolve the dispute, she may then refer the dispute to the Labour Court. If the Labour Court concludes, after having heard evidence, that her dismissal amounts to discrimination on the basis of her race, sex or gender (or any of the other listed grounds), the Court may order her reinstatement. If for any reason it is not feasible to order her reinstatement, the Labour Court may order that the employer pay her an amount of money to compensate her for the fact that she was dismissed unfairly.

Residual unfair labour practice

Item 2(1) of Schedule 7 of the Labour Relations Act, 1995 prohibits discrimination against women on the basis of race, sex and gender. This item also prohibits any unfair conduct by an employer towards an employee relating to the promotion, demotion or training of an employee or relating to the provision of benefits to an employee. Item 2(1) and (2) of Schedule 7 read as follows:

> '(1)For the purposes of this item, an unfair labour practice means any unfair act or omission that arises between an employer and an employee involving –
>
> (a) the unfair discrimination, either directly or indirectly, against an employee on any arbitrary ground, including but not limited to race, gender, sex, ethnic or social origin, colour, sexual orientation, age, disability, religion, conscience, belief, political opinion, culture, language, marital status or family responsibility;
>
> (b) the unfair conduct of the employer relating to the promotion, demotion or training of an employee or relating to the provision of benefits to an employee;
>
> ...
>
> (2) For the purposes of subitem (1)(a)
>
> (a) "employee" includes an applicant for employment;
>
> (b) an employer is not prevented from adopting or implementing employment policies and practices that are designed to achieve the adequate protection and advancement of persons or groups or categories of persons disadvantaged by unfair discrimination, in order to enable their full and equal enjoyment of all rights and freedoms; and
>
> (c) any discrimination based on an inherent requirement of the particular job does not constitute unfair discrimination.'

This provision of the Labour Relations Act, 1995 is referred to as the residual unfair labour practice provision. In terms of this provision it would constitute an unfair labour practice to discriminate unfairly, either directly or indirectly, against a woman (or any other employee) on any arbitrary ground, including, but not limited to: race, gender, sex, ethnic or social origin, colour, sexual orientation, age, disability, religion, conscience, belief, political opinion, culture, language, marital status or family responsibility. For the purposes of this item, 'an employee' includes a 'prospective' employee. This means that an employer is not allowed to discriminate against a woman when she applies for a job simply because she is a woman or black or practises a certain religion.

Notwithstanding this prohibition, an employer may discriminate against employees on the basis of race, sex, religion or any of the other listed grounds in the following two instances:

- The inherent requirements of a job: An employer may discriminate on the basis or race or sex (or any of the other listed grounds) if the inherent requirements of a particular job call for a person of a certain race or sex. The following example illustrates this point:

CASE STUDY

A film company advertises for actors to audition for the role of Bat Man in a film. One male actor and three actresses apply for the role. The director hires the male actor without even giving the three actresses an opportunity to role play for Bat Man. When the three actresses enquire about the reasons why none of them was hired, the director informs them that he specifically wanted a male for the role. The three actresses allege that they have been discriminated against on the basis of their sex. The director admits that he discriminated against the three actresses on the basis of their sex but argues that the inherent requirements of the job (the role of Bat Man) call for a male actor.

The director (the employer) in this example will probably defend himself successfully against a claim of discrimination on the basis of sex because the inherent requirements of the job calls for a male, not a female actor.

- In terms of an affirmative action programme: an employer may discriminate against persons on the basis of race or sex provided that such discrimination occurs in the context of an affirmative action programme. For example, where two people apply for a certain position and one is a white man and the other a black woman, the employer is allowed to discriminate against the white male on the basis of his sex and colour in favour of appointing the black woman. Affirmative action is necessary to correct the imbalances which exist in the workplace as a result of past discriminatory practices.

If a woman employee feels that she was unfairly discriminated against, she may refer the dispute (the fact that she was treated unfairly or discriminated against on the basis of her sex, race or gender) to the CCMA. If the Commissioner is unable to assist the parties to resolve the dispute, the woman who has been discriminated against can decide to take the matter further and refer the dispute to the Labour Court. If the Court comes to the conclusion that the employer discriminated against her on the basis of her race, sex or gender, it will make an order which is appropriate in the circumstances. If the case concerns the unfair conduct of the employer relating to the promotion, demotion, training or provision of benefits to the employee, the dispute must ultimately be referred to arbitration, not to the Labour Court.

Conclusion

In terms of the Labour Relations Act, 1995, unfair discrimination against women in the workplace is no longer tolerated. This is in accordance with the universal values of human dignity, freedom and equality of all human beings, irrespective of their gender or race, contained in our Constitution. These values create a whole new social philosophy in terms of which our society will be judged in future. It is no longer acceptable to discriminate between human beings on unreasonable grounds and it will certainly no longer be acceptable to discriminate against women on the basis of their gender: such discrimination would constitute a violation of the very values that form the cornerstone of the Constitution.

Notwithstanding legislation which outlaws discrimination, however, collective bargaining between employers and trade unions will also continue to play an important role in combating discrimination in the workplace. In South Africa, collective bargaining has, in the past, focused primarily on discrimination based on race. But the trade union movement also has the potential to play an important creative role in responding to the increased participation of women in the work force, and in increasing sensitivity towards gender issues in labour relationships.

CHAPTER TWELVE:
Equality for women in the workplace: affirmative action

Althought 40% of South Africa's labour force are women, in many instances they earn less than men. This is not only as a result of the type of work that they do, but also because women's average pay is generally lower than that of men. Furthermore, women are poorly represented in management and decision-making structures. Have you heard of many female managing directors?

Where discrimination results from social perceptions and practices and involves a class of persons rather than an individual, it is necessary to adopt a programme of affirmative action to remedy the situation. Broadly speaking, affirmative action involves redressing[†] the disadvantages of past discrimination by the provision of preferential treatment for the disadvantaged group. This means that if a certain group of people (such as women) has been treated unfairly in the past, then this group will now be given special privileges to make up for the unequal treatment of the past.

The achievement of equality is central to the new legal and constitutional order in South Africa. To this end, the Constitution recognizes affirmative action not as an exception to the principle of equality but as a central part of the achievement of equality.

Section 9 of the Constitution deals with equality. (See Chapter 11, above, where s 9 is quoted in full.) This section, inter alia, provides that every person is equal before the law and has the right to equal protection before the law and equal benefit of the law (s 9(1)). It also provides that no person shall be unfairly discriminated against, either directly or indirectly, for arbitrary reasons such as race, gender and sex (s 9(3)).

Section 9(2) permits affirmative action. It says that to promote the achievement of equality, legislative and other measures designed to protect or advance persons, or categories of persons, disadvantaged by unfair discrimination may be taken. Therefore, this section will help these disadvantaged groups to reach their full and equal enjoyment of all the rights and freedoms entrenched in the Constitution.

Different ways of implementing affirmative action

Essentially, there are two ways in which affirmative action can be implemented:
- first, it can be left to employers to implement on a voluntary basis, or,
- secondly, the legislature can intervene and introduce legislation to force employers to implement it.

Hitherto, affirmative action has been voluntary. A large number of affirmative action programmes were implemented for the wrong reasons and also in the incorrect manner. Employers experienced increasing pressure from potential investors and customers, particularly those from overseas, to do away with discriminatory practices. They also realized that a majority government would put pressure on them to make their employee and management structures more representative of South African society. In addition, they realized that their future consumer markets were among the black majority, and that greater credibility would be achieved if their staff and their managerial structures were more representative of South Africa.

CASE STUDY

A certain South African company, XYZ (Pty) Ltd, was looking for investments from the USA in the 1970s. Because of the political situation, however, many US companies were not willing to invest in a company that appeared to support apartheid.

This company quickly hired many new employees from different racial groups in order to call itself a multi-racial company. As a result XYZ (Pty) Ltd received substantial financial backing from the US company.

However, the new employees were temporary staff, with little opportunity for benefits or promotion.

After reading the example above, answer these questions:
- Do you think this was true affirmative action?
- Do you think the new employees were equal to the others?

Although some of the voluntary programmes were structured and implemented through collective bargaining,[†] most were management initiatives. The employers structured these programmes primarily to ensure and enhance the economic well-being and survival of their enterprises, not to redress discrimination. But, in creating these programmes, their emphasis was on race and not on sex. Most programmes were aimed at correcting employee and management profiles† to reflect the population profile, not the gender profile. Consequently, redressing discrimination usually meant the recruitment of 'suitably qualified' black men. Moreover, where an attempt was made to redress discrimination against women, management was influenced by society's negative perceptions of women in the workplace.

When it is suggested that the legislature must intervene and actively encourage affirmative action, we need to consider the extent and content of this 'encouragement'. In this regard, it is useful to consider how other countries have handled the matter. We shall look at how affirmative action programmes were introduced in the United States of America (US), the United Kingdom (UK) and Australia. Both the US and the UK came to consider affirmative action as inherently discriminatory† against the previously privileged groups. By this was meant that, since affirmative action programmes have the effect that a group of people (eg women) who were disadvantaged in the past come to receive preferential treatment under the new dispensation, this can constitute discrimination against the other groups (eg men) who had privilege in the past.

Affirmative action programmes from the First World

There are many different models of affirmative action programmes. Here we look at some models from First World countries and examine their strengths and weaknesses.

The United States of America

Title VII† of the Civil Rights Act of 1964† in the United States is the primary federal law that protects employees against discrimination based on sex. The Equal Employment Opportunity Commission (EEOC),† established in terms of Title VII, has the authority to ask the Federal courts to act on behalf of employees who believe they are the victims of discriminatory acts. Alternatively, individuals still have the right to start their own legal proceedings, even when the EEOC investigates a charge and determines that no violation has occurred.

In the US, affirmative action programmes are largely voluntary. However, where the EEOC or an individual believes that the affirmative action programme amounts to discrimination against the other side, the matter can be referred to a Federal court in terms of Title VII.

Look at the example below of Joseph and Anna, who both want to go to the Medical University to become doctors. Do you think Joseph was a victim of discrimination?

> **CASE STUDY**
>
> When Joseph applied to go to Medical School to become a doctor, he was sure his high grades and past academic achievement would be good enough. He had always been an excellent student, especially in mathematics and science courses, so he was shocked to find out that he had not been admitted!
>
> One of Joseph's high school friends, Anna, was accepted by the university, even though she had lower grades than Joseph. At the time, the university's medical school had an affirmative action programme in place to increase the number of women students. Joseph felt that he was a victim of discrimination because of that affirmative action, so he went to the EEOC and filed a claim in terms of Title VII.

In practice, therefore, it is left to the courts to define the limits of affirmative action programmes. The following limitations have been laid down:
- Voluntary affirmative action programmes do not necessarily violate Title VII;
- Voluntary affirmative action is permissible, provided that:
  - it should be a temporary measure designed to achieve rather than maintain a balanced work force;
  - it should not constitute an absolute bar to the employment of persons not covered by the affirmative action; and
  - it should not require the dismissal of persons.

The United Kingdom

The legal position in the UK does not present a useful example for our purposes because in that country legislation does not promote affirmative action in any real or specific terms. In fact, there is legislation which actually calls affirmative action 'unlawful'. Generally, the definition of 'discrimination' in the Sex Discrimination Act (SDA)[†] of the UK makes affirmative action unlawful. However, the SDA permits a measure of affirmative action by encouraging and enabling women to be candidates for jobs, while allowing an employer freedom to decide upon the person. This is done by permitting an employer to provide specific training for existing groups of employees (women), provided that the imbalance in the work force can be verified, as described in the SDA. The Act also allows an employer to provide training for women who are not yet employees.

Employers are prohibited from implementing affirmative action schemes that would go beyond what is allowed in the SDA. Still, some employers have implemented affirmative action schemes by identifying the unique features and problems of working women and trying to address them. In doing so, they have been able to entice women to work for them. Employers, for example, can do the following:
- increase promotion opportunities for part-time female employees;
- develop job-sharing schemes (a plan where two female workers share one job; one works mornings, the other afternoons);
- improve maternity and child-care facilities;
- retain contact with women who cease work for family reasons with the possibility of giving them some credit for the time they spend out of the work force (so that they don't lose seniority rights because of absence).

Neither the US nor the UK systems are good analogies for South Africa. The US legislation does not go far enough in the process of promoting affirmative action because there are too many regulations which allow employers to avoid it, or to keep it very simple. In the UK, they do not have specific legislation dealing with affirmative action; on the contrary, their laws actually label affirmative action as unlawful. Employers who want to help their women workers must use special schemes.

Of course, the social conditions in the US and in the UK are very different from those in South Africa. In the US, affirmative action is aimed at a minority black population, while in South Africa, it would be helping a majority of the population.

Australia

Comparison with Australia is more useful to us here than comparison with the US and the UK. Australia has an Act which specifically deals with affirmative action regarding women in the workplace. The Affirmative Action (Equal Opportunities for Women) Act of 1986[†] requires private-sector employers with more than a hundred workers to implement an employment equity policy[†] and programme. This Act imposes administrative, procedural and quota[†] targets requirements upon such employers.

The Act provides an eight-step programme for employers:
- they must develop a policy statement on affirmative action and communicate it to all their employees;
- a senior manager must be appointed to develop, implement and co-ordinate the affirmative action programme;
- trade unions must be consulted about the programme;
- all employees, particularly women, must be consulted about the programme;
- a statistical analysis and profile of the work force must be prepared;

- all existing personnel practices and policies must be reviewed;
- employers must then set out their own estimates and objectives;
- the programme must be monitored and evaluated.
- A public report must be prepared on the work force profile and outline of the programme and a separate confidential report must be prepared on the details of the programme.

AFFIRMATIVE ACTION PROGRAMMES IN SOUTH AFRICA

With the exception of s 9 of the Constitution, South Africa does not have any legislation which deals specifically with the question of affirmative action in the workplace.

The only statutory reference to affirmative action in the workplace is contained in schedule 7 to the Labour Relations Act, 1995. Schedule 7 is entitled Transitional Arrangement, and contains provisions which deal with certain labour and industrial relations aspects until such time as they are dealt with in specific legislation.

Item 2 of Schedule 7 deals with residual unfair labour practices. (See also the discussion in chapter 11 above, where the relevant parts of item 2 are quoted in full.) In terms of this item, 'unfair labour practice' includes the following:

- Any unfair act or omission that arises between an employer and an employee, involving unfair discrimination, either directly or indirectly, against an employee on any arbitrary ground, including race, gender and sex;
- Unfair conduct of the employer relating to the promotion, demotion or training of an employee or relating to the provisions of benefits to an employee.

In terms of item 2, a male employee may, for example, argue that the employer has committed an unfair labour practice against him by promoting a female employee instead of him. He will therefore be arguing that he has been unfairly discriminated against because of his sex. Item 2(2), however, allows an employer to implement an affirmative action programme. It states that:

'an employer is not prevented from adopting or implementing employment policies and practices that are designed to achieve the adequate protection and advancement of persons or groups or categories of persons disadvantaged by unfair discrimination, in order to enable their full and equal enjoyment of all rights and freedoms.'

The employer will thus be able to justify the promotion of the female employee on the ground that it was done in terms of an affirmative action programme.

As we have indicated above, the provisions contained in Schedule 7 are meant to be transitional. This means that they will remain in force only until legislation has been enacted which deals with unfair acts or omissions in the workplace, other than dismissals. (Unfair dismissals are specifically dealt with in the Labour Relations Act, 1995.)

Of particular importance in this regard will be legislation which deals with the abolition of discrimination against women, and affirmative action as a method of redressing the disadvantages of past discrimination. The process for the introduction of such legislation has been set in motion: on 1 December 1997 the Employment Equity Bill was published for comment in the *Government Gazette*. The purpose of the Bill is set out in s 1:

'The purpose of this Act is to achieve equality in the workplace by promoting equal opportunity and fair treatment in employment through the elimination of unfair discrimination; and

implementing positive measures to redress the disadvantages in employment experienced by black people, women and people with disabilities, in order to ensure their equitable representation in all occupational categories and levels in the work force.'

The purpose of the Bill is to achieve equality in the workplace. It aims to do this in two ways: first, by promoting equal opportunity and fair treatment through the elimination of unfair discrimination and, secondly, by implementing 'positive measures', such as affirmative action measures, to redress the disadvantages experienced by black people, women and people with disabilities.

The Bill regulates the implementation by the employer of positive measures for black people (a generic term which means Africans, 'coloureds' and Indians), women and people with disabilities (designated groups). The Bill's provisions regarding such positive measures are the following:

- The implementation of positive measures is restricted to employers who employ 50 or more employees (designated employers).
- Every designated employer must implement positive measures for people from designated groups in order to achieve employment equity. Positive measures must include affirmative action measures, including preferential treatment, to appoint and promote suitably qualified people from designated groups to ensure their equitable representation in all occupational categories and levels in the work force. However, the Bill does not require the employer, in implementing equity, to:

- appoint, train or promote a fixed number of people from designated groups;
- appoint or promote people from designated groups who are not suitably qualified;
- take any decision concerning an employment policy that would establish an absolute barrier to the employment prospects of people who are not from the designated groups; or
- create new positions in the work force.
- A designated employer must:
- consult with its employees.
- disclose all relevant information to its employees when consulting with them.
- conduct an analysis of its employment policies, practices, procedures and the working environment, to identify employment barriers which adversely affect people from designated groups. The analysis must also include a profile of the employer's work force within each occupational category and level in order to determine the degree of under-representation of people from designated groups in various occupational categories and levels in that employer's work force.
- prepare an employment equity plan which will achieve reasonable progress towards employment equity in that employer's work force. The plan must inter alia state the objectives to be achieved for each year of the plan as well as the duration of the plan. (Note that the Bill requires that the plan may not be shorter than one year or longer than five years.)
- annually report to the Director-General: Labour on progress made in implementing its employment equity plan. The report is a public document; in other words, the public will have access to it.
- assign one or more senior managers to take responsibility for monitoring and implementing an employment equity plan. The employer must also take reasonable steps to ensure that the managers perform their functions.
- make a copy of the employment equity plan available to its employees for copying and consultation.
- maintain records in respect of its work force and its employment equity plan.

CONCLUSION

Legislation on the promotion of equal opportunities for South African women in the work force is to be welcomed. The Employment Equity Bill complies with the requirements of the Constitution as well as with international standards, the most important of which is the International Labour Organisation's Convention concerning discrimination in respect of employment and occupation (Convention 111 of 1958). Although the Bill will undoubtedly spark a lot of debate between employers and employees, it is predicted that it will be passed by Parliament, perhaps in a somewhat different form, within the foreseeable future.

CHAPTER THIRTEEN:
'Equal pay for equal work'

'Equal pay for equal work' means when a male and a female employee are doing the same work, they must be paid the same remuneration. At this stage, a female employee who believes that she is not receiving the same remuneration as a male employee may proceed against her employer on the basis that it has committed an unfair labour practice against her in terms of item 2 of Schedule 7 of the Labour Relations Act, 1995. (The relevant parts of item 2 have been quoted in full in Chapter 11, above.) In terms of this item, 'unfair labour practice' includes the following:

'any unfair act or omission that arises between an employer and an employee, involving the unfair discrimination, either directly or indirectly, against an employee on any arbitrary ground, including race, gender and sex.'

In terms of item 2, a female employee who is being paid less than her male counterpart may argue that the employer is committing an unfair labour practice by unfairly discriminating against her on the ground of her sex or gender.

As mentioned earlier, Schedule 7 is only a temporary measure. It is the Legislature's intention that the question of equal remuneration should be dealt with in terms of the Employment Equity Act, which was still in Bill form at the time of going to press.

Talking about equal pay for equal work is not as easy as it seems, though, and the following issues need to be examined:
- the comparator;
- the basis of comparison;
- the meaning of 'equal pay';
- justifiable grounds for pay disparity

These issues are discussed below. Particular attention is paid to how other countries, such as the US and the UK, have dealt with these issues. These sources should provide us with some guidance as to the manner in which the various issues should be dealt with.

© JUTA & CO, LTD

The comparator

For a woman to claim equal remuneration, she needs to compare herself to someone in a similar position: a comparator, the male employee with whom the female employee compares herself.

This is one of the key issues in the remuneration debate.

In terms of the Equal Pay Act of the UK (the EQPA), a woman may compare herself to a man employed at the same establishment or at another company run by her employer. She may therefore compare herself with a man employed in another branch or factory of her employer. This could hold distinct advantages for the woman. If the other branch or factory is situated in an area which is economically more viable and active, her comparator's remuneration may be higher, not only because of his sex but also because of the better economic conditions of the area where the comparator works.

Who would be regarded as the women's employer? This may include subsidiaries or the holding company of the particular company for which the female is working. The EQPA appears to include such companies. It states that a woman may compare herself with a man employed at an 'associated employer'. Two employers are defined as 'being associated' if one is a company of which the other has direct or indirect control. They are also considered as 'being associated' if both are companies of which a third person has direct or indirect control.

The bases of comparison

The law must provide female workers with the basis on which they can compare themselves with male employees. The wider the basis, the more likely it will be that a woman will be able to find a suitable comparator. The EQPA provides for three categories (or bases) of comparison: like work, equivalent work, and equal value/comparable worth.

Like work

The first basis of comparison is generally referred to as the 'like work' criterion. The woman must compare herself with a man doing work which is either identical to hers or which differs only in small respects. It has a fairly limited effect, because men and women do not usually do 'like work'. In addition, an employer could simply change the content of a job in order to avoid two jobs being characterized as equal.

Equivalent work

A basis of comparison which provides the female worker with greater scope is that of 'equivalent work'. In this case, a woman can compare herself with a man employed in work which is rated as 'equivalent' to hers.

In order to establish whether two jobs are equivalent, they must be evaluated and compared. Often, employers have a system according to which jobs are evaluated and categorized into different grades. Job evaluation can be done in many ways. Different jobs can simply be compared, or they can be evaluated in terms of the demands made on employees. These demands can include things such as effort, skill and responsibility. Such an evaluation requires an analysis of the various tasks and skills involved in the work rather than a comparison of entire jobs.

The problem with this test is that people doing the grading are usually motivated and influenced by society's views on the following:
- women's role in life, and
- the importance and value of the jobs usually done by women.

In too many cases, the jobs traditionally done by women are categorized as low-grade jobs.

Equal value/comparable worth

The third basis of comparison is to decide whether the work is of 'equal value' or of 'comparable worth'. This basis is the widest, because an equal value claim is possible where the woman's work is neither like the comparator's work ('like work') nor rated as 'equivalent' to that of her male comparator. This basis allows a woman to compare herself with a man doing a job with a content completely different from her own.

The difficulty with this test lies in establishing the criteria to be used in evaluating jobs and the weight to be attached to each. In the US, the Federal courts have rejected the comparable worth criterion because they do not want to become involved in the process of evaluating work of equal value. Other opponents of the criterion have also criticized it for failing to allow employers to pay what the market dictates.

In the UK, in terms of the EQPA, the industrial tribunal first decides whether there are reasonable grounds for the woman's claim of discrimination. If there are, the tribunal calls for a report from a member of a panel of independent experts. It is for the independent expert, not for the tribunal, to determine the value of the relevant jobs of the woman and man. The woman is entitled to equal pay if the tribunal determines that the value of her work is equal to or greater than that of her comparator. Whether the woman's work is of equal value depends on the demands made on her under headings such as effort, skill and decision. Jobs must therefore be analysed under a number of headings. In this case, an employer would need to do a job evaluation study.

The meaning of 'equal pay'

Generally, when we talk about remuneration, we mean not only an employee's basic salary but also all the other benefits which she receives as an employee. In terms of the International Labour Organization's Equal Remuneration Convention, 100 of 1951, remuneration includes any additional benefits of the job which are directly or indirectly payable to an employee. The definition of 'remuneration' in the Labour Relations Act, 1995 is wide enough to include benefits such as pension scheme and medical aid contributions, housing subsidies, car allowances, bonuses, entertainment allowances, university bursaries for employees' children, and so forth.

> **CASE STUDY**
>
> In the UK Sally Jones is working at the same company as John Meyers. They work in the same department, doing almost exactly the same type of work. They are both working on marketing products of the company. Mrs Jones finds out that she is earning £3 000 a year less in salary than Mr Meyers, so she complains to her boss, Mr Smythe, and says she will file a claim of discrimination against the company.
>
> Mr Smythe tells Mrs Jones that John Meyers was hired as an assistant, and so earns more money. But Sally is sure that they actually do almost exactly the same type and amount of work in the office, so she files a claim.

Justifiable grounds for pay disparity

Just because a woman qualifies for equal pay because she does work of equal value does not mean that she will automatically get it. Sometimes there is a reason for this disparity or difference in pay. In certain cases or in special circumstances there may be a legitimate reason why the employer pays female and male employees differently. This is called justifiable pay disparity.

In the UK, for example, the EQPA provides that the equality clause will not operate where the employer proves that the difference between the terms of the woman's contract and that of her comparator are genuinely due to a 'material' factor which is not a difference of sex. The term 'material' has been interpreted as meaning 'significant' and 'relevant'. A relevant difference may include skill, qualifications and/or training. Also, the potential to exercise responsibility could constitute a material difference, as could length of service and working conditions. For example, in Sally and John's case above, the boss might claim that Mr Meyer's higher salary is due to his long experience of working in the company for 15 years, while Sally is a new employee.

SUGGESTIONS FOR IMPLEMENTING EQUAL REMUNERATION

In conclusion, legislation should provide for equal remuneration for men and women in the following instances:
- where a man and a woman do work that is the same;
- where the work done by the man and the woman have been rated as equivalent by an employer under a voluntary job evaluation scheme, and
- where their work is of equal value.

In those cases where a claim of discrimination can be made against an employer, the following issues should be remembered:

The usefulness of the 'equal value' test has been criticized on the grounds that such a claim is complex and that judicial bodies do not have the necessary expertise to decide it. Even so, this test would, at least, help in the negotiation of more equitable remuneration structures for women.

We can learn from the British law (EQPA) about how to evaluate the comparable worth of different work. The evaluation should not be done by the Court involved in the case, but by independent experts. The Court would not become involved in the process of evaluation, but would consider job evaluation studies as evidence against an employer accused of unfair pay practices.

The comparator should be employed in the same organization or by 'associated' employers as defined in the EQPA. We also need a clearer picture of what 'an organisation' is: the concept must be defined broadly to include the different undertakings which form part of that organization.

A woman should not need to find a male comparator currently working in the same organization, and comparison with a male predecessor should be permitted.

The concept of 'remuneration' must be defined widely enough to include any payment in money or in kind which is made or owing to any person by virtue of employment, including pension and medical benefits and any perks such as housing or travel allowance.

We have to have clear guidelines about what are considered to be justifiable grounds for pay disparity, similar to the guidelines found in the British and the American systems. Accordingly, personal characteristics, such as seniority, merit or productivity can be treated as justifiable grounds for differences in pay. However, only those merit and productivity criteria which are based on objective evaluations should be accepted by the judicial body. A pay difference based on market forces, such as skill shortages, should be permitted only where it corresponds to a real need on the part of the undertaking. This means that the employer has to prove that the difference in pay is appropriate and necessary in order to achieve a certain objective.

CHAPTER FOURTEEN:
Sexual harrassment in the workplace

Another very important issue in this part involves sexual harassment – the term for the making of sexual advances towards someone who doesn't want them. In other words, the sexual advances, whether of a verbal or a physical nature, are not encouraged or welcomed by the recipient. We attempt to offer a closer, more comprehensive definition of sexual harassment later in this chapter.

In the work environment, sexual harassment is not a rare or isolated occurrence. In fact, studies in the US and the UK have shown that more than 50% of working women have at one time or another been subjected to unwelcome sexual advances in the workplace. Some studies have shown that there may be an even greater incidence of harassment among working women in South Africa. Researchers argue that the percentage of women in South Africa who have been subjected to some form of harassment during their employment may even be as high as 70%. Since approximately 40% of South Africa's labour force is female, this is a sad and unacceptable state of affairs. Consider the case of Martha K below.

It is true that sexual harassment is not only directed against women or even limited to behaviour between members of the opposite sex. Still, female employees are far more exposed to harassment than their male colleagues. Millions of women all over the world are forced to deal with these unpleasant and humiliating experiences.

Sexual harassment is not only an attack on the equal rights of a woman, it also violates her right to the integrity of her body and personality – a fundamental right that belongs to every human being. In fact, s 10 of the Bill of Rights contained in our Constitution recognizes the fact that 'every person shall have the right to respect for and protection of his or her dignity'. There is no doubt that sexual harassment practices smack of a total disregard for the feelings and the integrity of the recipient.

Many victims of sexual harassment find the experience humiliating and embarrassing and it is not surprising that this often results in serious emotional and psychological effects for the victims. Moreover, sexual harassment creates an intimidating, hostile and offensive working environment for the victim. It often leaves the victims with no other option than to resign from their jobs. On the other hand, the work performance of the victim who decides not to resign may be seriously affected and after the harassment she may also be less loyal towards the organization or committed to her career.

CASE STUDY

The following is an example of sexual harassment. Note that Martha in our example is forced, against her will, to have a sexual relationship. What makes matters worse is the fact that Martha's financial position places her in a very vulnerable position. Martha K is a young woman working in a finance company in Port Elizabeth. After working hard for two years, she is happy to be promoted to a new department with a better office and salary. She also has a new boss, Joe M.

Joe likes Martha and he tells her this often. He likes the way she works and the way she dresses. He often talkes to her about her clothes and how attractive and sexy she lookes in her outfits. At first, Martha is flattered, but then she notices that Joe does not talk to his other workers in the same way. She begins to get nervous when Joe comes into her office and closes the door. He also likes to join her when she goes for coffee or to eat lunch. One day Joe closes the door and tries to kiss her. When she objects, he says that if she sleeps with him he will see that she gets a salary raise. Martha is confused. She is a single mother and desperately needs the money to send her child to a decent school. On the other hand, she resents being forced into having a sexual relationship with someone.

Martha tries to avoid Joe as far as possible. However, one day Joe gives Martha a lift to the station when she has to work late. As she gets out of his car, Joe asks Martha out for a date the next week. Martha, knowing what Joe wants, waits a bit, but she can't really say 'no' to her boss. Martha is extremely apprehensive about the date. As a result she starts making mistakes in her work. She also starts getting headaches. She tries to find other work just to get away from Joe, but with no luck.

TO THINK ABOUT

Put yourself in Martha's position. Think about how you would answer these questions:
- What do you think Martha should do?
- Should she go out on a date with her boss?

Definition of sexual harassment

Sexual harassment includes any unwanted sexual behaviour or comment which has a negative effect on the recipient. Such behaviour could range from inappropriate gestures, suggestions or hints, jokes or degrading remarks, or innuendo, to fondling a woman without her consent. The worst – and most extreme – example of sexual harassment is rape.

> **CASE STUDY**
>
> In *J Mampuru v PUTCO,* (unreported, Industrial Court No NH11/2/2136) the Industrial Court was faced with the following set of facts:
>
> A male store manager (Mr M) was dismissed by his employer for making suggestions to his female colleagues. These suggestions included calling these ladies 'skattie' and 'liefie' and suggesting that the ladies accompany him to a casino. He also touched and pulled them around.
>
> The Industrial Court confirmed his dismissal and had the following to say about sexual harassment practices:
> *'sexual harassment may take many forms. It may be trivial, it may be verbal but gross, or it may be physical, again varying from trivial or gross. It may be a single act or the act may be repeated. The actions as such disclose a total disregard for the feelings and the integrity of the recipient.'*

Note that a single act may be sufficient to constitute sexual harassment. The conduct need not be repeated. So if someone makes sexual jokes about a woman employee only once, this is sexual harassment. The case study of *J v M Ltd* (1989) 10 ILJ (IC) on page 4 is a classical example of an harassment situation:

Two categories of sexual harassment have been identified:
- *Quid pro quo*[†] harassment;
- Hostile environment harassment.

Both these forms have been identified by the Industrial Court in the example above as constituting sexual harassment.

> **CASE STUDY**
>
> In another case dealing with sexual harassment practices, *J v M Ltd* (1989) 10 ILJ (IC), there was a similar set of facts to those which prevailed in the *J Mampuru* case:
>
> J, a senior manager, was dismissed after allegedly fondling a female employee and making suggestive remarks to her. The Industrial Court held that the dismissal was fair.
>
> The Court made the following interesting and noteworthy remarks about sexual harassment:
>
> '...[I]n its narrowest form sexual harassment occurs when a woman (or a man) is expected to engage in sexual activity in order to obtain or keep employment or obtain promotion or other favourable working conditions. In its wider view it is, however, any unwanted sexual behaviour or comment which has a negative effect on the recipient ... Sexual harassment, depending on the form it takes, will violate that right to integrity of body and personality which belongs to every person and which is protected in our legal system both criminally and civilly.'

Quid pro quo harassment

The first category, *quid pro quo* harassment, refers to the situation where a female (or male) employee is blackmailed into surrendering to sexual advances against her (or his) will, or forced to grant sexual favours to the harasser for fear of losing a tangible job benefit such as a promotion or a raise in salary. The classic example is where a female employee is told by her superior to sleep with him if she wants to be promoted or get a raise in salary. Look at Martha's example again on the next page.

Hostile environment harassment

Hostile environment harassment refers to the situation in which an offensive or hostile environment is created by jokes or other sexual innuendoes that are offensive to the recipient and which result in a violation of her (or his) dignity. This form of sexual harassment does not involve the loss of any job-related benefit but nevertheless qualifies as sexual harassment. The most common response of victims of hostile environment harassment is to leave their employment, often at considerable cost to their career opportunities.

Pornographic pictures featuring nude women on the walls of the workplace may, for example, create a hostile working environment and therefore constitute discrimination.

> **CASE STUDY**
>
> Martha realises that she has no choice but to go on a date with Joe. After going on a few dates with her boss, Martha K is growing worried. She is afraid that the other workers in her office will find out about her 'friendship' with him. She is also worried about what will happen next ...
>
> After their third date, Joe asks Martha to have sex with him one night and promises that if she does she will get a salary raise. She tells him no, politely, and he doesn't force her. However, the date ends badly.
>
> Now Martha is worried about what will happen at the office. She knows that Joe will see to it that she does not get a salary raise. She is also worried that Joe will be angry with her.
>
> Martha is not therefore surprised when she finds out that the next promotion goes to Jim W, even though he hasn't done half the extra work she has.

The problem with hostile environment sexual harassment claims lies in deciding whether a hostile environment does indeed exist. Here we must bear in mind that some women are more sensitive than others: What would offend one woman would not necessarily offend another. Moreover, men's and women's perceptions about what constitutes hostile working environment sexual harassment might be even more divergent. What standard, then, should be applied in deciding whether a hostile working environment does exist? In some cases the Court applies what it terms the 'reasonable person' standard test in deciding whether something is an offence: would the reasonable person have been offended? A better approach in hostile environment sexual harassment cases, it is suggested, would be to apply the 'reasonable woman' standard and not the 'reasonable person' standard which would include the male viewpoint or position. Women experience sexual assault and rape differently from men. Moreover, far more women than men are victims in rape and sexual abuse cases (see *Elliso v Brady* 924 F2d at 878).

THE REQUIREMENT OF FAULT

If a man is accused of sexual harassment, he often denies that he committed such an act. Or he may admit that he did make sexual advances, but argue that he did not mean to harass the woman. Or he may even say that he thought the woman welcomed or wanted or encouraged his sexual advances. The question here is whether fault is a requirement for finding someone guilty of sexual harassment. In other words, does the complainant have to prove that the accused man knew that his behaviour or conduct would be unwelcome to her? Or would he still be guilty even if he didn't know?

This is an extremely controversial and emotional issue. There is an important general principle in our present law that says a person should not be held liable for his or her actions without fault. However, the counter-argument is that, if fault on the part of the harasser must be proved, a male harasser will easily escape liability by simply arguing that he believed the woman welcomed or wanted his intentions. In other words, all he has to do is to argue that he did not know that his attentions would be unwelcome.

The solution to the problem of fault might lie in accepting a standard form of fault amounting to less than actual knowledge, taken from Canadian law. In terms of this standard, the harasser does not have to have specific knowledge that a particular act is unwelcome. Merely because of his act, he may be found guilty of sexual harassment. According to the Ontario Human Rights Code, a person will be guilty of sexual harassment if he (or she) ought reasonably to have known that his (or her) conduct would be unwelcome. In other words, even negligent harassment may be sufficient for finding someone guilty of sexual harassment.

The law must protect all workers from sexual harassment. Every employer has a duty to ensure a working environment that is physically healthy and safe for its workers, including their being free from sexual harassment. From a business point of view, it is in the employer's interests to ensure that women work in an environment which is conducive to their productivity. This in turn must mean that his or her female employees are ensured of a working environment where their human dignity and human worth are protected and respected.

POLICIES TO PREVENT SEXUAL HARASSMENT

The South African Constitution places a high premium on human dignity and equality. In accordance with the spirit of the Constitution, we suggest that every employer, however small the business, should be required to adopt strict and express policies prohibiting any form of sexual harassment. These policies should, for example, state that all reasonable steps will be taken to ensure that a specified standard of conduct is observed. Such a code of conduct should serve to prevent members of either sex from being harassed, intimidated or subjected to any other form of discriminatory, unfavourable or humiliating practices on the basis of their gender.

To implement these measures effectively means that effective grievance procedures must be created which women in particular will feel comfortable to use. This is necessary because most women, despite the high incidence of sexual harassment current in our society, decline to lay charges against their harassers for fear of reprisal and rejection not only from the harasser, but possibly also from colleagues who are not sensitive to the situation. This point is illustrated by the fact that only two cases dealing with sexual harassment have been referred to our courts to date.

Furthermore, any person found guilty of conduct amounting to sexual harassment should be severely dealt with. Depending on the seriousness of the sexual harassment, the employer may, for example, consider transferring the sexual offender to another position or department. In appropriate instances, such a person should be dismissed. In addition, if the victim of sexual harassment feels that her (or his) legitimate complaints are not adequately attended to by her (or his) employer or that the sexual offender's actions warrant more serious action, she (or he) should consider going so far as to lay a criminal charge against him (or her).

CHAPTER FIFTEEN:
Pregnancy rights in the workplace

There is another area of the employment world where discrimination against women is common: maternity leave and pregnancy benefits. When a female worker finds out that she is going to have a baby, all too often this time becomes filled with anxiety about her job and future prospects, when, instead, it should be one of happiness and busy preparation for a new life. Look at the example below.

Giving birth is the way of ensuring renewal of the generations, the continuation of the human species. Since maternity has the function of continuing to build our society, it follows that our national health and family policies must be geared towards safeguarding women. When

> **CASE STUDY**
>
> When Mrs Anna T was told she was going to have a baby, she was so excited she wanted to tell everyone she knew! Of course, she told all her friends and colleagues at the office where she worked. Most of them were very happy for her, except for her supervisor, Ms J.
>
> Ms J called Anna into her office that afternoon and asked questions about her health and the due date of the baby. Anna told her that the baby was due sometime in early autumn, about 1 March. Ms J told Anna that she was glad that the baby was coming only after Christmas so that Anna would still be working over that busy time.
>
> Furthermore, Anna told Ms J that she intended to continue working after her baby was born, but was told by Ms J that it would be impossible. The company would have to hire someone to take Anna's place from the beginning of the year.
>
> Anna was dumbfounded! Not only would she have another mouth to feed, but now she would have to do so without her salary!
>
> What are Anna's rights?

working women wish to have children, special measures are needed to protect their rights, not least because their biological role in the reproduction process requires them physically to carry, give birth to and nurture their offspring. This biological role may not be used as grounds for discrimination against women nor may it be allowed to prohibit women from exercising their right to work.

The Legislature has attempted to address the plight of pregnant employees in a number of ways, for example by regulating issues such as:
- maternity leave;
- the payment of benefits during maternity leave;
- the protection of employees before and after the birth of a child, and
- protection against dismissal.

We consider these issues in greater depth in this chapter.

Maternity leave

Maternity leave is regulated by s 25 of the Basic Conditions of Employment Act, 3 of 1997. In terms of this section, an employee is entitled to a minimum of four consecutive months' maternity leave. Nothing prevents her and her employer from agreeing to more than four months maternity leave.

Section 25 also regulates when the employee may commence maternity leave. She may do so:
- at any time from four weeks before the expected date of birth, unless otherwise agreed, or
- on a date from which a medical practitioner or a midwife certifies that it is necessary for the employee's health or that of her unborn child.

The section affords the employee and her employer a measure of flexibility. If the employee is healthy and she and her employer have not reached any agreement, she may commence her maternity leave four weeks before the expected date of birth. However, the employee and her employer may agree that she will commence her leave earlier (eg five weeks before the expected date) or later (eg three weeks before the expected date). If the health of the employee or that of the unborn child demands it, the employee may commence maternity leave earlier (eg six weeks before the expected date of the birth).

Section 25 also regulates the length of time for which the employee may not work after the birth of her child. It stipulates that the employee may not work for six weeks after the birth of her child unless a medical practitioner or midwife certifies that she is fit to do so. In terms of this section, the employee cannot be obliged to commence work for six weeks after the birth of her child. However, she and her employer may agree that she will commence work before the expiry of the period (for example, four weeks after the birth of the baby) provided that a doctor or midwife has certified that she is fit to do so.

The section also makes provision for maternity leave in respect of an employee who has a miscarriage during the third trimester of pregnancy or who bears a stillborn child. Such an employee is entitled to maternity leave for six weeks after the miscarriage or stillbirth, whether or not the employee had commenced maternity leave at the time of the miscarriage or stillbirth. The flexibility of the section as regards the time when leave may be taken is to be welcomed.

The Basic Conditions of Employment Act does not regulate maternity pay. In other words, the Act does not oblige an employer to pay maternity pay. Consequently, those employees who are not paid by their employer during maternity leave may prefer or may be obliged to work for as long as possible before the expected date of birth and to resume work as soon as possible thereafter.

Payment of benefits during maternity leave

It was mentioned in the previous paragraph that the Basic Conditions of Employment Act does not regulate maternity pay. However, there is nothing to prevent an employer and an employee from agreeing that the former will pay the latter maternity pay. The employer may, for example, agree to pay the employee her full salary for the duration of her maternity leave. Or he or she may agree to pay only a portion of her salary for the full duration or a part of her maternity leave.

The payment of maternity benefits is regulated by the Unemployment Insurance Act 33 of 1966 and is fairly complicated. In terms of s 34 of this Act, an employee is entitled to receive maternity benefits out of the Unemployment Insurance Fund (UIF) when she becomes 'unemployed', that is when her employer does not pay her maternity pay or when she receives from her employer less than one-third of her normal earnings (s 37(6)). An employee is also entitled to benefits only if she was in employment for at least 13 weeks during the 52 weeks immediately preceding the expected date of her confinement or, where an application for benefits is made on or after the date of birth.

If she is deemed to be 'unemployed' in terms of the Act, an employee is entitled to maternity benefits for a maximum period of 26 weeks from the date on which she is deemed to have become unemployed (s 37(1)). The benefits payable to an employee are calculated at the rate of 45% of her normal weekly earnings (s 34(2)).

Let us summarize these provisions:
- An employee is entitled to maternity benefits if her employer does not pay her maternity pay or if she is paid less than one-third of her normal earnings.
- An employee is entitled to maternity benefits if she was in employment for at least 13 weeks during the 52 weeks before the expected date of birth of the child. Where an application for benefits is made on or after the date of birth, the employee must have been in employment for at least 13 weeks before the date of birth.
- The employee is entitled to maternity benefits for a maximum period of 26 weeks.
- The benefits are calculated at the rate of 45% of an employee's normal weekly earnings.

Protection of employees before and after the birth of a child

The Basic Conditions of Employment Act regulates the protection of employees before and after the birth of a child. In terms of s 26, no employer may require or permit a pregnant employee or an employee who is nursing her child to perform work which is hazardous to her health or the health of her child.

Furthermore, during the employee's pregnancy, and for six months after the birth of the child, her employer must offer her suitable, alternative employment on terms and conditions that are no less favourable than her ordinary terms and conditions, if:
- the employee is required to perform night work or her work poses a danger to her health or safety or that of her child, and
- it is practical for the employer to do so.

Protection against dismissal

The Labour Relations Act, 1995 regulates unfair dismissal. Section 186 of that Act defines 'dismissal' in very wide terms and the refusal by an employer to allow an employee to resume work after she has taken maternity leave in terms of the Basic Conditions of Employment Act or a collective agreement or her contract of employment, constitutes dismissal. In other words, an employer is obliged to allow an employee to resume her work if she reports for duty after the expiry of her allotted maternity leave.

Should the employer refuse to do so, then, for the purposes of the Labour Relations Act, 1995, such refusal will constitute dismissal.

Once the facts show that there has been a dismissal as described above, the onus is on the employer to prove that the dismissal was fair. However, the Labour Relations Act, 1995 provides that if the facts show that the employee was dismissed because of her pregnancy, the dismissal will be 'automatically unfair' (s 187(1)(e)).

The Labour Relations Act, 1995 also brands the dismissal of an employee because of her intended pregnancy, or for any reason related to her pregnancy, as automatically unfair (s 187(1)(e)).

The Labour Relations Act, 1995 regulates the enforcement of the employee's rights where she has been dismissed because of her pregnancy or her intended pregnancy or for any reason related to her pregnancy. In terms of the Act, the employee must:

Refer to matter to the Commission for Conciliation, Mediation and Arbitration (CCMA) established in terms of the Act. A commissioner must try to settle the dispute through conciliation.

If the dispute remains unresolved, the dismissed woman may refer the matter to the Labour Court for final adjudication.

If the Labour Court finds that the employee's dismissal was automatically unfair, it may order:
- reinstatement, or
- re-employment, or
- compensation.

A reinstatement order restores the contractual position between the employer and the employee as if it had never been broken. The employee is, in essence, given back the job and the position occupied by her before the dismissal. Consequently, rights such as seniority rights will be unaffected.

A re-employment order implies a new employment relationship which may be different from the old one. The employee may be given back her old job but without the rights, such as seniority rights, which had been acquired in terms of the old employment contract. It may also mean that the employee is given another job which differs from the old one.

The maximum compensation which the Court may order is 24 months' remuneration, calculated at the employee's rate of remuneration as at the date of dismissal.

In addition to the above remedies, the Labour Court may also 'make any other order that it considers appropriate in the circumstances' (s 193(3)). It may, for example, grant an interdict (ie an order forcing the employer to do something or to desist from doing something).

Conclusion

For the first time in South Africa's history, the right to equality has been made a principle on which our society will be built and by which it will be judged in the future. The challenges facing our country, in particular for the women of South Africa, remain daunting, however. Women should be made aware of their rights in terms of the Constitution, the Labour Relations Act, 1995, the Basic Conditions of Employment Act and the future Employment Equity Act and should demand that they be treated with dignity. If nothing else, they are entitled to such treatment in terms of the Constitution, which has laid the foundations for a non-sexist society.

However, it should be recognized that the law alone cannot change attitudes towards women. For this reason non-discriminatory education will play an indispensable role in the years to come in bringing about changes in social and economic attitudes and practices regarding women.

Fortunately, both society's and employers' perceptions can be changed and, indeed, are slowly changing. Undoubtedly, many women today are the joint breadwinners or, where their husbands have been retrenched, the sole providers for their households. There are also a large number of women who are, for various reasons, single parents having to provide for their children alone. It is important that these changes in society be recognized and accommodated by employers to enable women to fulfil their rightful place in society.

Lastly, it is essential that legislation providing for gender equality and the advancement of women, not only in society at large but also in the sphere of employment, be introduced. For it is only through legislative and educational efforts that social and economic attitudes towards women will change.

PART FIVE:
Women and health

INTRODUCTION

Many concerns of women relate to the family and their children, as we discussed in Part Two: Women and the family. In Part Four: Women and employment we discussed, inter alia, how their having children cannot be used as an excuse to discriminate against women in the workplace. In this part, we focus on those aspects of healthcare – of both women themselves and their families – and child care that concern women specifically. In particular, we concentrate on four important health or health-related issues: procreation rights (Chapter 16), surrogate motherhood (Chapter 17), unwanted procreation and abortion (Chapter 19), and the disease AIDS (Chapter 19).

CHAPTER SIXTEEN:
Procreation rights

One of the most important natural functions of women in our society is that of procreation, the having of children. Indeed many of society's beliefs about the roles of the woman as mother, caretaker and keeper of the home stem from this function.

When we speak of procreation rights, in general, we refer to a person's right to decide whether or not to have children. That decision must be as much the woman's as the man's. A woman may decide, for example, not to have children and can use some means of contraception, sterilization or even abortion to give effect to her choice. Or she may decide that she wants to have children. Nowadays, she may even decide to have children knowing that she is not physically able to conceive: she may be helped in various ways such as artificial insemination or *in vitro* fertilization, or she may even resort to using a surrogate mother.

Although all the procreation choices discussed in this section have important sociological, ethical and religious consequences, our emphasis is on the most important legal aspects. We pay specific attention to two of the ways in which a woman can be helped to have a baby: artificial insemination and *in vitro* fertilization.

ASSISTED REPRODUCTION

In some cases, despite the best efforts of a man and a woman to have children, they are unable to do so. The cause may be some physical problem to do with either the man or the woman. Fortunately, these days, there are ways to overcome these problems through assisted procreation,[†] in which a woman is helped to become pregnant by means of medical intervention. This can involve the woman taking certain medicine or it can amount to a surgical operation or procedure.

In South Africa, our law still requires the husband's consent when a wife uses assisted reproduction. This has recently been challenged through the efforts of the Human Rights Commision and amendments to the present law are expected soon. This will enable single women to also qualify for artificial insemination procedures. However, according to the feminist viewpoint, a woman should not have to obtain her partner's/husband's consent when making procreation choices. There are several medical choices that a woman can make if she needs help in falling pregnant, and one of these is artificial insemination.

Artificial insemination

The term 'artificial insemination' technically means a medical procedure in which a gamete is placed in the womb, uterus or Fallopian tubes of the woman who wants to have a baby. A gamete is defined in the Human Tissue Act 65 of 1983, as: 'either of the two generative cells essential for human reproduction' which means the egg of the woman and the sperm of a man. The Fallopian tubes are the tubes in the woman which the egg normally would pass through.

Artificial insemination is often used where the woman experiences some infertility problem. In other words, she is unable to fall pregnant in a natural way through sexual intercourse. If a male person is unable to bring about the pregnancy of his partner/wife, the sperm or semen may also be obtained from a donor. This is known as AID, artificial insemination with a donor's sperm. If the husband's sperm is used, it is known as AIH – artificial insemination, husband. AIH is often used where the husband's semen is unable to reach and/or to fertilise the egg on its own.

In the broad sense, artificial insemination includes *in vitro* fertilization (see below) and includes all forms of insemination which are not done by sexual intercourse between a man and a woman.

In vitro fertilization

In vitro fertilization refers to fertilization outside the human body. In this procedure, a needle is used to collect ripe eggs (ova) from the woman in a minor surgical procedure, called a laparoscopy. The eggs are fertilized by semen (from either a donor or the husband) in a laboratory dish, containing a growth medium.

Fertilization is thus effected outside the human body – *in vitro*. This is sometimes called 'test tube' fertilization because the egg and sperm are mixed in a test tube. Foetuses[†] conceived in this way are sometimes called 'test tube babies'.

Once the egg and sperm are mixed, the egg is fertilized and is called an embryo. Then the embryo may be transferred to the woman's own womb (or to a surrogate mother – see next section). If the procedure is successful, one or more of the embryos will attach to the mother's uterine wall and the embryo will develop and grow in the ordinary fashion. Then the baby will be delivered after nine months or so.

Regulation of Assisted Reproduction in South Africa

Artificial insemination and *in vitro* fertilization are strictly regulated by the Human Tissue Act and other regulations.

The Human Tissue Act regulates these forms of artificial reproduction and defines 'artificial insemination of a person' as the following:

'The introduction by other than natural means of a male gamete or gametes into the internal reproductive organs (which means the womb or Fallopian tubes) of a female person for the purpose of human reproduction, including:
- *The bringing together outside the human body of a male and a female gamete or gametes with a view to placing the product of a union of such gametes in the womb of a female person; or*
- *The placing of the product of a union of a male and a female gamete or gametes which have been brought together outside the human body in the womb of a female person.*

These procedures are mostly performed by doctors specializing in infertility problems at private clinics or large academic hospitals. There are 11 infertility centres in South Africa at present.

Artificial insemination with the husband's sperm (AIH) raises few legal obstacles, although the premises on which the procedures take place must be approved and the procedures may only be performed under conditions specified by the Director-General of Health and Welfare.

Artificial insemination with a donor's sperm (AID) is more carefully regulated and the procedures more complicated, because an 'outsider' is involved. There are detailed requirements regarding donor and recipient files, the artificial insemination procedure itself, confidentiality, registers and notification of the Director-General. Also, important policy issues and moral and ethical issues are addressed in the Human Tissue Act and Regulations.

Only doctors or persons acting under their supervision may perform artificial or *in vitro* fertilization and transfer of the embryo into the mother. The procedures may be performed only on married women, with the written consent of their husbands. 'Married' women include women who are married by customary law. A married woman can therefore be artificially inseminated with sperm of her husband or a donor.

Amendments to this provision will, however, be made soon. The Human Rights Commission recently challenged these provisions on the grounds that they discriminate against single women. They will be changed to make it possible for a single woman to legally choose to start a pregnancy by artificial insemination. It also means that women in lesbain relationships will legally be able to start a family.

In terms of the Human Tissue Act, artificial insemination and *in vitro* fertilization may be performed only 'for medical purposes.' In other words, if there is no infertility problem, a doctor may not merely artificially inseminate a woman for the sake of convenience. An example of this would be where a doctor places the product of artificial insemination (the embryo) in the womb of a surrogate mother (see below) who will carry the baby on behalf of a professional woman, who can then pursue her career without the physical inconvenience and interruption of her work which a pregnancy would entail.

In terms of the Children's Status Act 82 of 1987 children conceived by assisted reproduction are considered the legal children of the woman giving birth and her husband, provided he consented to the procedure in writing. The Act does not deal with the status or legitimacy or illegitimacy of a child born to an unmarried woman with the help of assisted reproduction.

CHAPTER SEVENTEEN:
Surrogate motherhood

The term 'surrogate motherhood' was practically unknown a decade ago. Unlike artificial insemination and *in vitro* fertilization, surrogacy is not a form of medical treatment although assisted reproductive techniques are usually used. Rather, it is an arrangement between the 'intended parents' and a surrogate mother. 'Surrogate' means a substitute: the surrogate mother acts as a substitute mother until the baby is born. The surrogate mother agrees to carry a baby for the intended parents and to give up her parental power over the baby at birth. Spiro (in *Law of Parent and Child*) defines parental power as:

> '*the sum total of rights and duties of parents in respect of minor children arising out of parentage.*'

One of the most important rights is custody of the child, while duties include support of the child. Therefore, when a surrogate mother gives up the parental power, she gives up her rights to custody of the baby after it is born.

REASONS FOR USING A SURROGATE MOTHER

There are many reasons why women would sometimes use a surrogate mother. After trying for many months or years to have children in the usual way, many couples become desperate to have children. Some decide to adopt children or to try assisted reproduction, mentioned in Chapter 16, above. However, some people regard surrogacy as the only option, mainly for the following reasons:
- The waiting period for a surrogate pregnancy is nine months, the same as a normal pregnancy term. This is much shorter than the long waiting period involved in adoption.
- When a surrogate mother is used, the child is usually biologically and genetically related to at least one of the parents.
- Surrogacy creates the possibility for people over 35 to have a child, whereas this is the cut-off age for adopting a child.

Although the process of surrogate motherhood is not directly regulated by legislation, its practice is influenced by the following acts and regulations:
- the Human Tissue Act 65 of 1983 and regulations;
- the Child Care Act 74 of 1983;
- the Children's Status Act 82 of 1987; and
- the Constitution of the Republic of South Africa Act 108 of 1996.

FORMS OF SURROGACY

Two forms of surrogacy may be distinguished – full (real) and partial. In full surrogacy, all the genetic material (sperm and eggs) is provided by the intended parents who are the commissioning couple.[†] In this case, the surrogate mother acts as a host or birth mother. A variation on full surrogacy is where one of the partners is unable to provide sperm/eggs and donor sperm/eggs are used. The surrogate has no biological link with the child.

In partial surrogacy the surrogate mother is artificially inseminated with sperm from the commissioning husband (intended father) but uses her own egg. In this case, the surrogate mother contributes biologically (genetically) to the child. The majority of surrogacy cases that have come before the American and English courts have been cases of partial surrogacy.

In South Africa, there was a famous case, called the Tzaneen surrogacy, in 1987. This was a case of full (real) surrogacy where a grandmother (Pat Anthony) acted as host mother for the triplets of her daughter and son-in-law. When these children were born, the incident caught the legal system unprepared in many ways.

In our legal system, it had never before been necessary to define 'mother' since the common law provided that the mother is always certain. This is known in Latin as *mater semper certa est*. As a result of this case, however, it became uncertain whether this 'legal rule' should also apply in a case of surrogacy where the birth mother had no biological (genetic) link to the child or children.

In fact, modern birth technology makes it possible for at least three women to claim that they are the mother of an artificially conceived child, as the following example illustrates:

Approximately two weeks after the birth of the Tzaneen triplets, the Children's Status Act became operative. This Act has placed some legal obstacles in the way of surrogacy. For instance it provides that the children conceived from donor sperm or eggs are considered to be the legitimate children of the birth mother and her husband – even in the case of full surrogacy, where the sperm and eggs (genetic materials) are provided by the commissioning couple.

CASE STUDY

Mrs A is unable to have a child because she is infertile. Mrs B agrees to provide eggs to be fertilized *in vitro* with semen from Mr A (Mrs A's husband). The embryos are transferred to Mrs C, who agrees to carry the baby until birth and hand it over to Mrs A and her husband after the birth.

To think about

- Who is the legal mother of the child?
- Is it Mrs A, to whom the legal and medical literature refers as the commissioning, infertile or social mother?
- Is it Mrs B, the biological (genetic) mother?
- Or is it Mrs C, the gestational or birth mother?

Thus, in the example given above, Mrs C (and her husband, if she has one) would be regarded as the legal parent of the child.

The effect of the Act on the surrogacy procedure is unsatisfactory and often not in the best interests of the child. In our opinion, it is strange to bestow the role of parent on a surrogate mother (especially where she is not the biological mother) and her husband. This legislation places the husband of the surrogate mother in a very powerful legal position, one that is superior to that of the biological parents. He is given parental rights to the child and can effectively block adoption of the child by the commissioning couple.

Under the present indirect legislation, adoption is the only way in which the commissioning couple can now secure parental rights to the child, even though the child may be conceived from their own egg and sperm.

To think about

- Do you think surrogacy is a good alternative to adoption?
- Is surrogacy fair to the child who is born as a result of the procedures?
- Should all forms of surrogacy (including commercial surrogacy) be permitted?
- Can one really distinguish clearly between commercial and altruistic surrogacy?
- Is legislation regulating surrogacy necessary?

Altruistic vs commercial surrogacy

The surrogate mother is often a friend or family member of the childless couple who, through her generosity, chooses to assist the couple by carrying a child for them. This is known as altruistic surrogacy. The commissioning couple usually pays for necessary medical and legal expenses, but the surrogate mother does not make a profit from her serivces.

In America, however, there is another type of surrogate mother, usually a stranger to the commissioning couple – who offers commercial or paid surrogacy. Besides being paid compensation for medical and legal expenses, the surrogate mother receives a large amount of money for her services. Moreover, the commissioning couple usually get into contact with a surrogate mother through a surrogacy agent or broker. The present rate for being a surrogate mother is approximately R120 000.

The commercial or paid type of surrogacy has been banned in many countries. An important concern with paid surrogacy is that wealthy women or couples may exploit those who are less fortunate or less advantaged by paying them for the use of their bodies.

It has also been argued that if surrogacy is permitted in law at all, the Legislature should prevent any form of payment to the surrogate mother – not even compensation for medical and legal expenses. This view seems unrealistic, however. We all know that medical care and hospitalization can be expensive. A surrogacy contract is usually drawn up by a lawyer, which is necessary because of the present uncertainty about the rights of the various 'mothers'. Also, if adoption proceedings have to be instituted, the procedure becomes even more expensive. Why should a surrogate mother have to pay for everything when she is helping the other couple? Furthermore, the surrogate mother will need maternity clothes and will have to make regular trips to a doctor. She should at least be compensated for such expenses.

Validity and enforceability of surrogacy contracts

Whether written surrogacy agreements are valid and enforceable are key issues in the debate on surrogacy. The surrogacy contract is valid if it has legal force; if the contract can be upheld in a court of law it is enforceable. A surrogacy agreement will be valid and enforceable only if it does not go against an Act of Parliament or other legal rule. In addition, it will be valid and enforceable only if it is not considered immoral or against public policy – *contra bonos mores*.

In South African law, one cannot merely agree to transfer parental power without intervention by the law. This means that there must be an adoption order or a transfer of parental power by the High Court as upper guardian of all minors.

Although it could be argued that altruistic surrogacy is not immoral, commercial surrogacy agreements are seen as immoral in most countries. Sometimes they are even referred to as 'baby selling' because the woman having the baby rents her body to the other couple to use for nine months, long enough to have the child. Another reason for caution in this area is the possibility of a wealthy commissioning couple paying a poor, often unmarried, desperate woman to have a baby for them. In other countries the only way a poor woman can sometimes survive is to sell her body as a 'baby factory' for the wealthy. There have also been cases where surrogate mothers decided to keep their children, rather than give them to the commissioning parents.

An attorney should therefore always be asked to help draw up the surrogacy contract. This is essential because of the many controversies and uncertain areas in the legislation. The law is interested in protecting the new baby from legal battles and also in protecting all the people involved: the surrogate mother, the genetic parents, and the commissioning couple.

Breach of contract

As with any type of contract, there are legal complications when one of the people decides to change her or his mind, and break the contract. This is called a breach of contract. The most important kind of breach of contract in surrogacy arrangements is that the surrogate mother may refuse to hand the baby over to the commissioning couple. Because no law regulates the procedure at this time, the Courts will be asked to intervene and they will reach their own decision.

The Courts will decide who should have custody of the child on the basis of what is in the 'best interests of the child.' The best interests of the child is a criterion also considered in divorce and adoption proceedings to guide the presiding judge who has to make a decision on parental rights.

Recommendations of the Law Commission

Because of the complicated issues involved with surrogacy, the Law Commission has completed a report on this issue. The following are some of the recommendations of the Commission:
- Surrogate motherhood should only be utilized as a final option.
- A clear medical reason should be present – it may for instance not be utilized for mere convenience (eg furthering a career).
- All the people should be screened for physical and psychological suitability.

- The gametes (sperm and egg) used, should be provided by both or by at least one of the commissioning parents, so that a biological (genetic) link exists between the child and at least one of the parents. (The gametes of the surrogate mother and her husband may not be used. The child will thus have no biological (genetic) link with them and the surrogate acts as a true 'host' mother.)
- Surrogate motherhood for financial gain (commercial or paid surrogacy) should not be permitted, but the surrogate mother may be compensated for actual expenses.
- The surrogate mother should be married, divorced or widowed. She should at least have given birth to a child prior to entering into a surrogacy agreement.
- The written and informed consent of all the parties concerned (ie the commissioning husband and wife and the surrogate mother and her husband, is required.)
- The surrogacy agreement must receive prior approval by a court. This is to ensure that the best interests of the child are considered before its birth.
- Where necessary and legal, the decision to abort the foetus will lie with the surrogate mother, although the commissioning parents will have the right to be informed of the circumstances and to consult with the surrogate mother before the abortion.
- The child born as a result of the surrogate pregnancy will be the legitimate child of the commissioning couple. They will obtain all rights and duties of parenthood towards the child.
- The surrogate mother should have no claim to or legal obligation towards the child.

> **TO THINK ABOUT**
>
> Of course these decisions are never easy. There are many questions which should be considered:
> - Who is the 'real mother' of the child?
> - Why did the commissioning parents need to use a surrogate mother?
> - Which type of surrogacy was arranged?
> - How can someone who has carried a baby for nine months be forced to give up a child?
> - What type of life will the child have with either mother?
> - Which mother would be better for the child?
> - Can you think of some other questions that must be asked?

Besides these recommendations, the Law Commission also discussed ways to prevent abuse of surrogacy and to discourage illegal surrogate motherhood by establishing penalties:
- Those who assist in the (illegal) fertilization of the surrogate mother will be guilty of an offence and liable on conviction to a fine not exceeding R20 000 or up to one year's imprisonment or both.
- The identity of the parties will not be published without the written consent of all concerned.

The report of the Law Commission was handed to the Minister of Justice in 1992. A special committee was subsequently appointed to discuss the proposals of the Law Commission and to make recommendations regarding surrogacy. A Parliamentary Committee is now considering surrogacy and its legal implications.

Legislation affecting artificial insemination/*in vitro* fertilization and surrogate motherhood:
- Human Tissue Act 65 of 1983
- Regulations No R 1182 *GG* 10283 regarding the Artificial insemination of Persons and related matters (in terms of the Human Tissue Act 65 of 1983)
- Children's Status Act 82 of 1987
- Child Care Act 74 of 1983
- Constitution of the Republic of South Africa Act 108 of 1996

CHAPTER EIGHTEEN:
Unwanted procreation

Another aspect of health that is a concern to many women is what to do in order not to have children, or more children. For many women, especially in poverty situations, the announcement that they are going to have another baby is sad news. It may mean another mouth to feed with the same low income. It may mean increased poverty, without adequate shelter and protection for the family. It may mean increased health risks for the mother, especially if she is older and if she has already had many children. For women working in part-time jobs, it may mean losing another job since many employers do not grant maternity leave for part-time workers (see Part Four).

Some women are willing to do almost anything to prevent an unwanted pregnancy, using contraception without telling their husbands, sterilisation so that they will never have another child, or even an abortion. Many of us have heard of illegal operations, performed in some dark, unsafe, unsanitary, back street 'clinic' where desperate women went as a last resort. However, with the passing of the Choice on the Termination of Pregnancy Act 92 of 1996 (see below) this picture has now changed.

ABORTION

Abortion has been one of the most hotly debated issues in South Africa, involving not only women's groups and organizations, but religious groups, medical practitioners, lawyers, politicians and policy makers. The South African legislature responded to the strong call for abortion reform (the Abortion and Sterilisation Act 2 of 1975 came into force in 1975, with minor amendments in 1976, 1980 and 1982) and made history when those provisions of the latter act having to do with abortions were repealed, and the new Choice on the Termination of Pregnancy Act was promulgated on 1 February 1997. The provisions of this new Act will be discussed shortly. It is important to to note at this stage that the new Act differs vastly from the previous Abortion and Sterilization Act, as the most important feature of the new Act is the fact that abortion has been made available upon request by the pregnant woman if her pregnancy does not exceed 12 weeks. More about this later.

Although the emphasis is on legal aspects in this discussion, you must keep in mind that for centuries there have been numerous heated debates about abortion. Many of the questions centre around the question of the precise moment when life begins. Does life start at conception? Or at birth?

The two sides on this issue are sharply divided. Those people in favour of abortion call themselves pro-choice because they believe that women should have the choice of what to do with their bodies, including whether or not to have children. The people who are against abortion are called pro-life because they believe that abortion is murder, or the killing of an unborn baby.

Pro-abortion supporters have consistently argued that the foetus is not 'human' since it is merely a live organism consisting of a number of cells. However, some of these pro-choice supporters do believe that once brain activity is detectable, after 10 to 12 weeks, the foetus is worthy of protection.

On the other hand, pro-life supporters have generally argued that life begins at conception and that a human embryo should not be aborted under any circumstances.

As a general rule, the law has avoided arguments about the precise moment when life begins, as these arguments are considered largely philosophical, religious and medical in nature. The law is primarily concerned with the question of when and how life should be protected. Apart from the abortion legislation discussed here, human life is protected in our legal system only from the moment a live birth occurs.

The present abortion law in South Africa: Choice on the Termination of Pregnancy Act 92 of 1996

Introduction

In South Africa, where women have suffered severe discrimination and hardship on the grounds of sex, race and class in the past, it is no small feat that the Termination of Pregnancy Bill was passed by the National Assembly on Wednesday, October 30, 1996. The Act became operative on 1 February 1997, and greatly facilitates the process of obtaining reproductive rights for women. You may well ask what reproductive rights are and how they are protected.

Reproductive health and health care

Reproductive rights in general and abortion in particular should be seen against the backdrop of international recognition of the reproductive rights of men and women and the struggle to have states recognize and protect those rights, even against infringement by a government itself or by pressure groups such as the pro-life movement.

Paragraph 7.2 of the International Conference on Population and Development (ICPD), held in Cairo on 5-13 December 1994 defines reproductive health as:

> ... *a state of complete physical, mental and social well-being and*

not merely the absence of disease or infirmity, in all matters relating to the reproductive system and to its functions and processes.

It goes on to say that reproductive health implies that people are able to have a satisfying and safe sex life and that they have the capacity to reproduce and the freedom to decide if, when and how often to do so. Implicit in this condition are:

... the right of men and women to be informed about and to have access to safe, effective, affordable and acceptable methods of family planning of their choice, as well as other lawful methods of their choice for the regulation of fertility, and

the right of access to appropriate health-care services that will enable women to go safely through pregnancy and childbirth and provide couples with the best chance of having a healthy infant.

The rights to health and health care are usually classified as second generation, socio-economic rights or positive rights (See Part Six). Individuals can ask the State to protect these rights, but it is difficult to hold governments accountable if the rights are breached. In the international community, socio-economic rights are often not taken as seriously as first generation or civil/political rights, even though it is often said that all human rights are universal and indivisible. The international community has not paid much attention to these rights nor tried very hard to ensure that these rights are realised. Instead of treating them as fully-fledged rights, they are often seen as mere aspirations. Nevertheless civil/political and economic, social and cultural rights are interrelated, interdependent and indivisible. Thus, a person who is denied access to proper health services may die, which means that his or her right to life (a so-called first generation right) has been ignored. Also, if medical procedures which only women require are criminalized, this is unequal treatment of and discrimination against women.

The origin of reproductive rights in international conventions can be traced back to the 1945 United Nations Charter which encouraged respect for human rights and fundamental freedoms for all without distinction as to sex (see also Part Six). The UN Charter prepared the ground for further universal and regional international instruments, such as the 1948 Universal Declaration of Human Rights, and the right to health and health care has been emphasized in various international legal documents and conventions.

Apart from the ICPD document cited above, reproductive rights are protected in other international conventions. The Vienna Declaration and Programme of Action (12 July 1993) emphasized that the full and equal enjoyment by women of their human rights was a priority of the international community. It declared as follows:

The human rights of women and the girl-child are an inalienable, integral and indivisible part of universal human rights. The full and equal participation of women in political, civil, economic, social and cultural life, at the national, regional and international levels, and the eradication of all forms of discrimination on the grounds of sex are priority objectives of the international community.

As mentioned already, despite all these international documents and conventions, it has been difficult to make governments uphold these rights. Individual persons cannot approach the International Court of Justice for the protection of their rights. However, a major breakthrough in holding governments accountable, was achieved with the Convention on the Elimination of all Forms of Discrimination against Women (CEDAW) (see Chapter 21).

From a very reluctant beginning, international law has increasingly come to recognize women's human rights in general and reproductive rights, in particular. Women, in turn, are increasingly placing their hopes on international human rights law to protect them against all forms of discrimination, particularly in respect of health and health care.

From the legal aspects discussed above, it is clear that the present South African abortion legislation was desperately needed, not only to effectively protect women against unsafe or 'backstreet' abortions, but also to assist those who were financially unable to travel to foreign countries to obtain legal abortions. Financial restraints prevented a vast majority of South African women from following this route. The lengthy and cumbersome procedures of the previous Act (the Abortion and Sterilisation Act,) prevented many women from obtaining safe and legal abortions. Moreover, statistics indicated that the majority of abortions in terms of the previous Act were performed on white women. Poor and disadvantaged women did not have access to these procedures.

The Abortion and Sterilisation Act provided for abortion on very narrow grounds. Although abortion was allowed in cases of incest and rape, the procedures which had to be followed were very slow, and women were often treated very harshly under these circumstances (see Part Three, Women and violence).

In the Bill of Rights (chapter 2) of the new 1996 Constitution, women's rights to life (s 11), dignity (s 12), privacy (s 14), equality (s 9) and freedom of religion (s 15) are constitutionally protected. Women are also protected from an environment which may be detrimental to their health or well-being (s 24).

The Choice on Termination of Pregnancy Act

The circumstances and conditions under which a pregnancy may be terminated in terms of our new Choice on Termination of Pregnancy Act are the following:

- upon request by the pregnant woman during the first 12 weeks of her pregnancy;
- if the woman is between 13 and 20 weeks (including the 20th week) pregnant, her pregnancy may be terminated if a medical doctor, after consulting with the pregnant woman, believes that
- the woman's health and mental state will be affected (injured) if her pregnancy continues; or
- there is a risk that the foetus will suffer from a physical or mental abnormality; or
- the woman is pregnant as a result of rape or incest; or
- the woman's social or economic circumstances will be significantly affected if her pregnancy continues.

> **TO THINK ABOUT**
>
> Note that the Act does not define what an abortion is. It refers instead to the 'termination of a pregnancy.' This term is fraught with problems, since a termination of a 'pregnancy' does not necessarily mean the death of the foetus, as the emphasis is clearly on pregnancy.
> - Can you perhaps think why the legislator used this phrase? Can you foresee any problems with the use of this phrase?

If the woman is more than 20 weeks pregnant, the pregnancy may be terminated if a medical doctor, after consulting with another medical doctor or a registered midwife believes that
- the woman's life will be endangered if the pregnancy continues;
- the foetus will be severely malformed if the pregnancy continues;
- there is a risk of injury to the foetus if the pregnancy continues.

> **TO THINK ABOUT**
>
> - What strikes you when studying the time limits laid down by the above Act?

The new Act contains three trimesters of limits allowing abortions to be performed under various circumstances. In this respect, the Act differs vastly from the previous Abortion and Sterilisation Act under which no gestational limits were specified.

These limits differ from those laid down in the well known American case of *Roe v Wade* 410 US 118 (1973) in which the Court divided pregnancy into three trimesters. Therefore the first trimester is the first three months of pregnancy, the second trimester is months 4–6, and the third trimester is the last three months of pregnancy.

It is important to note that a registered midwife, who has completed the required training course, is also allowed to perform an abortion, at the request of the pregnant woman, but only if she is still less than 12 weeks pregnant. A midwife may not perform an abortion at the request of the woman if she is more than 12 weeks pregnant. The reasons listed above are the only grounds on which a medical doctor may carry out an abortion if the woman is more than 12 weeks pregnant.

The termination of a pregnancy by means of surgery may only take place at a state hospital or facility.

A very important feature of the Act, apart from the fact that abortion on demand has become available to any woman (if she is less than 12 weeks pregnant), is that a woman of any age may ask for an abortion in terms of this Act if she is less than 12 weeks pregnant, which means that a pregnant minor may request an abortion without her parent's consent. The Act, however, states that the doctor or midwife must advise the minor to tell her parents, guardian or other family members before the pregnancy is terminated. If the minor chooses not to tell her parents, friends or relatives of her plan to end the pregnancy, the doctor or midwife may not refuse to

> **TO THINK ABOUT**
>
> Consider the following situation:
> Rebecca suffers from a medical condition which puts her foetus at risk of injury. She hears that she qualifies for a lawful abortion on this ground and is booked in for the following week because she is already 22 weeks pregnant. However, Rebecca spontaneously goes into labour and delivers a premature baby at the hospital.
> - Does she have the right to terminate the life of the infant by unplugging the incubator which is keeping it alive?

perform the abortion as requested by the girl, that is if she is still less than 12 weeks pregnant.

The Act also provides for the termination of pregnancies of mentally disabled women, or of women who are unconscious without a reasonable prospect of regaining consciousness at the request of their natural guardian, spouse or legal guardian.

Any woman who requests that her pregnancy be terminated before 12 weeks, must be informed of her rights under this Act. The Act also provides that the identity of the woman who has requested the abortion must be kept secret at all times, unless she herself chooses to disclose it.

As far as offences and penalties in terms of the Act are concerned, the Act states that any person who is not a medical doctor, or a registered midwife who has completed the required training course, and who performs the abortions referred to in the Act, is guilty of an offence and may be fined or imprisoned for a period not exceeding 10 years. Moreover, a person who prevents a lawful abortion or prevents the woman from

> **TO THINK ABOUT**
>
> If Miss X's boyfriend tries to stop her from obtaining an abortion by locking her up in his flat, he may be guilty of an offence under the Act, apart from any other offence of which he may be guilty.

going to hospital to have the abortion, may also be guilty of the same offence.

A critical evaluation of the new Act

The new Act can be described as a big improvement on the previous Act. It seems to be consistent with the new Constitution (s 12(2)(a)) which provides for reproductive autonomy. Some of the problems arising out of the previous Act were squarely addressed. There are, however some questions which need to be addressed.

The following aspects can be singled out as being problematic: a pregnant girl of 13 does not need to obtain her parents' consent for the abortion. Deciding to have an abortion is definitely not easy, especially for a very young girl. She will need counselling and assistance to overcome this traumatic experience. You will also remember from the previous sections that minors under the age of 16 can in law not consent to sexual intercourse, so that a girl of 13, who is in the eyes of the law not able to consent to sexual intercourse, may decide on a much more critical matter, namely to terminate a pregnancy!

What about the consent of the woman's husband or partner? Surely the biological father of an unborn child should have a say in the matter – or don't you agree? Remember that s 12(2)(a) of the Constitution provides for the right to make decisions in respect of reproduction. This right applies to every person, that is both the wife and the husband or woman and her partner. Do you think that it is possible to reach a compromise in such a case?

Although every person's right to freedom of conviction, belief and opinion is protected in our Bill of Rights, our Constitutional Court has not

> **TO THINK ABOUT**
>
> Jane (17 years old and in Grade 11) discovers that she is pregnant. Her boyfriend, Tim, also in grade 11, refuses to acknowledge that he is the father of the unborn child. Jane lives with her mother, a widow, who works full time and struggles to make ends meet. Jane knows that they will not be able to afford to look after the baby. She does well at school, and had hoped to study further. She does not want to quit school.
> - How would you advise Jane about the options available to her?

yet answered the question whether a state doctor may refuse upon this ground to perform an abortion on a woman. Consider this problem in the light of the fact that no person may sign away his or her fundamental rights in any contract of employment.

STERILIZATION

The Abortion and Sterilisation Act still applies to the sterilization of persons. This includes those people who themselves are incompetent and/or incapable of consenting to sterilization, for example, seriously brain damaged persons. There is no provision in the Abortion and Sterilisation Act for sterilization as a method of birth control.

> **CASE STUDY**
>
> Mr and Mrs T have just had their second child in two years. Mr T drinks a lot and seems to have no intention of getting a job. Mrs T is the manager of a small clothing store in Benoni, and she does not want to have any more children. She already has to support her husband and the two babies, and her work situation demands a lot of her. Trying to take care of her home, and still working an 8-hour day, Mondays through Saturdays, is no easy task.
>
> Mr T refuses to wear a condom and he refuses to have a vasectomy. Both of these make him 'less of a man', he says. He also refuses to let his wife be sterilized. This will make her 'less of a woman' in his eyes.
> - What should Mrs T do?

In terms of the Child Care Act, all persons over the age of 18 years are competent to consent, without the assistance of their guardians, to the performance of any operation on themselves. In other words, any person over the age of 18 years may decide on a sterilization.

Consider the following question and then look at the example below:
- Do you think a woman or a man in a marriage or stable relationship should be able to obtain a sterilization or vasectomy without the consent of her or his partner?

Consider the following questions about abortion, even if you are not able to give a definite answer:
- Do you think that the previous abortion legislation was adequate in protecting women against so-called 'back street' abortions?
- Do you think that abortion legislation should also provide for abortion on social grounds?

Conclusion

The new abortion legislation, although welcomed by many, is criticized by others, many of whom feel that the Act permits women to 'murder the unborn'. The question of the status of the human embryo and foetus has been raised by these groups which intend to go to Court to test the constitutionality of the present Act. They claim that human life starts at conception, and because the Bill of Rights protects the right to life (s 11), that the unborn is also entitled to this protection.

The Court will have to test whether the legislation complies with the requirements and values in the Constitution. The decision of the Court will be decided by carefully balancing the rights – in this case procreation rights – of the individual against the rights of society. One must not forget that society is entitled to see its values reflected in legislation, in general, and in the Constitution, in particular. This is because the Constitution is supposed to be 'the mirror of the nation's soul'.

CHAPTER NINETEEN:
AIDS and women

HIV† infection and AIDS† have become a serious health problem in South Africa. The latest estimate is that every day more than 1 500 people are being infected with HIV (the virus which causes AIDS) and that more than half a million South Africans are already carriers of the virus. If medical projections are correct, the rate of infection will increase considerably in the near future. If no drastic changes take place in behavioural patterns and no cure or vaccine is developed, it is estimated that 21% of South Africa's adult population will be infected by the year 2010.

Because of various physiological factors, women – especially those in the 15 to 34 year age group – are much more at risk of HIV infection than men. The rate of infection among South African women who attended antenatal clinics of the public health services in 1996 was 14,07%, which represents an increase of 3,63% in the prevalence of HIV infection since 1995. Overall, the level of HIV infection increased from 10,44% in 1995 to 14,07%.

The prevalence rate in women under 20 years of age is also alarming, at 12,78%. Using a mathematical model, this statistic is projected to a figure of 2,4 million South Africans who are now HIV positive.

The most alarming of the results is the increase in infection in the North West Province, where 25% of pregnant women are HIV positive in sharp contrast to 8,3% in 1995.

Note that in South Africa neither AIDS nor HIV infection is a condition that people are compelled to report to the health authorities. The cases on which the abovementioned statistics are based were reported voluntarily and anonymously to the health authorities and give only some indication of the spread of AIDS in South Africa.

BACKGROUND TO AIDS

'Acquired Immune Deficiency Syndrome' (AIDS), is the condition that is 'acquired' in the sense that it is caused by a virus, called Human Immuno-deficiency Virus (HIV), which enters the body in body fluids such as blood, semen and breast milk. The term syndrome indicates that various characteristic symptoms appear simultaneously; in the case of AIDS, as soon as the HIV virus has weakened the body's immune system, certain 'opportunistic' illnesses, such as tuberculosis (which in Africa, in particular, is increasing alarmingly), pneumonia, certain cancers (amongst women cancer of the cervix especially), and neurological and psychiatric problems such as dementia, manifest themselves. It is from these that AIDS sufferers die.

People who are infected with HIV are carriers of the virus for the rest of their lives and can infect other people. To be infected with HIV does not necessarily mean that one is ill. Infected people may show no visible signs of infection for years and may lead productive lives. During this phase these people do not yet have AIDS. The average period of infection until full-scale AIDS develops is less than 10 years, although some people remain healthy for much longer than that.

The life expectancy of people with AIDS varies according to their general health, the circumstances of their lives and the specific opportunistic illnesses which develop. People become known as AIDS sufferers only once they start suffering from one of the opportunistic illnesses. AIDS therefore becomes the final phase of HIV infection, one that lasts on average one to two years.

There is, at present, no cure for HIV infection or for AIDS. The best-known remedy used to treat people with HIV is the drug called AZT (Zidovudine). This is not a cure, but it does afford temporary relief and usually improves the quality of life of infected persons. It does have unpleasant side-effects, however, and is very expensive. New developments include protease inhibitors and combination treatments (so-called 'cocktails' of drugs).

HIV has been identified in various body fluids, but only blood, semen, vaginal secretion and breast milk contain a sufficient concentration of the virus in order for it to be to transmitted. There is no scientific proof that HIV is transmitted by any other means than the following:

- sexual intercourse between heterosexuals, between bisexuals and between homosexuals;
- the reception of or exposure to HIV-infected blood products, the sperm or the organs of an HIV infected person, and
- a baby's reception of or exposure to HIV-infected blood products of an HIV-infected mother before or during birth, or by breast-feeding.

Moreover, the risk of HIV transmission increases when other sexually transmitted diseases are present. A recent case in which a woman was infected through a kiss by her HIV-infected husband raised many concerns. It has, however, been suggested that the high prevalence of blood in the husband's mouth, due to his illness, was a contributing factor which facilitated the spreading of the infection. Kissing has largely been ruled out as a means of HIV transmission.

The statistics mentioned above make it clear that heterosexual intercourse is the principal means by which HIV is being spread in South Africa at present. This is in sharp contrast to the period 1982–86, when HIV infection and the spread of AIDS in South Africa were confined largely to the male homosexual community.

Exposure to infected blood is currently responsible for relatively few cases of infection. This may be because in South African all blood donations are subject to strict tests and blood which is supplied by South African blood banks is considered among the safest in the world: to date, only 29 of the South African cases of AIDS stem from infected blood transfusions. In South Africa, only two known cases of AIDS stem from the sharing of needles by drug-takers.

In addition, in the health system universal measures to prevent exposure to infected blood are emphasized. For example, health care workers wear gloves and masks and handle needles very carefully.

High-risk behaviour therefore consists principally of unprotected sexual intercourse with an infected partner. Although condoms do not offer complete protection, using them whenever one's sexual partner is infected or where one is uncertain of the partner's HIV status is the only way of reducing one's risk of becoming infected with HIV (and with sexually transmitted diseases).

About one-third of the babies of HIV-infected mothers are infected with the virus. The more advanced the mother's infection, the greater the likelihood of her transmitting the virus to her baby. It must nevertheless be remembered that the vast majority of babies of HIV-infected mothers are not infected.

Infected children usually develop full-scale AIDS at a very young age, but recent studies show that some infected children remain free of symptoms up to the age of seven. Studies also show that a Caesarean operation halves the risk of HIV infection, but it is unlikely to become a standard procedure, since that operation is riskier for the mother than a normal birth and is probably too expensive to be done routinely. Experiments have also demonstrated that if pregnant HIV-infected women are treated with AZT during their pregnancy and during the birth process, and they do not breastfeed their babies, the rate of transmission of HIV to their babies declines dramatically. However, it is probably impossible to provide AZT as part of a public health strategy because of its high cost, and to advise women not to breastfeed their babies will probably give rise to other serious health problems, such as malnutrition.

DETECTION AND PREVENTION OF AIDS

Is it possible to determine whether someone is infected with HIV by using blood tests which trace the antibodies caused by the infection in the blood? The antibodies are usually present in the blood six to eight weeks after exposure to the virus, but before that there is a period known as the 'window period' when infected persons can transmit the virus without knowing that they are infected.

The above brief survey makes it clear that not only women but also children are increasingly being threatened by AIDS. AIDS orphans (whose parents have died of AIDS or who have been abandoned by their parents) represent a growing problem. The first South African orphanage for HIV-infected babies was completed in 1993, and will presumably soon be inadequate to cope with the growing numbers of orphans.

As far as the spread of AIDS is concerned, the problem of prevention and detection is compounded by the fact that by far the majority of South Africa's women often do not have access to basic health care and information. This problem can possibly be addressed by providing better guidance in schools, not only on health matters and sexuality but also in respect of life-skills, which should include the ability to say no to high-risk sex or even better, to practise abstinence until marriage and to live monogamously after marriage. Family planning clinics and other information centres disseminate information about AIDS and other health matters, and help in the early detection and treatment of sexually transmittable diseases, which unfortunately are fairly widespread amongst the South African population.

Because of physiological factors, women are more susceptible to HIV infection than men. In addition sociological factors contribute to women's risk of HIV infection. As a result of their subordinate role, especially in customary relationships, women are often not in a position to prevent infection. Because of their lack of empowerment, it is sometimes not possible for them to assert themselves in sexual relationships and to insist, for example, on the use of condoms. Cultural and social practices which place women in such a position ought therefore to be openly scrutinized and questioned.

Empowerment in the spheres of work opportunities and education will naturally improve the position of women in society. Our Constitution makes express provision for the elimination of inequalities in society (see Part Six, below), and to this end it permits affirmative action. This means that measures may be taken to protect and advance certain persons or groups of persons – including women – who received unequal treatment in the past.

The Constitution prohibits unfair discrimination of various kinds, including discrimination against those suffering from a disability. Our Courts may perhaps find that the definition of 'disability' includes AIDS and infection with HIV, especially if they follow certain overseas court cases, particularly some United States judgments. In particular, discrimination in the workplace against those suffering from HIV or AIDS is likely to prove as indefensible as forcing employees or prospective employees to undergo HIV testing.

Prostitution and HIV/AIDS

Today many people argue that sex work (jobs in which sex is used to make money) and homosexual intercourse between consenting adults ought to be decriminalized. The reason given is that, because they risk criminal prosecution, people who engage in these practices are hesitant to come forward for HIV testing, which makes it more difficult to combat AIDS. A man who commits an immoral or indecent act with a boy under the age of 19 is, in terms of the Sexual Offences Act, guilty of an offence for which heavy sentences can be imposed. A woman who commits an immoral or indecent act with a girl under the age of 19 is also committing a punishable offence.

But none of this legislation outlawing sexual offences was drafted with HIV or AIDS in mind, especially not their detection or prevention. On the contrary, the existing legislation could arguably be contributing to the pandemic among certain sections of the population. For example, since prostitution is also still punishable, there is not much chance that persons who engage in it will come forward for testing or for education on AIDS. Sex workers also have no recourse to the law should they be abused by their clients or should they become infected with HIV. The Sexual Offences Act makes it difficult for a prostitute to ply her trade, but it is not a crime to be a prostitute *per se*. In terms of the Act, it is an offence to keep a brothel, to live partially or wholly on the proceeds of prostitution, to commit indecent acts with someone for reward, to entice someone in a public place for indecent purposes, or display oneself deliberately and openly in improper clothing in a place to which the public has access.

It is sometimes said that people who want prostitution to be decriminalized and regulated are less concerned with the moral objections to prostitution than they are with public health. Regulation of prostitution would mean, for example, that:

- prostitutes could be tested at regular intervals;
- they would be licensed to work as prostitutes only if they were free of infection;
- the use of condoms would be made compulsory, and
- if they were infected they would be forbidden to work as prostitutes.

Pleas for the regulation of prostitution have often been made in South Africa, and continue to be made. If prostitution were regulated, health authorities would be able to exercise better control over the sex work industry and therefore also over the spread of AIDS.

Marriage and HIV/AIDS

As early as the 1920s it was held in court that a wife might lawfully refuse to have sexual intercourse with her husband if he had a venereal disease. In the same way a wife can refuse to have intercourse with her husband if he is infected with HIV. It is likely that she could refuse even if he took steps to prevent the transmission of the infection. Remember that condoms do not offer absolute protection. Furthermore, our law now provides that a man may be found guilty of raping his wife. It follows that an infected man who forced his wife to have intercourse with him could be found guilty of rape.

Pregnancy and HIV/AIDS

A doctor or gynaecologist who suspects that a pregnant woman is infected with HIV must advise her to be tested for it. If she is infected, the doctor must inform her of the chances that her unborn child may also be infected and that, if it is, it will probably die within a few years. The doctor must also point out to her that her pregnancy and the birth process may damage her own health too and may hasten the onset of full-blown AIDS in her case. The mother's untimely death would mean that the child, whether it were infected or not, would not have a mother to raise it. Such a woman is entitled to an abortion in terms of the Termination of Pregnancy Act, (see Chapter 18, above).

If the woman wishes to proceed with the pregnancy to full term, the doctor may inform her of the latest medical experimentation with AZT to prevent the transmission of HIV to babies. She should however be warned that this treatment does not guarantee success and that AZT could have serious side-effects for her. It should also be explained that AZT should in any event not be taken during the first 16 weeks of pregnancy because its effect on the development of the foetus has not yet been fully researched.

A doctor who is told by an infected patient that she wishes to fall pregnant, should also give her the above information. If she is not told that there is a risk that she may give birth to an infected child and she then does so, she will be able to institute an action for damages against the doctor for negligently failing to give her the necessary warning. An infected mother will also be able to sue the doctor if, as a result of the pregnancy and of giving birth, she develops full-blown AIDS sooner than she would otherwise have done. Although this will naturally be difficult to prove, the doctor who negligently failed to give the necessary information could in principle be held liable for the early onset of the harmful results. If a woman has been warned of the risks and has accepted them, it will not be possible for her to hold the doctor liable if an infected baby is born.

Of course the woman should still have the choice whether to become pregnant or to continue with the pregnancy: to compel women to be tested or not to fall pregnant or not to continue with a pregnancy would probably be in conflict with the Constitution. This is because the Constitution provides that all persons are entitled to respect for and protection of their dignity and to freedom of their person, that no person may be subjected to torture of any kind, whether physical, mental or emotional, that all persons are entitled to personal privacy and that all persons have the right to freedom of conscience and religion. These rights may sometimes be limited, but only if to do so is reasonable and justifiable in an open and democratic society based on human dignity, freedom and equality.

In arriving at a decision, all relevant factors should be taken into account, including the following factors:

- the nature of the right;
- why it is important to limit the right;
- what the purpose of the limitation is, and
- what the nature of the limitation is and whether there are not perhaps less restrictive means of achieving that purpose.

It will be very difficult to prove that a woman's rights should be limited by, for example, compelling her to have an abortion or to undergo compulsory tests because this would be necessary or reasonable.

Conclusion

Since 1993, the South African Law Commission has been investigating the reform of the law affecting AIDS and HIV. A discussion document (Working Paper 58) was published for general information and comment during 1995. The comments received on the Working Paper showed differences of opinion between interest groups. A committee is helping the Commission to resolve differences and in addition to develop final recommendations.

Early in 1997 the Commission adopted the committee's first interim report (which deals with condom standards; universal infection controls in occupational safety regulations; the prohibition of the use of non-disposable syringes; a national policy on HIV testing; and the repeal of measures making HIV testing compulsory). The report has been presented to the Minister of Justice for tabling in Parliament soon.

A discussion paper on pre-employment HIV testing was distributed for comment in July 1997. A discussion paper on HIV/AIDS and Discrimination in Schools will be distributed soon.

Women's procreation rights are now protected in the Bill of Rights (s 12(2)(a)). Strengthened by the international human rights law, women's rights to reproduction have slowly but surely gained momentum and recieved the attention they urgently need.

This is borne out by the fact that the old conservative abortion legislation has now been replaced by a very liberal Act (see also Chapter 18 above).

The right to privacy is also relevant as decisions about procreation and having children are private matters. Privacy is also important to the questions of abortion and AIDS. In the past, it has usually been believed that the government should not interfere in those decisions. However, in protecting women's equality, dignity and privacy, the Constitution has served to strengthen women's struggle for complete autonomy and freedom.

Selected reading

Case law: *Roe v Wade* 410 US 118 (1973)

Winnie Koppers (ed). (1994) 17(5) *SALUS Health/Gesondheid* Department of National Health and Population Development, Private Bag X828, Pretoria, 0001

ML Lupton. 'The right to be born: Surrogacy and the legal control of human fertility' 1988 *De Jure* 36–58

D Pretorius. *Surrogate Motherhood – A Worldwide View of the Issues.* Chicago, Illonois, Thomas Publishers, 1994

E Spiro. *Law of Parent and Child.* Juta, Cape Town, 1985

SA Strauss. *Doctor, Patient and the Law – A selection of Practical Issues.* Pretoria, Van Schaik, 1991

PART SIX:
Women, human rights and democracy

INTRODUCTION

In this part we discuss three main topics: Women and the Constitution (Chapter 20); International human rights conventions dealing specifically with the Rights of Women, and the Beijing Platform for Action (Chapter 21); and National machinery for the advancement of women (Chapter 22). In this way, we hope to cover some of the broad range of women's human rights issues and constitutional issues in South Africa. Much has been done to eradicate discrimination and obtain equality for women, but substantive equality has not been attained yet. In this part we shall try to empower women with some tools to continue the struggle for equality, be it in the workplace, at home or in public life.

CHAPTER TWENTY:
Women and the Constitution

Human rights are not reducible to a question of legal and due process ... In the case of women, human rights are affected by the entire society's perception of what is proper or not proper for women.

Ninotchka Rosca

It is common knowledge that the movement to recognize fundamental/human rights has developed largely since the end of the Second World War. But until recently, women's rights were not a central issue, even in the international sphere – the adoption of the Convention on the Elimination of all Forms of Discrimination against Women (CEDAW) took place only in 1979. CEDAW came into force on 3 September 1981. From that date, women's rights have begun to receive some attention, but women's issues are generally still viewed as separate from the mainstream of human rights. This is in spite of the 'mobilization' of women to have their rights recognized as having more than incidental value.

The Vienna Declaration and Programme of Action, adopted on 25 June 1993 at the World Conference on Human Rights held in Austria (14–25 June 1993), is the first firm commitment to the rights of women, giving these rights their pride of place as an important part of human rights and not as 'lesser' issues separate from general human rights.

Article 18 of the Declaration deals with women and states:

The human rights of women and of the girl-child are an inalienable, integral and indivisible part of universal human rights; the full and equal participation of women in politics, civil, economic, social and cultural life, at the national, regional and international levels, and the eradication of all forms of discrimination on grounds of sex are priority objectives of the international community.

What follows is a discussion of the position of women in South Africa under its first democratic government. In this chapter we shall be introducing you to the legal compact called the Constitution of the Republic of South Africa Act 108 of 1996. This Constitution has a key role to play in the lives of all citizens of this country, especially of women.

> **TO THINK ABOUT**
>
> Think about and try to answer these questions before reading further:
> - What is a democracy or a democratic state?
> - What is a constitution?
> - What would you write into a constitution if you were to draw one up? (How is it structured and what is provided for in it?)
> - How can the Constitution be used to help women in South Africa in their struggle against inequality? (What are the implications for women?)
> - What do you think 'equality' means?

WHAT IS A CONSTITUTION?

To refresh your memory, page back to Part One: Introduction to women and the law and read again what was written about the position of women in South Africa. Keep that information in mind while reading through this chapter.

The terms below need to be studied especially carefully (you also need to understand the concepts):
- democracy
- constitution
- State authority
- bill of rights
- human rights
- equality
- enforcement mechanisms.

Therefore in the first part of this section we examine each of them in turn.

Democracy

Before we can discuss what a constitution is, we need to examine the concept of democracy. The word itself comes from the Greek words *demos*, meaning 'the people' and *kratos*, meaning 'authority' or 'strength'. Therefore democracy means 'the strength/authority of the people'. According to the *Concise Oxford Dictionary*, democracy is

> 'government by all the people, direct or representative; a form of society ignoring hereditary class distinctions and tolerating minority views'.

Direct democracy is totally unattainable in today's world, because it requires that all the citizens (people) of the country must have a direct say in the governing of the country. The sheer number of people makes this impossible. In a representative or indirect democracy, matters are streamlined by allowing the citizens to elect representatives who carry out the day-to-day activities of governing the country for the people.

The most important feature of a democracy is that it is a government by the people through their representatives. Representatives are people who are chosen to represent others by bringing their concerns to the attention of the government. When a country is ruled by the people, this is demonstrated by certain basic features or characteristics of the democratic state (or constitutional state). Some people prefer to call these basic features 'markers' or 'signposts' of democracy. (See McQuoid-Mason *et al* 16.) Ten of the important signposts are listed below, although there could be more than just these 10. Those marked in bold type are discussed in detail in this chapter and you should study them carefully:

- Participation in the government by the citizens. They vote for people, they stand for election, they become informed, they can debate issues, etc.
- Regular, free and fair elections.
- A multi-party system (where there are two or more political parties in elections, such as the ANC, CP, DP, NP, IFP, PAC, etc).
- Acceptance of the results of the elections, even by those who lose.
- Political tolerance† of other parties.
- **Open, transparent and accountable government.**
- Control of the abuse of power by government.
- **Equality**.
- **Fundamental/human rights.**†
- A bill of rights (a statement/list of fundamental/human rights in the Constitution).

Constitution

A great deal has been written about what 'constitution' means in the legal sense. Constitutions have been classified into various types:

- supreme;
- ordinary (constitutions which are not supreme, without special status);
- written;
- unwritten, etc.

For the purposes of this work, we say that a constitution is usually a written document that comprises the legal rules and principles governing the exercise of state authority (see below). This collection of rules also governs the relationship between the citizens of the State and the organs of the State (ie the institutions governing the State), as well as the relationship between the organs of the State themselves.

A constitution also describes the following:
- how the government will be elected;
- what powers it may and may not have, and
- what rights the citizens are entitled to.

However, the powers of the State are not unlimited, and one function of a constitution is to define the limits on the powers of government.

When a country has a supreme constitution, an added feature comes to the fore: the supreme constitution is the most important law of the land, and no other law may conflict with it. When a constitution is supreme, the Courts have a so-called 'testing power' (that is, the power to enquire whether the laws are in accord with the constitution) over legislation (the Acts passed by a national Parliament, provincial assembly or a local council). This is not the case when a country has an ordinary constitution. South Africa and the United States of America are examples of states that have a supreme constitution.

State Authority

State authority is the power of a government to govern a country at the highest – ie national – level. In a democracy, State authority has to be limited by counterbalancing it against the wishes of the citizens of the State, otherwise it runs the risk of becoming autocratic or authoritarian. In other words, the State must be answerable to the people.

Constitutional history of South Africa

South Africa has traditionally been a male-dominated country, even after the country became a union in 1910. This fact is evident in all walks of life, but especially in public life. Women today still remain largely 'invisible' in public life, even though no law has ever been passed to limit the status or role of women *per se* in South African society. Female representation in the public sector does not reflect the composition of the population (more than half the people in South Africa are women). For example, at present, very few directors-general in the civil service are women. Moreover, it is only in recent times that a few women have been appointed as ambassadors to represent South Africa overseas. State commissions also tend to be male-dominated.

The right to vote

In 1930 the Hertzog Government enfranchized white women, giving them the power to vote. Black women (like all black people) were granted the vote only in 1994. To have the right to vote means that a citizen has the right to express a preference for a candidate of a political party of his or her choice to represent him or her in Parliament.[†] This right is not only a very important human right, but it is also one of the markers or 'signposts' of democracy.

The rights of women

As has often been stated by women themselves, the struggle against racial oppression and discrimination in South Africa meant that the battle for gender equality and the true emancipation of women was often neglected. In other words, racial issues resulted in women's issues being downplayed. Albertyn (*Gender* 42) puts it thus:

> *It has only been in the immediate past, with the onset of the transition and the breaking down of the racial divisions of apartheid, that equality for all women has been identified as an autonomous aspect of the achievement of democracy.*

After 1990

In 1990 the African National Congress (ANC) was unbanned and a process of ongoing negotiations started to transform South Africa into a democratic state. One of the most important aspects of the process of transformation was the acceptance of the Interim Constitution by the role-players in this process. As a group these role-players were the people in the Multi Party

---

TO THINK ABOUT

- What were your own experiences during the elections from 26 to 28 April 1994?
- Had you ever voted before in South Africa?
- Did you vote during that election?
- How did it feel to vote?
- If it was your first opportunity to vote, think about how you felt during that time.
- Think about the months leading up to the election. What changes were taking place in the country during the period before the elections? Think about how different people felt about the elections.

Negotiating Process (MPNP). They agreed to the Interim Constitution on 17 November 1993 at the World Trade Centre in Kempton Park.

During a short session of the South African Parliament in November and December 1993, the Interim Constitution was adopted into statute (Act 200 of 1993) – the proper law-making body (Parliament) made the document a legitimate law of the land.

The elections of 1994

The Interim Constitution came into effect on 27 April 1994. Elections for the transitional Parliament took place from 26 to 28 April 1994. This was the first South African election in which the franchise[†] was enjoyed equally by all South Africans over the age of 18, the first occasion on which all adult citizens had the right to vote.

Women in the process

Before we leave the discussion of constitutional history, we have to mention one aspect relevant to women, that is the input of women (as a group) at the MPNP in Kempton Park. From a women's perspective, it is important for us to recognize the part played by women in the negotiating process and the writing of the interim or transitional Constitution. Women played important roles, 'both as delegates and as a social movement' (Albertyn *Gender* 60). For example, there was a compulsory requirement that one of each negotiating party's two representatives in the Negotiating Council had to be a woman. Although there was some criticism that these women were only token representatives, women's influence on the process should not be underestimated. Du Plessis & Corder (*Understanding* 38–9) summarize this force:

> [T]he input of female negotiators in debates on the making of Chapter 3 certainly had a visible impact on important aspects of the product. It also showed that the plight of women has become irrevocably part of the public *(their emphasis)* human rights debate in South Africa – a tendency which augurs well for the advancement of women's rights in the future.

STRUCTURE AND FRAMEWORK OF THE FINAL (1996) CONSTITUTION

The words 'interim' or 'transitional' have been used repeatedly in the discussion of the Constitution. The 1993 South African Constitution was an interim or transitional one, a temporary document, one intended to serve the new democratic state between the 1994 elections and the formation of a final Constitution for the nascent democracy. Therefore in the interim Constitution there were important provisions dealing with the establishing and functioning of a Constitutional Assembly – the National Assembly and Senate in joint sitting. The Constitutional Assembly's task was to write and adopt a final constitution which was in line with certain constitutional principles.[†]

These constitutional principles are a series of 34 rules which were set out in the interim Constitution. Note that these principles could not be changed or amended under any circumstances whatsoever. Moreover, they were the requirements that the final constitutional text had to meet in order to be valid.

The Constitutional Assembly completed its task on 10 May 1996. Once the Constitutional Court had declared that the final constitutional text met with the requirements of the constitutional principles, the final Constitution became law in February 1997.

Framework of the Constitution

The Constitution is an exceptionally detailed legal document that spells out the rules by which the country is governed and the limits on the powers of government. It also provides for the necessary 'structures' of government. These structures include a Parliament (to make laws); an Executive (to carry out the laws), and a Judiciary (who settle disputes). These are the three main structures at national level.

The Constitution consists of the following parts:
- A Preamble, which is an introductory statement setting forth the purpose of the document as well as the reasons for its adoption;
- 243 sections spread over 14 chapters (note that Chapter 2 of this Constitution contains the Bill of Rights, which is discussed below), and
- seven schedules (in legal terms a schedule is an annexure to a statute in which items are listed or in which matters to do with the statute are spelled out in greater detail: for example, Schedule 3 deals with election procedures).

In the case of the Constitution, the seven schedules regulate various matters, amongst them the procedure for the election of the president.

The Constitution is the supreme law of the land (s 2 of the Constitution) and the government is therefore not above the Constitution.

The Constitution provides for the State authority or power to be divided into three branches:
- Legislature: Parliament;
- Executive: the President and Cabinet of Ministers, and
- Judiciary: the Courts, including a Constitutional Court, a Supreme Court of Appeal, High Courts and magistrate's courts.

© JUTA & CO, LTD

Do you remember our reference to 'control of the abuse of power by government' as one of the signposts of democracy?

Having a supreme constitution is one way of checking and controlling the exercise of power by a government, since government must act in accordance with the Constitution. The government derives its powers from the Constitution and is at the same time bound by the Constitution.

The division of authority or power prevents an excess of power or a concentration of power in one particular branch which may lead to the abuse of power. Note that the separation of powers† is another way of checking and controlling the government, and is therefore also a signpost of democracy.

Legislature

In terms of s 43 of the Constitution it is Parliament that has legislative authority. The main function of Parliament is to make laws, or legislate.

Parliament consists of two chambers,† or groups of people. The first is called the National Assembly† and consists of no more than 400 members elected on the basis of proportional representation. Proportional representation is a special way of electing members of Parliament so that even small political parties in a multiparty system are able to have representatives in the chamber. Representation is in proportion to the number of votes cast for each party by the people. For example, since the ANC obtained the most votes in the 1994 election, this party has the majority of representatives in the National Assembly.

The second chamber is called the National Council of Provinces. It is composed of 90 members, 10 delegates from each of the nine provinces. Detailed provisions regarding the qualifications of members of Parliament (both the National Assembly and the Council of Provinces), their powers, control over them, etc, are set out in Chapter 4 of the Constitution.

Executive

The Executive consists of the President, the Deputy President and the Cabinet. The rules governing the function of this branch are set out in Chapter 5 of the Constitution. The head of the executive is the President who is elected by the National Assembly from among its members. Provision is also made for the office of Deputy President.

The Constitution also provides for ministers of State. The ministers, together with the President and Deputy President, form the Cabinet. The work and responsibilities of a Cabinet Minister are known as that Minister's portfolio. For example, the Minister of Health's portfolio is health matters. The Ministers may be assisted by deputy ministers. In the Constitution there are detailed provisions about a Minister's powers, and about the control of the Ministers. In the Constitution this is called the 'accountability' of the Ministers: in their deeds and decisions they have to be accountable to the electorate, and cannot behave irresponsibly, dishonestly or secretly without explaining their behaviour.

The President may select any number of Ministers from among the members of the Assembly and no more than two Ministers from outside the Assembly.

The President is both head of State and head of the government (ie executive President). In the first role, the President has mostly ceremonial functions. For example, President Mandela spoke at the World Hindu Conference in Durban in July 1995. When he delivered his speech, he acted as the head of State of South Africa and was therefore representing the people of the country. In the second function, the President plays an active role in governing the country. Note that even the President is bound by the Constitution and must act according to its provisions. The Constitution states that the President must act 'in consultation' with the Ministers – he or she must seek the advice of the Ministers and must follow their advice. This is an important way of keeping the President in check (remember 'checks and balances'?).

The executive function is to put into practice the laws made by Parliament as well as to carry out any other legal rules. The cabinet initiates legislation, which is then adopted by Parliament to become law. The executive's work also includes the planning, co-ordination and management of a great variety of government activities, as well as executing or implementing policy.

Judiciary

The judicial branch of the government (the Judiciary) is dealt with in Chapter 8 of the Constitution. It is made up of the Courts of the country which have judicial authority. These Courts are:

- the Constitutional Court
- the Supreme Court of Appeal
- the High Courts
- the magistrate's courts
- any other courts established in terms of an Act of Parliament.

The Judiciary's main function is to decide disputes concerning the interpretation and the application of legal rules. The Constitutional Court is the highest Court in South Africa in all matters having to do with the interpretation, protection and enforcement of the Constitution. To use a legal phrase, the Constitutional Court is 'the Court of final instance' in constitutional matters (which include the interpretation and application of the Bill of Rights). The Constitutional Court also has a very special function, but we shall return to its role below.

Chapter 2 of the Constitution is of crucial importance for the citizens of South Africa. It contains the Bill of Rights, which is tested in the Constitutional Court as citizens and or organizations try to bring its loftier provisions to life.

Other matters which are discussed in the Constitution are provincial and local government, the public and police services, the role and status of traditional leaders, finance and the national defence force.

IMPLICATIONS OF THE 1996 CONSTITUTION FOR WOMEN

General implications

The first thing we notice when reading the Constitution is that it is 'woman-friendly'. This means that the rights of women are not ignored or considered inferior to the rights of men. This did not happen in the past – for example, according to the Interpretation Act, reference to the masculine was presumed automatically to include the feminine, so that women were left 'hidden' in legislation. The Constitution refers throughout to both men and women, thereby setting an example to be followed in all future legislation. (See also the introduction to Part One, above.)

At the practical level, the political transition has also brought about changes as far as women are concerned. According to the latest figures obtained from Parliament more than a quarter of the Members of Parliament (MPs) are women, compared to only 2,8 percent under the previous government.

The Bill of Rights and the principle of equality

For the women of South Africa in particular, the Constitution has brought benefits through the prominence given in both the Constitution and the Bill of Rights to the principle of and the right to equality.

Before we go any further with the discussion of the principle of equality, we need to address two questions first:
- What is a bill of rights?
- What are fundamental/human rights?

A Bill of Rights

In the relationship between government and the individual, the individual is usually subordinate. The relationship is therefore one of inequality. The three branches of State authority (the Legislature, the Executive and the Judiciary) 'exist to manage and protect the common interests of the people' (Rautenbach & Malherbe *Rights* 2). In order that the three branches may perform these functions, the Constitution confers certain powers on the government. These powers sometimes include the power to compel a person to do something. For example, we are all forced to pay taxes and to obey certain rules. This explains the State's stronger position compared to the individual's.

However, it is possible that this power may be abused by the State. In a democratic state, rights (written into a bill of rights) are the most important constraint on the possible abuse of government power. But it is important to note that

> ... *the purpose of a bill of rights is not to paralyse the state so that it is unable to perform important functions* ... *(Rautenbach & Malherbe 2)*

Therefore, although a bill of rights permits the State to limit certain rights, in the bill of rights itself rules are set out governing how and when the State may limit an individual's rights.

A bill of rights, then, is a document which sets out the rights of the individual. It may also provide for the enforcement of such rights, and for their limitation in certain circumstances. Note that the State (or government) itself does not have rights in terms of a bill of rights. It does, however, have the power to limit or suspend rights. This distinction is important to remember.

> **TO THINK ABOUT**
>
> Remember what we said about the relationship between the rights of the individual and the government.
>
> Can you think of any situation where the government is more important than an individual? Can you think of any cases where the individual is more important than the government?

Fundamental Human Rights

But what is the difference between a bill of rights and human rights? According to the doctrine of fundamental human rights, each and every person has certain inalienable rights which are inviolable or inherent. This means that every person automatically has these rights – they are not something an individual has to work for or which he or she deserves, nor are they a privilege conferred by the State or the government. Furthermore, the rights may not be encroached upon or invaded by the State, unless the bill of rights allows this. It is also important to understand that no right is absolute: all rights have to be 'weighed' against the rights of other individuals, and weighed against the public interest.

Below is a list of the human rights protected in the South African Bill of Rights.

The Human Rights established in terms of the Bill of Rights in the Constitution (Note: Please read these rights together, not in isolation – they fit together to form a complete picture.) The right (to) or (of)

1. Equality (s 9);
2. Human dignity (s 10);
3. Life (s 11)
4. Freedom and security of the person (s 12);
5. Freedom from servitude and forced labour (s 13);
6. Privacy (s 14);
7. Religion, belief and opinion (s 15);
8. Freedom of expression (s 16);
9. Assembly, demonstration, picket and petition (peacefully and unarmed) (s 17);
10. Freedom of association (s 18);
11. Political rights (s 19);
12. Citizenship (s 20);
13. Freedom of movement and residence (s 21);
14. Freedom of trade, occupation and profession (s 22);
15. Fair labour practices (s 23);
16. A healthy environment (s 24);
17. Property (s 25);
18. Housing (s 26);
19. Health care, food, water and social security (s 27);
20. Children's rights (s 28);
21. Education (s 29);
22. Language and culture of choice (s 30);
23. Freedom to belong to cultural, religious and linguistic communities (s 31);
24. Access to information (s 32);
25. Just administrative action (s 33);
26. Access to Courts (s 34);
27. Detained, arrested and accused persons (including the right to:
    - employ a lawyer and be provided with a lawyer by the State in certain circumstances;
    - be informed of reasons for arrest;
    - remain silent and to be presumed innocent;
    - be brought before the Court within 48 hours of arrest;
    - bail unless the interests of justice require otherwise;
    - a fair trial (s 35).

Equality is one of the cornerstones of the South African Constitution and is the first human right mentioned in the list above. In this regard Du Plessis & Corder (*Understanding* 139) write that 'equality rights ... hold a position of pre-eminence ...'. Albertyn & Kentridge (*Equality* 149) say that 'Equality is a value fundamental to the Constitution'. Not only is the right to equality listed first in the Bill of Rights, but throughout the document 'equality' is featured as one of the aspirations of the Constitution (Albertyn & Kentridge 150). One of the aims of the Constitution is to ensure that people are treated equally and enjoy their rights as equals.

Even in the Preamble, the importance of equality is established when it is stated that one of the purposes of the Constitution is to lay the foundations for a democratic and open society in which government is based on the will of the people and every citizen is protected equally by law.

The protection of the 'rights of *every person* (ie every man, woman, child, ...) throughout Chapter 2 implies *equal* protection under the supreme Constitution' (Du Plessis & Corder 139). Moreover, although we stated previously that rights can be limited, the limitation of rights must be 'justifiable in an open and democratic society based on freedom and equality' in terms of s 36 of the Constitution.

The section of the Constitution which deals with 'equality' (s 9) reads:

[1] *Everyone is equal before the law and has the right to equal protection and benefit of the law.*

[2] *Equality includes the full and equal enjoyment of all rights and freedoms. To promote the achievement of equality, legislative and other measures designed to protect or advance persons, or categories of persons disadvantaged by unfair discrimination may be taken.*

[3] *The State may not unfairly discriminate directly or indirectly against anyone on one or more grounds, including race, gender, sex, pregnancy, marital status, ethnic or social origin, colour, sexual orientation, age, disability, religion, conscience, belief, culture, language and birth.*

[4] *No person may unfairly discriminate directly or indirectly against anyone on one or more grounds in terms of subsection (3). National legislation must be enacted to prevent or prohibit unfair discrimination.*

[5] *Discrimination on one or more of the grounds listed in subsection [3] is unfair unless it is established that the discrimination is fair.*

But what does this mean? This section of the Constitution guarantees the right to equality before the law and the right to equal protection of the law. This section also seeks to ensure equal treatment; equality before the law mandates (or authorizes) the equal treatment of all persons by a Court of law, as well as by the State administration, whereas equal protection of the law requires that the rights of all persons should enjoy equal protection.

Section 9(3) forbids *unfair* discrimination against anyone for the reasons of race, colour, language, gender, sex, pregnancy, marital status, etc. The question of what constitutes 'unfair discrimination' is quite difficult to address. The answer is one based on the concept of 'differentiation' or 'differential treatment'. To explain what this means, Du Plessis & Corder argue as follows (at 141):

> ... *differentiation is acceptable, but discrimination is unjustified differentiation which is either based on a personal quality not related to the object sought to be achieved (race is, for instance, used as a criterion to determine the amount which pensioners are to receive) or which pursues an untenable object or purpose (for instance 'to keep a residential area white').*

Section 9(4) forbids any person to discriminate unfairly against anyone on one or more of the grounds mentioned. Note, too, that 'sex' and 'gender' are mentioned separately as protected conditions under this section.

The reason advanced for this distinction is the following: 'sex' refers to the physical qualities of an individual, those qualities determining whether a person is male or female. 'Gender', on the other hand, refers to what is called the 'sex-role stereotypes' or 'social constructs' associated with masculinity or femininity' (Du Plessis & Corder 143; see also Part One: Introduction). An example of discrimination on the basis of sex could be to exclude a woman from a position because she can become pregnant. This is sex discrimination based on the woman's physical ability to bear children. An example of gender discrimination, on the other hand, would be paying a woman a lower wage or salary than a man simply because she is a woman. Among the reasons given for this is that 'women are not breadwinners' or 'women do not have the strength or staying power of men'. These reasons are gender discrimination based on sex-role stereotyping.

> **TO THINK ABOUT**
>
> Think about yourself or about other women you know who have suffered from discrimination.
>
> Can you think of some more examples of sex discrimination? Can you think of some more examples of gender discrimination? Remember what we discussed earlier in Part Three: Women and violence and Part Four: Women and employment about sex and gender discrimination. This would be a good time to go back and review those chapters.

In short then, as far as the right to equality is concerned, the State must treat people equally. When the State does not do so, its treatment must comply with the general requirements for the limitation of rights as set out in the Bill of Rights (as discussed above). For example, it is not unequal or unfair to state a minimum age for a driver's licence or to require an academic qualification for a job that demands a certain level of expertise or knowledge.

Note that the equality principle is a little different in the case of affirmative action because affirmative action is aimed at assisting people who have been discriminated against in the past to 'enjoy their rights fully and equally' (Rautenbach & Malherbe 31). The Constitution makes it clear that the equality clauses should not stand in the way of affirmative action. The equality and non-discrimination clauses should therefore not be interpreted as forbidding measures designed to achieve the adequate protection and advancement of persons and groups or categories of persons who have been disadvantaged by unfair discrimination in order to enable their full and equal enjoyment of all rights and freedoms (s 9(2)).

Some people argue that affirmative action is actually discrimination in reverse, and is therefore a denial of the principles of equality and of non-discrimination. Others believe that the very purpose of affirmative action is to redress existing inequalities, arising from the unjust policies of the past. This means that because affirmative action is helping people who were disadvantaged in the past, it is not discrimination.

Women are a case in point in this regard. While representation by women in the national government has shown an increase since 1994, the situation is not as good in other fields. In a Report on the Status of SA Women, for instance, it was mentioned that female representation in 'both the public and private sectors [is] far out of line with the composition of the population of which more than half are women'. Many more women still need to find their rightful place in our society.

Up till now we have heavily emphasized the right to equality and this right's central position in the Bill of Rights. However, it is important to remember that, even with this emphasis, we are not saying that the right to equality is more important than the right to liberty, for example. The issue of conflicting rights is an extremely difficult area of the law and one that will keep lawyers occupied for many years to come.

Control and enforcement

We have referred to rights and listed those rights protected by the Bill of Rights in the Constitution. But a bill of rights which cannot be enforced means very little, so enforcement is crucial. There are many institutions which have to ensure that there is adequate enforcement of these rights.

Rautenbach & Malherbe (at 43), for instance, refer to the media as an important source of public control. They say that the freedom of expression enjoyed by the media plays a role that should not be underestimated. Private organizations also have an important task to fulfil in controlling the government. Such organizations may be formed for the promotion of human rights, and especially for the purposes of control over the activities of government bodies. In this regard the role of non-governmental organizations (NGOS) is of vital importance.

But what is the most effective way of enforcing one's rights? Control and enforcement by the Courts is the best way to ensure that the Bill of Rights is observed and a person's rights are enforced. For this reason the Bill of Rights also guarantees freedom of access to the Courts. Therefore, when you feel that your rights are being violated or threatened, the Courts are the institutions to approach. The only difficulty is that often individuals cannot afford to go to court.

A question which arises is the following: who may approach a Court about violations of rights in the Bill of Rights? The individual whose rights are violated or threatened has access, but the Constitution provides that access to a Court is not restricted to those people.

Over and above the individual (a person acting in his or her own interest), the Constitution allows the following persons and institutions to take a matter to court:

- an association in the interest of its members (for instance, an association looking after the interests of mentally handicapped persons, in the interest of such a person if that person's right is infringed);
- a person acting on behalf of somebody who is not in a position to approach the Court in his or her own name (for instance, when a person is detained without any reason and another person approaches the Court for his or her release);
- a person acting as a member of a group or class of persons, or on behalf of a group or class of persons, even if he or she is not a member of it (for instance, a group of parents acting on behalf of their children if the children's rights are infringed);
- a person taking the matter to Court in the public interest (for instance, a person acts in the public interest when he or she complains about noise or other forms of pollution) (s 38).

Anther important question is: which Courts may deliver judgments in connection with the Bill of Rights? We stated above that the Constitutional Court is one very important institution protecting human rights. In terms of s 167 of the Constitution, the Constitutional Court is the highest court for the interpretation, protection and enforcement of the Constitution, and a decision by that Court binds all persons and government insitutions, including all other courts.

Please take note of the following important point pertaining to the role of the Judiciary as 'watchdog' over the Constitution: the Judiciary can perform this role only if it is independent. This means that 'nobody may exert pressure on the Courts to influence their judgments' (Rautenbach & Malherbe at 46).

Even the Cabinet Ministers or the President of the country cannot make the Courts change their minds. The Constitution itself states that the Courts are independent and impartial and subject only to the Constitution and the law.

The Constitutional Court is also more representative of the population than other courts, and it remains a matter of great concern that the judicial system does not reflect the realities of the composition of the population of South Africa. At present, only two out of the 11 members of the Constitutional Court are women.

Normally, the Constitutional Court will hear a case only after an appeal has been lodged against the judgment of another Court or when a matter has been referred to the Court by another court. In other words, the Constitutional Court functions as a higher court. When it is the only court that may give a decision in a matter, we say the Constitutional Court has 'exclusive jurisdiction'. Note that provision is made in the Constitution for parties to agree (to save time, for instance) to the alternative jurisdiction of a provincial or local division of the High Court. Appeals on constitutional matters nevertheless still go to the Constitutional Court.

We have mentioned the Supreme Court of Appeals. This Court may not decide constitutional cases, and therefore, if a case before it involves a constitutional matter or an issue requiring a decision on that constitutional issue or matter, the question must be referred to the Constitutional Court.

The High Courts may deliver judgments in all constitutional cases, except those on which only the Constitutional Court may decide. Other courts include the magistrate's courts and they are also bound by the provisions of the Constitution and must apply them.

May a person enter the Constitutional Court in Braamfontein, Johannesburg and insist that the Court hears his or her complaint? The answer is a definite no.

The person whose rights have been infringed – the aggrieved party – must lodge her or his complaint with a lawyer. However, many people cannot afford to go to a lawyer. In larger cities, organizations such as Lawyers for Human Rights, Legal Resources Centres and legal aid clinics at universities may come to the assistance of such persons. (See the Appendix to Part Three for lists of various legal aid bodies in the different regions.)

After hearing the case, what can a Court do? If the Constitutional Court or a High Court finds that a law is invalid because it infringes a right in a way that conflicts with the Constitution, the Court may tell the Legislature to correct the defect in the law within a certain time. The decision must be in the interests of justice and good government, however. If the Legislature fails to act within the period set by the Court, the law is invalidated. If the Constitutional Court or a provincial or local court finds that an executive action is invalid, the Court may require the relevant body not to do this again, or to correct the act on certain conditions and within a specified period (Rautenbach & Malherbe 45).

Although we have stated that our courts are the most important protectors of human rights, the Constitution itself provides for other 'enforcement mechanisms' also. We shall mention them with only a brief reference to their function(s):

- the Public Protector: his or her main function is to enquire into complaints about civil servants and to try to solve problems relating to them (see also Chapter 22, below);
- the Human Rights Commission: its main task is to act as a guardian ('watchdog') to protect fundamental/human rights. Any complaints about fundamental rights can be lodged with this Commission (see also Chapter 22, below);
- the Commission on Gender Equality: the object of this institution is to promote respect for gender equality and the protection, development and attainment of gender equality (s 187 of the Constitution) (See also Chapter 22, below);
- the Commission on Restitution of Land Rights: its task is to resolve disputes over land claims and, where necessary, to prepare reports on claims for a Court to consider.

We must emphasize, though, that the judiciary remains the main guardian, 'watchdog' or protector of fundamental/human rights. However, these other bodies (institutions), which are supported by the Constitution, also have a valuable role to play in the protection of human rights and freedoms.

The position of women in general can be summarized as follows:

[L]iberation secured in political manifestos or legal compacts such as the 1993 Constitution does not necessarily mean liberation in practice. It is the way in which legal rights are translated into reality and the way in which they are supplemented by social change that determine whether they change women's lives. (Kaganas & Murray Gender 1)

But women themselves must become more conscious of the need to make their own specific contribution from grassroots level up to the development of the protection and promotion of their rights. One way of attaining this goal is to keep asserting that human rights are universal – not in the geographical sense only, but more particularly in the sense that all human rights belong to all people, irrespective of sex, race, sexual orientation, gender, language, colour, etc. A human right is a human right, irrespective of who the human being is.

CHAPTER TWENTY-ONE:
International conventions of particular importance to women

Section 39 of our Constitution provides that, when interpreting the chapter on fundamental rights a Court must have regard to international human rights law. South Africa is therefore committed to taking cognizance of international trends and standards regarding human rights, including women's rights.

Our Courts are therefore obliged to consider international human rights law when dealing with issues such as the right to equality, the right to life, the right to human dignity and the right to privacy. Part of international human rights law is to be found in international documents such as United Nations Conventions. In the booklet, CEDAW in South Africa, the writers define a convention as: 'an international agreement which must be obeyed by all of the nations which accept it'.

We could also look at regional human rights documents such as the African Charter, the American Convention on Human Rights and the European Convention on Human Rights. However, here we deal with only those United Nations Conventions of specific importance to women which were signed by the South African government in January 1993.

A country becomes a party to a United Nations Convention only when it accepts that Convention as part of its law. The technical process which ensures that a Convention becomes part of a country's law is referred to as 'ratification'. Usually a country signs a Convention and then ratifies it only later: it normally does not form part of a country's law if it is signed but not yet ratified. However, human rights activists argue that a government becomes morally bound to the ideals of a convention when it signs it.

In January 1993 the South African government signed the United Nations Convention on Consent to Marriage, Minimum Age for Marriage and Registration of Marriages; the Convention on the Nationality of Married Women; and the Convention on the Elimination of All Forms of Discrimination Against Women (CEDAW).

On 15 December 1995, CEDAW became the first of these conventions to be ratified by the South African government. For our purposes, CEDAW is the most important of these Convention and therefore the only one to be discussed in some detail below.

Convention on the Political Rights of Women

This United Nations Convention came into force on 7 July 1954. It was signed by the South African government in January 1993, but has not yet been ratified. Its aim is '[t]o implement the principle of equality of rights for men and women which is contained in the United Nations Charter'.

It recognizes that men and women should have equal opportunities to execise their political rights, for instance, participating in the government of their country, directly or indirectly, through freely chosen representatives.

Article 1 states that women are entitled to vote in all elections on equal terms with men.

Article 2 declares that women must be eligible for election to all publicly elected bodies on equal terms with men.

Article 3 guarantees women an equal opportunity for holding public office and exercising public functions.

Convention on Consent to Marriage, Minimum Age for Marriage and Registration of Marriages

This United Nations Convention came into force on 9 December 1964. The South African government signed it in January 1993, but it has not yet become part of our law through ratification.

The broad aim of this Convention, in accordance with the United Nations Charter, is the following:

> *To promote universal respect for, and observance of, human rights and fundamental freedoms for all, without distinction as to race, sex, language or religion.*

The Convention recognizes that certain customs, ancient laws and practices relating to marriage and the family are inconsistent with the principles of equality and fundamental rights in the Charter. States (meaning the countries) which sign this Convention and make it part of their law are expected to take all appropriate steps to abolish these customs, ancient laws and practices. For instance, a nation would be expected to do the following:

- ensure complete freedom in the choice of a spouse;
- eliminate child marriages and the betrothal of young girls before the age of puberty;
- establish appropriate penalties if necessary, and
- establish a register in which all marriages will be recorded.

These aspects are explained in the Articles of the Convention:

Article 1 provides that no marriage may be legally entered into without the consent of both people in the marriage.

The people must consent of their own free will and consent must be given in the presence of the person who has been authorized to solemnize the marriage.

In terms of Article 2, countries which make this Convention part of their law must ensure that they have laws that specify a minimum age for marriage.

A marriage may not be legally entered into by any person under this age, except where the authorities decide to allow an exception to this rule for serious reasons. An exception may be granted only if it is in the interests of the persons who intend to marry.

Article 3 provides that all marriages must be registered in an appropriate official register by the competent authority or agency which has been set up specifically to do these registrations.

Convention on the Nationality of Married Women

This Convention came into force on 11 August 1958. It was signed by the South African government in January 1993, but has not yet become part of our law through ratification.

This Convention recognizes the principle contained in the Universal Declaration of Human Rights, namely, that every person has a right to nationality. This principle also implies the following:
- persons may not, without good reason, be deprived of their nationality, or
- be denied the right to change their nationality.

In practice, laws in certain countries ignore these principles. Depending on the country in which they live, women may lose or acquire nationality as a result of marrying. A woman may also lose her nationality as a result of divorce or of the dissolution of her marriage.

Article 1 of this Convention explains that countries which make this Convention part of their law agree that neither the beginning nor the ending of a marriage between one of its citizens and someone who is not one of its nationals, nor a change of nationality by the husband during the marriage, will automatically affect the nationality of the wife.

This means that if a South African woman marries a man from Zimbabwe, for example, she will not automatically lose her South African citizenship.

In terms of Article 2, states have to agree that a wife may decide to retain her nationality of a particular country even though her husband may have given up his nationality of that country or may have acquired the nationality of another country.

This means that if a woman's husband moves to the United Kingdom, for example, and changes his nationality, hers does not automatically change.

In terms of Article 3, states must agree that the foreign wife of one of its nationals (or citizens) may, at her request, acquire the nationality of her husband through special naturalization procedures.

Laws may also be introduced by countries which make it possible for the alien (or foreign) wife to acquire her husband's nationality at her own request.

Convention on the Elimination of All Forms of Discrimination against Women (CEDAW)

This Convention came into force on 3 September 1981. It was signed by the South African government in January 1993, ratified on 15 December 1995 and became operational 30 days later. CEDAW is the most important and comprehensive international document dealing with equality for women.

This Convention 'envisages its aims being achieved by means of legislative as well as/or other measures' (Delport 1). These 'other measures' will, for instance, include provisions in the Constitution, the Beijing Platform for Action, and National Machinery for the Advancement of Women (discussed below).

Many international documents such as those discussed above say that men and women should have equal rights. However, discrimination against women still exists. CEDAW goes further than these other documents by requiring states that sign this Convention to do the following: 'to embody the principle of equality of men and women in their national constitution or other laws; to ensure the practical realization of the principle of equality.'

States which make CEDAW part of their law must take action, through laws as well as other measures, to address inequality in all aspects of women's lives in order to ensure that women may enjoy and exercise their human rights on a basis of equality with men. CEDAW points to various areas of inequality which have to be addressed.

CEDAW provides a framework for addressing gender discrimination and inequality by explaining what steps should be taken by the countries which adopt it.

Article 1 begins by explaining discrimination against women.

In order to eliminate discrimination states should make the principle of equality of men and women part of their constitution and laws. Governments themselves may not discriminate against women and must ensure that no public authorities or institutions do so either. Furthermore, they must ensure that no private person, organization or business does so either. All existing laws, regulations, customs and practices which constitute discrimination against women must be changed.

Article 2 deals with policy measures that should be taken by a state which accepts CEDAW as part of its law.

Article 3 gives the guarantee of basic human rights and fundamental freedoms.

States must agree to ensure that women have opportunities to develop and advance fully in any field – whether it be political, social, economic or cultural. If necessary, laws must be passed which ensure that women may exercise their human rights and fundamental freedoms on a basis of equality with men.

Article 4 provides for the use of affirmative action.

Using affirmative action for this purpose is not discrimination even though affirmative action programmes treat women and men differently (see Chapter 20, above).

Article 5 addresses sex-role attitudes and prejudice.

Programmes must be developed to teach people and society that both child-bearing and child-rearing are important social functions and are vital to the development of a healthy, balanced society. Both women and men must share responsibility for the upbringing of children.

Article 6 deals with prostitution.

This Article provides that states must take all appropriate steps to ensure that women are not treated as objects that can be bought and sold.

Article 7 deals with women's equality in politics and government.

Article 8 covers women's participation in international affairs.

Article 9 provides that states must recognize that women must have the same rights to citizenship as men. (Note that CEDAW overlaps here with the Convention on the Nationality of Married Women.)

Article 10 deals with equal rights in education.

Women must be assured of equal rights with men with regard to equal access to:
- the same courses of study;
- the same examinations;
- teaching staff with the same qualifications;

- school buildings and equipment of the same quality;
- the same kinds of career and vocational guidance;
- equal opportunities to receive bursaries and other study grants;
- equal access to adult education and literacy programmes;
- equal opportunities to participate in sport and physical education.

Article 11 deals with employment issues.

Men and women must have equal rights to all kinds of training, to job choice, promotions, job security, job benefits and conditions of employment. Of great importance is the requirement that men and women must have the right to equal pay and equal benefits for work of equal value (see Part Four: Women and employment).

Governments must ensure that employers do not discriminate against women on the grounds of marriage or maternity. In addition, paid maternity leave must be introduced. A woman who takes maternity leave should not lose her job, her seniority or any special social allowances she might be entitled to receive (see Part Four: Women and employment).

Article 12 ensures that women are not discriminated against in the areas of health care, including family planning.

Women must have access to appropriate health care services during pregnancy, at the time of giving birth and after the birth of the baby. Women must have adequate nutrition during pregnancy and while they are breastfeeding. These services must be provided by the State free of charge, if necessary.

Article 13 addresses the economic needs and social benefits of women.

Article 14 expresses special concern for rural women.

States must pay special attention to the problems of rural women and the important role that they play in the economic survival of their families. This would include the work that many rural women do without receiving any money, for example, growing food for their families.

Article 15 ensures that women will be equal with men before the law.

For instance, women must have the same rights as men to sign contracts and to administer property. Women must be treated equally at all times during a court trial. Any contract or agreement that tries to restrict the legal powers of women will not be enforced.

Article 16 obliges states to take steps to eliminate discrimination against women in all matters relating to marriage and family relations.

Regardless of whether they are married or single, women and men must have the same rights and responsibilities as parents. Both women and men must have the right to decide freely and responsibly on the number and spacing of their children. They must have equal access to information about family planning and to methods of contraception.

With regard to matters such as guardianship and adoption of children, women and men must have the same legal rights and responsibilities.

The law must set a minimum age for marriage and must also require all marriages to be registered in an official registry (see above; see also Part Two: Women and the family, above).

Enforcement of CEDAW

CEDAW Committee and the report-back system

An International Committee on the Elimination of Discrimination against Women monitors the progress of nations which have ratified the CEDAW Convention – the members of this Committee are selected by the participating nations.

This committee meets every year to consider the reports that the different nations have submitted and in turn submits these to the General Assembly of the United Nations in order to monitor progress made in eliminating discrimination against women in each of these nations. Delport ('An Overview ...' 68–9) discusses some of the problems faced by this committee:

> *Unfortunately the limited authority of, and inferior procedures followed by the Committee, interfere with the Convention on the Elimination of All Forms of Discrimination Against Women's effectiveness as an international force for the elimination of discrimination against women.*

Delport goes on to list the main problems faced by the committee:
- the committee cannot consider complaints by state parties or the individual. It also cannot go beyond the limits of the reporting system;
- the committee lacks information from non-governmental organizations (NGOs). Even though many NGOs attend meetings and observe, they have no specific role to play in CEDAW;

One of the most serious criticisms against CEDAW is its inability to force states to obey the provisions set out in CEDAW. There is no international court which deals specifically with discrimination against women and which may punish countries if they do not comply with their obligations in terms of CEDAW.

The report-back system mentioned above depends entirely on a specific country's willingness to co-operate. A state is supposed to submit a report to the committee within one year after CEDAW has come into force in that country. After that, countries must submit a report at least once every four years.

In practice, however, very few of the countries which have signed and ratified CEDAW have submitted any reports – unfortunately, no mechanisms exist to force them to do so.

Also, many countries have placed reservations on the Convention. In fact, at least 25 states have made a total of 68 reservations to important provisions of the Convention (Delport 70).

Despite these serious flaws, CEDAW may be applied in South Africa with good effect. It can be used to provide some substance and guidance to gender policies and development programmes. It 'needs to be used creatively in order to ensure that it becomes a framework and a tool for the delivery of real equality' (Delport 'An Overview ...' 71). Furthermore, it can serve as a yardstick to indicate how far we have come and how far we still have to go.

Draft optional protocol to CEDAW

We have already mentioned one of the drawbacks of the CEDAW Convention: when countries do not take their obligations under the Convention seriously people in these countries cannot bring their individual complaints to the CEDAW Committee. Early in 1996 the United Nations Commission on the Status of Women adopted a resolution aimed at remedying this situation and making it possible for individual complaints to be brought to the CEDAW Committee. The Commission proposed that a draft optional protocol to the Convention be drawn up to make an individual complaints procedure available to women and interest groups whose countries had ratified CEDAW but had in some way failed to give effect to it. Countries that signed the Optional Protocol would not be allowed to enter reservations against it. Both a Communications and an Enquiry Procedure were proposed. If the United Nations adopted the Draft Optional Protocol, this is what would happen:

Communications procedure

Communications (that is to say, complaints) would have to be in writing and be submitted to the CEDAW Committee by an individual or group claiming to have suffered from a violation of any right in the Convention or to be directly affected by the failure of their government to comply with its obligations under the Convention. Before people or groups did this, however, they would have to try to solve their problems by using remedies available to them in their own country. When the CEDAW Committee received a communication, it would have to inform the government concerned, but it would not tell that government who it was that had complained unless the complainants agreed to this. The Committee would have to be willing to act as a facilitator† between the parties.

Inquiry procedure

If it received a complaint that a government (which had agreed to the Optional Protocol) had committed a serious and systematic violation of rights set forth in the Convention, the Committee would have to ask that government to cooperate with it so that the complaint could be examined. One or more members of the Committee might hold an inquiry and report back to the Committee, and there might also if necessary be a visit to the government concerned, but only if that government agreed to the visit. After the Committee told the government about its findings, that government would have to respond within three months. Inquiries would be confidential. It is hoped that the Protocol may be adopted by the United Nations General Assembly soon. The chief difficulty in the way of its adoption is that certain countries are happy for individuals to have the right to complain, but not so anxious for groups to have the same right.

The Beijing Declaration and Platform for Action

In the Beijing Declaration and Platform for Action, which came out of the United Nations Fourth World Conference on Women held in Beijing, People's Republic of China, in September 1995, the women of the world once again urged governments to realize the goals expressed in the CEDAW Convention as quickly as possible. All governments which took part in the Conference, including South Africa, adopted the Platform, which named key obstacles to the advancement of women worldwide and set priorities for action by governments and the United Nations between 1996 and 2001. It was emphasized that it is governments, particularly, which must see to it the the Platform is implemented (Beijing Platform for Action 123). The South African Government undertook to adopt all parts of the Platform, so government departments must ensure that all their policies and actions are in accord with it, and must take steps to ensure women's empowerment (South Africa: Summary Report of 4th World Conference on Women iv and v).

CHAPTER TWENTY-TWO:
National machinery for the advancement of women

We have seen that to have equality written into the Constitution is not enough – what is needed is real or substantive equality for every woman – in the words of the Beijing Platform for Action. After the South African government adopted the Platform for Action, it followed the example of other countries such as Australia which, for a long time, have had National Machinery for the Advancement of Women, and set about creating national machinery here.

'National machinery' is a network of structures both inside and outside the government which together must create a gender policy aimed at transforming the country. Once this policy is in place, gender awareness ought to be seen in all decisions which government takes on budget, policy, employment and promotion practices, for example; and all government departments should make regular reports on steps they have taken towards gender equality.

The aim of the national machinery is to 'achieve equality for women as participants, decision-makers and beneficiaries in the political, civil, social, economic and cultural spheres' (*National Machinery for Women in South Africa: a Policy Document for Discussion*. Gender Research Project, Centre for Applied Legal Studies, 1995). National machinery should be 'the central policy co-ordinating unit inside government and it should operate at the highest level in government', according to the Beijing Platform for Action (1995, para 201). This is to ensure that national machinery will not be marginalized, as it has been in some countries. Further problems which have arisen have been 'unclear mandates, lack of adequate staff, training, data and sufficient resources' (Beijing Platform for Action para 196). Machinery should, of course, also be introduced at departmental, provincial and local level.

THE OFFICE ON THE STATUS OF WOMEN

As we have seen, the Beijing Platform for Action urged governments to vest the responsibility for the advancement of women in the highest possible level of government, perhaps at the level of a Cabinet Minister (*Summary*

Report on 4th World Conference on Women Beijing, 36). This suggestion was closely followed when the South African Office on the Status of Women was established in January 1997 as 'the manifestation of the nation's commitment to the constitutional imperative regarding gender mainstreaming' (press release, 12 February 1997). The office is housed in the Office of the Deputy President and is headed by a Chief Executive Officer. It is seen as a 'key feature in South Africa's national machinery aimed at advancing gender equality' and as 'the driving force for mainstreaming gender into all government activities' (press release, 12 February 1997).

Its functions are:
- to advance the National Women's Empowerment Policy;
- to advise and brief the Deputy President on all matters having to do with the empowerment of women;
- to find ways of measuring progress to gender equality; to liaise between NGOs which deal with women's issues and the Office of the Deputy President and between international bodies and that office;
- to arrange for training in gender analysis and gender sensitization and for awareness training and confidence building among women at all levels;
- to encourage affirmative action;
- to work with line ministries, provinces and all publicly funded bodies in mainstreaming gender in all policies and programmes;
- to initiate and promote cross-sectoral action on issues (such as violence against women) that cut across all sectors;
- to co-ordinate structures at the provincial level;
- to prioritize key concerns and initiate policy and action-oriented research;
- to consult and liaise with civil society and Parliament (press release, 12 February 1997).

Especially in the spheres of training and research, there appears to be some overlapping with the functions of the Commission on Gender Equality, which is discussed below, so the two bodies need to co-operate closely in order that they do not waste time on projects that are too similar.

The Women's Budget

One of the projects in which the Office on the Status of Women is likely to be closely involved is the Women's Budget. The first Women's Budget Initiative was started in 1995 by the Parliamentary Joint Standing Committee on Finance: Gender and Economic Policy Group in conjunction with various NGOs. It 'provides the first serious South African attempt to examine the gender impact of key aspects of the total budget' (D Budlander (ed) *The Women's Budget* (Idasa, 1996) 8) and focuses on welfare, education, housing and work on taxation and public sector employment. The project emphasizes the economy's impact on the poor and the disempowered and focuses on their needs.

The Women's Budget is not a separate budget for women but tries to ensure that every programme of each government department is examined for its impact on women (Govender in Budlender op cit).

COMMISSION ON GENDER EQUALITY

The Commission on Gender Equality was established by the Commission on Gender Equality Act 39 of 1996. The Commission's objects are:
- To promote gender equality.
- To advise and make recommendations to Parliament or any other law-making body on any laws or proposed laws which affect gender equality and the status of women.

The Constitution lists the Commission on Gender Equality as one of the State institutions supporting constitutional democracy and prescribes that it 'must promote respect for gender equality and protection, development and attainment of gender equality'. The Commission is a juristic person and is independent. In their work for the Commission members should therefore be guided by broad gender interests rather than party political affiliations.

The Commission commenced its work in 1997. It comprises a chairperson and no fewer than seven and no more than 11 members, who must have a record of commitment to the promotion of gender equality and must also have knowledge or experience of matters which fall into the ambit of the Commission's objectives (s 3(1)). Members of the Commission may be full-time or part-time and are appointed for a period of not more than five years.

Powers and functions of the Commission

The Commission:
- must monitor and evaluate policies and practices of government bodies and officials and public and private bodies;
- must develop, conduct or manage information and education programmes;
- must evaluate all existing and proposed law, which does or is likely to affect gender equality or the status of women, and make recommendations to Parliament or other law-making bodies;
- may recommend the introduction of appropriate new laws to Parliament or other legislatures;

- must investigate gender issues, either when it decides itself to do so or after receiving a complaint. It must use mediation, conciliation or negotiation to try to resolve disputes or to put things right. It may also, however, refer any matter to the Human Rights Commission, the Public Protector or any other authority, whichever is the best to deal with the matter.

  When the Commission on Gender Equality conducts an investigation, it must try to liaise with other bodies with similar aims to its own. Close co-operation with the Office on the Status of Women, as suggested above, as well as the Human Rights Commission is therefore essential. The Human Rights Commission has very similar aims and powers to those of the Gender Commission: both are committed to promoting, protecting and monitoring human rights. Co-operation is especially necessary because both Commissions have very limited resources;
- must also, in order to further its aims, liaise with other organizations promoting gender equality and with civil society;
- must monitor the government's compliance with international conventions and other international documents which South Africa has agreed to or has ratified which concern gender equality. It must also submit reports to Parliament on these conventions, etc. The most important international convention with which the Commission will have to concern itself is CEDAW. It will have to make sure that the government complies with its duty to send periodic reports to the United Nations on its progress towards compliance with that Convention. It would seem that the Commission should not only have to campaign for full and timely reporting, but should also scrutinize reports for omissions and inaccuracies. It will have to ensure that these reports are indeed an accurate reflection of the progress or lack of it in the striving towards gender equality in South Africa;
- may conduct research or have research conducted to further its objects;
- may consider recommendations, suggestions and requests concerning the promotion of gender equality.

Entry and search of premises

For the purpose of exercising its powers and functions under the Act the Commission has wide powers of search and entry. These powers have been questioned as perhaps being too wide but they are very similar to those of the Human Rights Commission. After investigating a matter, the Commission may make known its finding, point of view or recommendation to any person. If it deems it fit to do so, it must make known the finding of an investigation to the complainant and any implicated person.

Reports by the Commission

The Commission must at least once a year report to the President on its activities and the attainment of its objectives and the President must have the report tabled in Parliament. However, the Commission may also at any time submit any other report to the President and Parliament (s 15(2)).

An assessment of the Commission's powers of enforcement

Although the powers and functions of the Commission are extremely wide-ranging, its powers of enforcement are weak. The lawmakers seem to have seen the Commission's role as one of monitoring progress in the attainment of gender equality, evaluating legislation, and of educating people on gender rights, rather than as one of taking action to enforce gender equality. When the Commission has conducted an inquiry, it may conciliate, mediate or arbitrate, and/or it may refer a matter to the Human Rights Commission or the Public Protector. The Human Rights Commission Act 54 of 1994 gives the Human Rights Commission the specific power to bring an action on behalf of a person or group of persons, but there is no such provision in the Commission on Gender Equality Act. However, there is nothing to stop the Commission, being a juristic person, from bringing court actions if it so chooses.

THE HUMAN RIGHTS COMMISSION

The Human Rights Commission, although not strictly speaking part of the national machinery for women, has to concern itself with the human rights of all people, including women. Besides, the Gender Equality Commission may refer matters to the Human Rights Commission (see above). Before the Human Rights Commission was established, it was stressed, in a report on what Parliament had done to improve the quality of life and status of women (Report on what the SA Parliament has done to improve the quality of life and status of women in South Africa (1995) 13), that the Commission must integrate women's human rights into its work.

The Commission has to promote respect for human rights and a culture of human rights, see that human rights are protected and developed, and make sure that they are respected. In this sphere it can carry out investigations and produce reports, take steps to secure redress[†] where human rights are violated, carry out research and educate people. Each year, government bodies must report to the Commission about progress being made in respect of the rights relating to housing, health care, food, water, social security, education and the environment.

The Commission:

- must develop and conduct information programmes so that the general public understands the Bill of Rights and the Commission's own role and activities;
- must maintain close liaison with bodies similar to itself;
- may consider recommendations, suggestions and requests on fundamental rights;
- must carry out studies concerning human rights if the President requires it to do so;
- may take a matter to court in its own name, or on behalf of a person or a group or a class of persons;

The Commission is also allowed to mediate, conciliate and negotiate on human rights matters.

THE PUBLIC PROTECTOR

Like the Human Rights Commission, the office of the Public Protector does not, strictly speaking, form part of the national machinery for the advancement of women; but women should be aware that it is an important informal avenue for bringing complaints against the government. In addition, as we have seen above, the Commission on Gender Equality may refer matters to it. Since the Public Protector must be accessible to all persons and communities, there is nothing to prevent individual complaints being brought to its attention. These will relate to matters such as government maladministration, improper conduct by public functionaries, improper acts with respect to public money, and improper or unlawful enrichment of public functionaries (see the Preamble to the Public Protector Act 23 of 1994). Any person may approach the Public Protector by means of a written or oral declaration under oath or by affirmation.†

THE TRUTH AND RECONCILIATION COMMISSION

At the 1993 United Nations World Conference on Human Rights in Vienna, a Global Tribunal on Violations of Women's Human Rights was held at which a number of women from all over the world who had suffered human rights abuses were given the opportunity to tell their story. Following this example, in South Africa women's groups lobbied the Truth and Reconciliation Commission to hold similar sessions for women, and this has been done in the main centres of the country.

How women's human rights issues may be brought to Court

Often a lack of financial resources means that complaints concerning the breach of women's human rights do not reach the Courts. One way of overcoming this difficulty is to bring a group action – a number of women who all have the same problem should unite in bringing an action to Court. One method is for them to approach organizations that have legal expertise and ask them for their assistance. Preferably, South Africa should have an organization such as the Canadian Women's Legal Education and Action Fund (LEAF) which not only educates the public about gender issues but also sponsors test cases† on gender issues.

Conclusion

Discrimination against women goes against the aspirations and goals of the Constitution. As long as discrimination continues, as long as South African women are oppressed, the ideal of equality cannot be achieved.

We have pointed to international conventions which are important to women, especially CEDAW. We have shown that a concerted effort was made by the writers of our Constitution to overcome the inherent inequality that existed in South Africa in the past. Many South African women have suffered from double discrimination – on the grounds of both gender and race. We also described the debates that took place while the South African Constitution was being compiled.

We have shown that the problem of inequality of women as human beings, worthy of dignity and equality before the law, is a global problem and an issue that is being actively debated internationally. The fact that this is such an issue indicates that there is still much to be done.

Lastly, in this chapter we have described the national machinery that has been created to ensure that theoretical equality becomes real.

We have attempted to extract from the Constitution – and the debates surrounding constitutional issues – those matters which relate uniquely to women (not forgetting that the Constitution deals with much wider issues than women's rights). The Constitution presents a vision of a society which is sincere in its attempt to create justice, democracy and equality. However, its ramifications have to reach all areas of that society. A Constitution is meaningless if, while guaranteeing equality and dignity, it still permits a woman to be subjected to violence, abuse and disregard in the privacy of her own home, especially if she lacks access to assistance.

At the core not only of our Constitution but also of the national machinery for women lies only one idea – you, the individual. No one, no institution, no law can operate properly unless individuals play their part, by being aware of their rights, and aware of issues and of centres of help and assistance that are available to women and by using their own knowledge in order to assist others.

The President, Nelson Mandela, in his State of the Nation Address in May 1994, had this to say:

> *It is vitally important that all structures of government, including the President himself, should understand this fully: that freedom cannot be achieved unless women have been emancipated from all forms of oppression. All of us must take this on board that the objectives of the RDP will not have been realized unless we see in visible and practical terms that the condition of the women of our country has radically changed for the better, and that they have been empowered to intervene in all aspects of life as equals with any other member of society.*

SELECTED READING

C Albertyn and J Kentridge 'Introducing the Right to Equality in the Interim Constitution' 1994 *South African Journal on Human Rights* 149–78

C Albertyn '*Mainstreaming Gender*' National Machinery for Women in South Africa: A Policy Outline (1995). A Report on what the SA Parliament has done to improve the quality of life and status of women in South Africa

D Budlender (ed). *The Women's Budget* Idasa, 1996

CEDAW in South Africa: The United Nations Convention of the Elimination of All Forms of Discrimination Against Women (CEDAW) 1995, NIPLAR Taj Printers, Johannesburg

H Corder 'Towards a South African Constitution' 1994 T*he Modern Law Review* 491–533

E Delport. *An overview of the United Nations Convention on the Elimination of All Forms of Discrimination Against Women: How does South Africa Measure up?* (June 1995) LLM Dissertation, University of Pretoria

Department of Foreign Affairs. *Fourth World Conference on Women: Action for Equality, Development and Peace 4-5 September 1995* Beijing, China Background document

'*Draft Policy for Women's Empowerment: Documentation for the Advancement of Women in South Africa*' 1995 August policy document/4/8/95, Ministry in the Office of the President, Cape Town

Draft Policy on Women's Empowerment Office of the President (1995) para 16.3

K Engle 'International Human Rights and Feminism: When Discourses Meet' 1992 *Michigan Journal of International Law* 13

E Evatt 'Eliminating Discrimination Against Women: The impact of the UN Convention' 1991 *Melbourne University Law Review* 18

Z Illic *The Convention on the Elimination of All Forms of Discrimination Against Women* 1991, New York

S Liebenberg *The Constitution of South Africa from a Gender Perspective* 1995

D McQuoid-Mason et al *Democracy for all: Education towards a Democratic Culture* 1994, Juta, Cape Town

D Meyerson 'Sexual Equality and the Law' 1993 *South African Journal for Human Rights* 9

C Murray (ed) *Gender and the New South African Legal Order* 1994, Juta, Cape Town

National Machinery for Women in South Africa: a Policy Document for Discussion. Gender Research Project, Centre for Applied Legal Studies (1995)

© JUTA & CO, LTD

LA Rehof. *Guide to the Travaux Preparatiores of the United Nations Convention on the Elimination of All Forms of Discrimination Against Women* 1993, Martinus Nijhoff Publishers, Dordrecht
Summary Report on Fourth World Conference on Women 1995, Beijing
CW van Wyk & H van Oosten (eds) *Nihil Obstat: Essays in Honour of WJ Hosten* 1996, Durban, 257–71
D van Wyk, J Dugard, B de Villiers and D Davis (eds) *Rights and Constitutionalism: The New South African Legal Order* 1994, Juta, Cape Town

Appendix

Resources and contacts

Advice desk for abused women
University of Durban-Westville, E Block
Department of Social Work
Private Bag X54001
Durban 4000
(031) 820-2862

AGISANANG
c/o Alexandra Health Clinic
PO Box 175
Bergvlei 2012
(011) 440-1231

Baragwanath Medico-Legal Clinic
Baragwanath Road
Soweto
(011) 933-1100 (x 2864)

Border Rape Crisis
East London
PO Box 11061
Southernwood 5231
(0431) 43-7266

Cape Town Rape Crisis
4 Bishop Road
Observatory
(021) 47-1467

Centre for Peace Action
25-7 Calvinia Street
Eldorado Park Extension 4
(011) 342-3840

Centre for the Study of Violence and Reconciliation
(Trauma Clinic)
49 Jorisson Street
PO Box 30778
Braamfontein 2017
(011) 403-5650

Guguletu Rape Crisis
Ilitha Labantu
Guguletu
(021) 440-4016

Isipingo Support Group for Abused Women (ISGAW)
(031) 902-5578

Lifeline
Actonville	(011) 421-8614
Benoni	(011) 422-4242
Cape Town	(021) 461-1111
Durban	(031) 23-2323
East London	(0431) 22-000
Empangeni	(0351) 92-2222
Grahamstown	(0461) 31-8180
Johannesburg	(011) 728-1347
Klerksdorp	(081) 462-1234
Krugersdorp	(011) 953-4111
Mafikeng	(0140) 81-4263
Namibia	(09264) 61-23-2221
Nelspruit	(01311) 55-3606
Pietermaritzburg	(0331) 94-4444
Pretoria	(012) 343-8888
Rustenburg	(0142) 97-2000
Secunda	(0136) 31-1612
Shelley Beach	(03931) 75-4447
Sun City	(01465) 73-777/8
Transkei	(0471) 2-5691
Vanderbijlpark	(016) 33-7333
Welkom	(057) 352-2212

Lungelo
Chiawelo Clinic
Soweto
(011) 933-1100 (x 2006)

NICRO
Bloemfontein	(051) 447-6678
Cape Town	(021) 47-4000
Durban	(031) 304-2761
East London	(0431) 24-123
Germiston	(011) 873-6976/7
Kimberley	(0531) 811-715
Pietermaritzburg	(0331) 45-4425/2
Pretoria	(012) 326-5331/2
Port Elizabeth	(041) 542-611/2/3
Queenstown	(0451) 81-602
Soweto	(011) 986-1020/1/2

Standerton   (01771) 21-092
Tygerberg   (021) 949-2110
Umtata   (0471) 31-0598
Vaal   (061) 422-5019
Zululand   (0351) 2-1574

NICRO Women's Support Centre
4 Buitensingel
Cape Town
(021) 22-1690
Bloemfontein   (051) 47-6678
Durban   (031) 304-2761
East London   (0431) 812-2475/43-7266
Kimberley   (0531) 2-6392
Pietermaritzburg   (0331) 45-4425/45-4442
Port Elizabeth   (041) 54-2611
Pretoria   (012) 32-6533
Soweto   (011) 986-1020/1/2
Zululand   (0351) 2-1574

NISAA Women's Institute
Suite 105, Mafa Manzil
104 Gemsbok Avenue
Lenasia
(011) 854-5804

People Against Human Abuse (PAHA)
(012) 805-7416

Port Elizabeth Rape Crisis
Alfin House, Room 506
5th Floor, 510 Main Street
North End
Port Elizabeth 6056
(041) 54-6284/54-3804

POWA
PO Box 93416
Yeoville 2143
(011) 642-4345/6

Sexual Harassment Education Project (SHEP)
PO Box 30778
Yeoville 2143
(011) 403-5650

Soweto Crisis Centre
(011) 473-2505

Vista Rape Crisis
Vista University
Mamelodi
Private Bag X1311
Silverton 1027
(012) 323-1020

Women Against Women Abuse (WAWA)
PO Box 1476
Johannesburg 2000
(011) 836-5656
Laudium Advice Office
Laudium
Pretoria 1000
(012) 374-4792

GENERAL COUNSELLING AND ADVICE

Black Sash Advice Offices
5 Long Street
Mowbray 7700
(021) 685-3814

Durban	(031) 301-9215
East London	(0431) 43-9206
Grahamstown	(0461) 2-8091
Johannesburg	(011) 834-8372
Knysna	(0445) 2-4458
Pietermaritzburg	(0331) 42-6368
Port Elizabeth	(041) 54-6274
Pretoria	(012) 322-3969
Umtata	(0471) 32-0226

Legal Aid Clinics
The following universities have Legal Aid Clinics which render a service to the public

Rand Afrikaans University Law Clinic	(011) 489-2633
Rhodes University Law Clinic	(0461) 2-2023 (x 434)
University of Bophuthatswana Law Clinic	(0140) 2-1171
University of Cape Town	(021) 650-2678
University of Natal Community Law Centre, Durban	(031) 816-2446
University of Natal, Pietermaritzburg	(0331) 6-3320
University of Port Elizabeth Legal Clinic	(041) 53-2433
University of Potchefstroom	(0148) 93-0045
University of Pretoria	(012) 43-5404
University of South Africa, UNISA	(012) 320-8570
University of Stellenbosch	(021) 808-3195

University of the North Law Clinic, Sovenga	(01522) 4300
University of the Orange Free State	(051) 47-9915
University of the Western Cape	(021) 959-2414
University of the Witwatersrand, Campus Law Clinic	(011) 716-5650
University of Zululand Centre for Legal Services	(0351) 9311 (x 194)

Glossary

An asterisk (*) indicates that the word or expression it follows is itself defined or explained in this Glossary.

abeyance state of being suspended or put aside temporarily
action legal proceeding
adversarial of a situation in which there are opposing parties or views
affirmation statement made by a person who does not wish to take the oath*
affirmative action act promoting the interests of people who have been disadvantaged in the past
Affirmative Action Act of 1986 Australian law which sets up affirmative action policies in the workplace
AIDS Acquired Immune Deficiency Syndrome; the stage by which the body's immune system has been sufficiently weakened to allow opportunistic diseases to develop unchecked
allegation unproved statement or assertion
annulment act if declaring void; formal invalidation (of a marriage)
antenuptial contract contract made by engaged people before they marry in which they agree about property arrangements for their marriage (*see also* marriage settlement*)
arrear late in paying debt or meeting an obligation
arbitration procedure where people ask a third person to settle their dispute
artificial insemination impregnating a woman by introducing semen into her Fallopian tubes without sexual intercourse
assault unlawful use of violence against another person; threat of violence against another
assess estimate value
attach to take property with lawful authority (*see also* writ of execution*)
assisted procreation alternative means of conceiving a child when sexual intercourse is unsuccessful, eg *in vitro* fertilization, surrogacy

chambers in constitutional law the meeting place of a country's legislature – usually called parliament; also the rooms from which a legal practitioner works
Civil Rights Act of 1964 United States law that deals with the recognition of civil rights for all persons
Code of Zulu Law KwaZulu Code of Zulu Law Act 16 of 1985 and the Natal Code of Zulu Law; written accounts of the customary laws of KwaZulu-Natal

collective bargaining　negotiation between the employer, on the one hand, and the trade union, on the other, in which the union strengthens its bargaining power by acting for a number of employees

commissioning couple　the man and woman (couple) who want to use a surrogate mother in order to have a child *(see also* natural parents*)

conception　the moment that a human egg (ovum) is fertilized by a human sperm in the womb

constitutional principles　standard rules of conduct or set values in the Constitution which state how the country is supposed to be governed

consummation　completing a marriage by sexual intercourse

contempt of court　disobeying the court's order

continuous　prolonged without interruption

criminal law　law relating to conduct that the State considers to be unlawful and which the State punishes

custody　control of the child and his or her daily life, including the child's education, physical care, protection and physical and mental development

damages　money to be paid as compensation to a person for injury, loss, etc

disabled　having a disability, such as a limp or a broken arm; can also mean lacking physical, moral or intellectual strength

debt　obligation to pay; liability

defaulter　person who fails to act as required, eg who does not pay

discrimination　different treatment based on a certain aspect of a person; sex discrimination, for example, means less favourable treatment of a woman only because she is a woman

domestic abuse　violence in the family; emotional and/or physical or sexual abuse of people in the family or in an intimate relationship, usually in the privacy of the home

employment equity policy　policy which states that women are to be treated fairly and equally – the same as their male counterparts – in the workplace

Equal Employment Opportunity Commission　United States government agency which helps people who think they are victims of discrimination in the workplace

equal franchise　when all people have the same right to vote, regardless of race, sex, colour, language, etc

equality before the law　when the law applies universal standards to every person

equality of opportunity　all people must be treated equally and must receive the same opportunities in areas such as education and employment

equality of outcome granting men and women the same rights will not necessarily result in equality between the sexes. It is sometimes necessary to grant one group (eg women) special rights to ensure that, in the end, men and women are equal (in contradistinction to equality of opportunity)

estate all the property (movable and immovable) and debts pertaining to a person

exempt free from or not subject to obligation

facilitator person who assists the progress of negotiations (*see also* mediation*)

feminist jurisprudence study of the law from a woman's point of view

financially prejudiced disadvantaged in money matters (eg women being paid less than men for the same work)

foetus human embryo from the end of the second month of pregnancy until birth

forfeiture act of forfeiting or paying a penalty

fosterage act of caring for or bringing up a child who is not the biological or adopted child of the foster parents (in Islam, usually a woman who has nursed a child)

franchise right to vote

gender state of being male or female

gender fairness equality between men and women

get documentation in Jewish marital law necessary for divorce

gratuity reward for services rendered

guardian person legally appointed to manage the affairs of one incapable of acting for himself or herself (eg a child)

heir person who inherits property from another

habitual regularly and repeatedly; eg a habitual criminal is someone who breaks the law repeatedly

HIV Human Immuno-deficiency Virus; virus that attacks and weakens the body's immune system, laying it open to opportunistic diseases such as tuberculosis, cancer, etc

human right basic right that belongs to all people, regardless of their sex, gender, race, colour, language, national origin, age, class, religion or political beliefs

illegitimate illegal, unlawful; also (a child) born of parents who did not have a valid marriage (*see also* legitimate*)

impediment obstruction, eg to contract of marriage by reason of closeness of blood or affinity

impotence inability to perform sexual intercourse

in community of property marriage system in which the husband and wife share their property (*see also* out of community of property*)

indigenous coming from a certain place or region; in the case of traditional Africans, indigenous law = customary law

informal dispute settlement settlement of disagreements without going to court (the formal route)

inherently discriminatory discrimination as an integral feature or element (of affirmative action programmes); this is because the less-favoured side (women) becomes more-favoured (which is discriminatory against men)

invariable consequences effects or results that cannot be changed

in vitro fertilization fertilization of ovum outside the human body by mixing sperm and ripe ova in a test tube (*see also* surrogacy*)

irreconcilable uncompromising; incompatible

irretrievable breakdown of the marriage marriage relationship is no longer normal and it is most unlikely that there can be a normal relationship again

judicial body court or commission that administers justice, eg court of law

judicial order instruction issued by a judge or a court of law

jurisdiction area over which a court has authority

law of delict law relating to the private wrongs which cause harm

legal literacy knowing something about the law, especially as it affects one personally; being able to understand one's rights within the law

legal status position and rights under the law

legitimate legal, lawful; also (a child) born of parents who have a valid marriage (*see also* illegitimate*)

legitimize make lawful or legal; make an illegitimate child legitimate

liable legally obliged

litigation legal proceedings

maintenance creditor person liable for maintenance payment

major adult in the eyes of the law; 21 years of age or older (*see also* minor*)

majority status of being a major; being of legal age to be considered an adult under the law

malicious desertion abandoning a spouse or family

marginalization being pushed out to the edges of something; not in the mainstream; eg working mothers who are able to work only part-time

marital power husband's power to make the decisions in the marriage; husband's power over the person and property of his wife

marriage contract contract between a man and a woman (and/or their families) dealing with the terms of the marriage

marriage settlement specific donation of an asset or a sum of money promised by one of the spouses to the other in their antenuptial contract*

maternity benefits benefits received from an employer when a woman is pregnant; also called pregnancy benefits

means money or other resources; financial ability

mediation procedure where two people try to resolve their problems through the intervention of a third person, but not in court (*see also* facilitator*)

minor person who is not an adult under the law (*see also* major*)

National Assembly first (representative) chamber of the South African Parliament, comprising 400 members (the National Council of Provinces is the second chamber)

natural parents biological mother and father (*see also* commissioning couple*)

notice of motion formal legal document required to begin civil proceedings which cannot be started by summons* for various technical reasons

offence violation or breach of law

out of community of property marriage system where the husband and wife's property is regarded as separate (*see also* in community of property*)

Parliament highest legislative authority in the country; the institution which has the power to make laws

paternity fact or state of being a father

patriarchal society society structured round the man as the head of the family and other institutions

pension interests matters or benefits affecting a person's pension

political tolerance recognition that people from opposing political parties are entitled to organize and to speak out in opposition without interference from anyone

polyandry marriage system where a woman may have more than one husband at a time

polygymy marriage system where a man may have more than one wife at a time

precedence act of preceding; order of priority

pregnancy benefits *see* maternity benefits*

pro rata 'by rate'; dividing something based on criteria rather than equal shares; each according to his or her contribution

profile overview of the workers in a company or institution, showing the different types of people working there (gender, age, race, etc); often used to show up discrimination or where affirmative action is needed

property unit collection of the property or assets in a customary marriage

puberty age of sexual maturity; age at which a youth is able to have children

putative marriage marriage in which one or both of the partners were unaware that the marriage was invalid or not legal

quid pro quo 'this for that'; an exchange where both sides should be equal; a trade-off

quota proportional part of the total; share of the total; eg when a certain percentage of the workers in a company must be women

rape sexual intercourse with a woman when she had not consented to it

reciprocal rights and duties rights and duties that two people give to each other

redress put right, especially through compensation; remedy* or cure

redistribution order legal order to divide property; instruction to redistribute assets

remedy anything that serves to put a fault to rights, cure defects or improve conditions

repudiation rejection of the validity or authority of something

revocable able to be cancelled

rite formal act or procedure prescribed or customary in religious ceremonies

Roman law body of law developed by the Romans during the period from about 753 BC to AD 565

Roman-Dutch law system of law derived from the ancient Romans and adapted/codified by Dutch jurists during the Middle Ages

separation of powers division of the powers of a government into three separate branches: Legislature, Executive, and Judiciary (keeping these branches separate helps keep each one in check)

service legal delivery of a legal document by an officer of the court

Sex Discrimination Act United Kingdom law which deals with discrimination based on sex

social constructs beliefs of a society

summons formal legal document used to institute civil proceedings; formal legal document given to the accused to bring him or her to court in criminal proceedings (*see also* notice of motion*)

surrogacy arrangement between intending parents and a surrogate (or substitute) mother in which the surrogate carries a baby for the intending parents and gives up her parental power over the baby at birth (*see also in vitro* fertilization* and natural parents*)

tacit consent silent consent; agreement that is inferred from a person's behaviour

take the oath swear to tell the truth (an oath is binding on a person's conscience) (*see also* affirmation*)

terms of a marriage legal settlement reached before a couple marries (*see also* antenuptial contract*)

test case court case in which is decided a question of law that is of interest to many people, not just the people involved in a particular case

testator person who dies leaving a will*

Title VII part of the American Civil Rights Act of 1964, dealing specifically with discrimination based on sex (in South Africa part of an Act is a 'section' not a 'title')

tolerance state or quality of being tolerant of others or their viewpoints

unilaterally involving one party of several; performed by one party without consulting others

victim person against whom a crime has been committed, eg someone who has suffered abuse or violence

ward person under the protection of another

will written expression of a person's wishes regarding the disposal of his or her property in the event of death

writ of execution court order for property to be seized (*see also* attach*)